3-

SATiRE

Wadsworth Guides to Literary Study
Maurice Beebe, General Editor

APPROACHES TO *WALDEN*
  edited by Lauriat Lane, Jr., University of New Brunswick
CONRAD'S *HEART OF DARKNESS* AND THE CRITICS
  edited by Bruce Harkness, University of Illinois
CONRAD'S *SECRET SHARER* AND THE CRITICS
  edited by Bruce Harkness, University of Illinois
CRIME AND PUNISHMENT AND THE CRITICS
  edited by Edward Wasiolek, University of Chicago
DARWIN AND HIS CRITICS: The Darwinian Revolution
  edited by Bernard R. Kogan, University of Illinois, Chicago
J. D. SALINGER AND THE CRITICS
  edited by William F. Belcher and James W. Lee,
  North Texas State University
THE *KING LEAR* PERPLEX
  edited by Helmut Bonheim, University of California, Santa Barbara
LITERARY CENSORSHIP: Principles, Cases, Problems
  edited by Kingsley Widmer, San Diego State College,
  and Eleanor Widmer
LITERARY SYMBOLISM: An Introduction to the Interpretation of
Literature
  edited by Maurice Beebe, Purdue University
MELVILLE'S *BILLY BUDD* AND THE CRITICS
  edited by William T. Stafford, Purdue University
OEDIPUS REX: A MIRROR FOR GREEK DRAMA
  edited by Albert Cook, Western Reserve University
THE RIME OF THE ANCIENT MARINER: A HANDBOOK
  edited by Royal A. Gettmann, University of Illinois
SATIRE: THEORY AND PRACTICE
  edited by Charles A. Allen and George D. Stephens, California State
  College at Long Beach
A *SCARLET LETTER* HANDBOOK
  edited by Seymour L. Gross, University of Notre Dame
VOLTAIRE'S *CANDIDE* AND THE CRITICS
  edited by Milton P. Foster, Eastern Michigan University
WHITMAN THE POET: Materials for Study
  edited by John C. Broderick, Wake Forest College

SATiRE
theory and practice

edited by
Charles A. Allen
and
George D. Stephens

CALIFORNIA STATE COLLEGE
AT LONG BEACH

wadsworth publishing company, inc.
belmont, california

First printing, May 1962
Second printing, July 1964

L.C. Cat. Card No.: 62-11238

Printed in the United States of
America

Manufactured by American Book-
Stratford Press, Inc., New York

PREFACE

Satire is a form of writing—or of speech or behavior—that has both delighted and repelled men throughout history. In some periods of history it has flourished; in others it has been subdued or forced into disguise or driven underground. In primitive times, satire involved mockery and ridicule and was connected with ritual and magic, as in the rites of fertility and Dionysian revelry. As civilization developed, it became a literary form used by poets and dramatists and essayists. The Greeks practiced it; the Romans defined and in a sense refined it. Horace and another Roman, Juvenal, who lived a hundred years later, have exerted a tremendous influence on the development of Western satire; in fact, many literary historians classify *all* satire into two traditions: the embittered Juvenalian and the cheerful Horatian.

Satire appeals to certain deep-laid elements of human personality—to anger and contempt, to the love of mockery and of laughter; but wit and intellect are also directly and strongly involved. It may and often does have moral or social correction as one of its primary objectives. As a glance at the Table of Contents of this volume will indicate, the editors prefer an inclusive rather than an exclusive view of satire. Certainly they do not believe that it is a definable genre with its own method of establishing scene, character, and action. They would argue that much of the world's best satire is not totally satiric in tone and intent. The line between satire and comedy or humor is often difficult to establish with any degree of certainty.

This book does not attempt to survey the history of satire (although, to provide the student with an introduction to the subject, Richard Garnett's essay has been placed out of chronological order at the beginning of Part One) but to provide ample materials for the study of satire, both with regard to critical theory and to practice of the art as found in the writings of certain excellent satirists. It is designed as a source book for freshman composition, for courses in satire, and as a supplementary text for introductory classes in English, American, or world literature.

The selections dealing with critical theory in Part One are not exhaustive, but they are representative of many of the ideas and problems connected with the subject. Although the critical selections are arranged chronologically, they are also arranged in ascending order of complexity, with the more sophisticated treatments appearing toward the end of Part One. With this material as a starting point, the student can explore further the depth and variety of the subject as dealt with by the critics and, of course, by the satirists. As a second step in such an exploration, he may wish to consult the Bibliography at the end of the book.

Although a few of the selections at the beginning of Part Two are brief and simple, for the most part the editors have weighted that section with pieces of considerable length and complexity. If the student and the instructor wish to read further among the satirical poems, plays, stories, novels, and essays of the past twenty-five hundred years, they will, again, find suggestions in the Bibliography.

The glossary at the end of Part One includes key terms for the discussion and understanding of satire. Definitions of these terms are taken from Meyer Abrams' excellent handbook, *A Glossary of Literary Terms,* based on the original version by Dan S. Norton and Peters Rushton (New York: Rinehart, 1957). Together, the selections and the glossary in the Theory section should give the student the vocabulary and technique for dealing with the materials in the Practice section.

In the Suggestions for Study we have included comments on the authors in the Practice section and their works; questions for discussion and writing; and topics for research papers. These we offer with the object of stimulating close reading and discussion, and also with the hope that instructor and student will be encouraged to formulate questions and topics of their own.

The Bibliography is in two parts: a listing of important essays, articles and books about satire; and a chronological list of many famous satirists, with some of their works, not mentioned in the Suggestions for Study. Because satire may range in tone from indignation to whimsy, and because it may turn in the direction of tragedy rather than comedy, we have included in the second part of the Bibliography a few controversial works. Are Shakespeare's *Troilus and Cressida,* Eugene O'Neill's *Marco Millions,* or Franz Kafka's *The Trial* and *The Castle* really predominantly satirical in tone? The reader is invited to examine these works and formulate his own conclusions.

To give the student the feeling that he is using original sources, we have interpolated in superior brackets the pagination of the works from which we derived our selections. Whenever a page of the source concluded with a divided word, we have placed the page reference after the complete word. We have transcribed the texts as accurately as possible; we have, however, corrected obvious misprints, eliminated footnotes where feasible, and renumbered the remaining ones. Unspaced ellipses (...) are by the original author; spaced ellipses (. . .) indicate an editorial omission from the text.

We are grateful to everyone who offered suggestions for this book, particularly to Merton Rapp, editor, satirist, and friend.

C. A. A.

G. D. S.

CONTENTS

vii

PART ONE

THEORY

RICHARD GARNETT

Satire

FROM   *Encyclopaedia   Britannica,*
14th ed. Chicago: Encyclopaedia
Britannica, Inc., 1959. 24 vols. Reprinted by permission from *Encyclopaedia Britannica,* Vol. XX, pp.
5–6, © 1959.

Satire, in its literary aspect, may be defined as the expression in adequate terms of the sense of amusement or disgust excited by the ridiculous or unseemly, provided that humour is a distinctly recognizable element, and that the utterance is invested with literary form. Without humour, satire is invective; without literary form, it is mere clownish jeering. The first exercise of satire no doubt consisted in gibing at personal defects. To dignify satire by rendering it the instrument of morality or the associate of poetry was a development implying considerable advance in the literary art. In the accounts that have come down to us of the writings of Archilochus, the first great master of satire, we seem to trace the elevation of the instrument of private animosity to an element in public life. Simonides of Amorgus and Hipponax were distinguished like Archilochus for the bitterness of their attacks on individuals, with which the former combined a strong ethical feeling and the latter a bright active fancy. The loss of their writings, which would have thrown great light on the politics as well as the manners of Greece, is to be lamented. With Hipponax the direct line of Greek satire is interrupted; but two new forms of literary composition, capable of being the vehicles of satire, almost simultaneously appear. Although the original intention of fable does not seem to have been satirical, its adaptability to satiric purposes was soon discovered. A far more important step was the elevation of the rude fun of rustic merry-makings to a literary status by the evolution of the drama from the Bacchic festival. The means had now been found of allying the satiric spirit with exalted poetry, and their union was consummated in the comedies of Aristophanes.

A rude form of satire had existed in Italy from an early date in the shape of the Fescennine verses, the rough and licentious pleasantry of the vintage and harvest. As in Greece, these eventually were developed into a rude drama. Verse, "like to the Fescennine verses in point of style and manner," was added to accompany the mimetic action, and these probably improvised compositions were entitled *Saturae*, a term denoting *miscellany*, and derived from the *satura lanx*, "a charger filled with the first-fruits of the year's produce."

The Roman people thus had originated the name of satire, and, in so far as the Fescennine drama consisted of raillery and ridicule, possessed the thing also; but it had not yet assumed a literary form among them. The real inventor of Roman satire is Gaius Lucilius (148–103 B.C.). The fragments of Lucilius preserved are scanty, but the verdict of Horace, Cicero and Quintilian demonstrates that he was a considerable poet. It is needless to dwell on compositions so universally known as the Satires of Lucilius's successor Horace, in whose hands this class of composition received a new development, becoming genial, playful and persuasive. The didactic element preponderates still more in the philosophical satires of Persius. Yet another form of satire, the rhetorical, was carried to the utmost limits of excellence by Juvenal, the first example of a great tragic satirist. Nearly at the same time Martial, improving on earlier Roman models now lost, gave that satirical turn to the epigram which it only exceptionally possessed in Greece, but has ever since retained. About the same time another variety of satire came into vogue, destined to become the most important of any. The Milesian tale, a form of entertainment probably of Eastern origin, grew in the hands of Petronius and Apuleius into the satirical romance, immensely widening the satirist's field and exempting him from the restraints of metre. Petronius's "Supper of Trimalchio" is the revelation of a new vein, never fully worked till our days. As the novel arose upon the ruins of the epic, so dialogue sprang up upon the wreck of comedy. In Lucian, comedy appears adapted to suit the exigencies of an age in which a living drama had become impossible. With him antique satire expires as a distinct branch of literature.

In the Byzantine empire, indeed, the link of continuity is unbroken, and such raillery of abuses as is possible under a despotism finds vent in pale copies of Lucian. The first really important satire, however, of the middle ages, is a product of western Europe, recurring to the primitive form of fable, upon which, nevertheless, it constitutes a decided advance. *Reynard the Fox* . . . , a genuine expression of the shrewd and homely Teutonic mind, is a landmark in literature. It gave the beast-epic a development of which the ancients had not dreamed. About the same time, probably, the popular instinct, perhaps deriving a hint from Rabbinical literature, fashioned Morolf, the prototype of Sancho Panza, the incarnation of sublunar mother-wit contrasted with the starry wisdom of Solomon; and the *Till Eulenspiegel* is a kindred Teutonic creation, but later and less significant. *Piers Ploughman*, the next great work of the class, adapts the apocalyptic machinery of monastic and anchoritic vision to the purposes of satire. The clergy were scourged with their own rod by a poet and a Puritan too earnest to be urbane. The Renaissance, restoring the knowledge of classic models, enlarged the armoury of the satirist.

Partly, perhaps, because Erasmus was no poet, the Lucianic dialogue was the form in the ascendant of his age. Erasmus not merely employed it against superstition and ignorance with infinite and irresistible pleasantry, but fired by his example a bolder writer, untrammelled by the dignity of an arbiter in the republic of letters. The ridicule of Ulric von Hutten's *Epistolae obscurorum virorum* is annihilating, and the art of putting the ridicule into the mouth of the victim is perhaps the most deadly shaft in the quiver of sarcasm. It was afterwards used with even more pointed wit though with less exuberance of humour by Pascal. Sir Thomas More cannot be accounted a satirist, but his idea of an imaginary commonwealth embodied the germ of much subsequent satire.

In the succeeding period politics take the place of literature and [5] religion, producing in France the *Satyre Ménippée,* elsewhere the satirical romance as represented by the Argenis of Barclay, which may be defined as the adaptation of the style of Petronius to State affairs. In Spain, where no freedom of criticism existed, the satiric spirit took refuge in the *novela picaresca,* the prototype of Le Sage and the ancestor of Fielding; Quevedo revived the mediaeval device of the vision as the vehicle of reproof; and Cervantes's immortal work might be classed as a satire were it not so much more. About the same time we notice the appearance of direct imitation of the Roman satirists in English literature in the writings of Donne, Hall and Marston. The prodigious development of the drama at this time absorbed much talent that would otherwise have been devoted to satire proper. Most of the great dramatists of the 17th century were more or less satirists, Molière perhaps the most consummate that ever existed; but, with an occasional exception like *Les Précieuses ridicules,* the range of their works is too wide to admit of their being regarded as satires. The next great example of unadulterated satire is Butler's *Hudibras.* Dignified political satire, bordering on invective, was carried to perfection in Dryden's *Absalom and Achitophel.* In France Boileau was long held to have attained the *ne plus ultra* of the Horatian style in satire and of the mock-heroic, but Pope was soon to show that further progress was possible in both. The polish, point and concentration of Pope remain unsurpassed, as do the amenity of Addison and the daring yet severely logical imagination of Swift; while the *History of John Bull* places their friend Arbuthnot in the first rank of political satirists.

The 18th century was, indeed, the age of satire. Serious poetry had for the time worn itself out; the most original geniuses of the age are decidedly prosaic, and Pope, though a true poet, is less of a poet than Dryden. In process of time imaginative power revives, but meanwhile Fielding and Smollett have fitted the novel to be the vehicle of satire and much beside, and the literary stage has for a time been almost wholly engrossed by a collossal satirist, a man who has dared the universal application of Shaftesbury's maxim that ridicule is the test of truth. The world had never before seen a satirist on the scale of Voltaire, nor had satire ever played such a part as a factor in impending change. As a master of sarcastic mockery he is unsurpassed; his manner is entirely his own; and he is one of the most intensely national of writers, notwithstanding his vast obligations to English humorists, statesmen and philosophers. English humour also played an important part in the literary regeneration of Germany, where Lessing, imbued with Pope but not mastered by him, showed how powerful an auxiliary satire can be to criticism. Another great German writer, Wieland, owes little to the English, but adapts Lucian and Petronius to the 18th century with playful if somewhat mannered grace. Goethe and Schiller, Scott and Wordsworth, are now at hand, and as imagination gains ground satire declines. Byron, who in the 18th century would have been the greatest of satirists, is hurried by the spirit of his age into passion and description, bequeathing, however, a splendid proof of the possibility of allying satire with sublimity in his *Vision of Judgment*. Two great satiric figures remain—one representative of his nation, the other most difficult to class. In all the characteristics of his genius Thackeray is thoroughly English; his satire is a thoroughly British article, a little solid, a little wanting in finish, but honest, weighty and durable. But Heine hardly belongs to any nation or country, time or place. In him the satiric spirit, long confined to established literary forms, seems to obtain unrestrained freedom.

In no age was the spirit of satire so generally diffused as in the 19th century, but many of its eminent writers, while bordering on the domains of satire, escape the definition of satirist. The term cannot be properly applied to Dickens, the keen observer of the oddities of human life; or to George Eliot, the critic of its emptiness when not inspired by a worthy purpose; or to Balzac, the painter of French society; or to Trollope, the mirror of the middle classes of England. If *Sartor Resartus* could be regarded as a satire, Carlyle would rank among the first of satirists; but the satire, though very obvious, rather accompanies than inspires the composition. The number of minor satirists of merit, on the other hand, is legion. James Russell Lowell's *Biglow Papers* represent the highest moral level yet attained by satire. Mallock, in his *New Republic,* made the most of personal mimicry, the lowest form of satire; Samuel Butler *(Erewhon)* holds an inverting mirror to the world's face with imperturbable gravity; the humour of Bernard Shaw has always an essential character of satire—the sharpest social lash. One remarkable feature of the modern age is the union of caricature . . . with literature.[6]

HORACE

FROM *Satires*, First Series, IV [*c.* 35
B.C.]. In *The Works of Horace*,
translated by C. Smart. London:
George Bell & Sons, 1888, pp. 154–
159.

. . . Now I shall only consider this point, whether this satiric
kind of writing be deservedly an object of your suspicion. . . . You, says
he, delight to hurt people, and this you do out of a mischievous disposition. From what source do you throw this calumny upon me? Is any
one then your voucher, with whom I have lived? He who backbites
his absent friend, who does not defend, at another's accusing him;
who affects to raise loud laughs in company, and has the reputation
of a funny fellow who can feign things he never saw; who can not
keep secrets; [157] he is a dangerous man: be you, Roman, aware of
him. . . .

But do I appear malignant, if I have laughed because the fop Rufil-
lus smells all perfumes, and Gorgonius, like a he-goat, appears invidious
and a snarler? If by any means mention happen to be made of the
thefts of Petillius Capitolinus 1 in your company, you defend him after
your manner: [as thus] Capitolinus has had me for a companion and
a friend from childhood, and being applied to, has done many things
on my account: and I am glad that he lives secure in the city; but I
wonder, notwithstanding, how he evaded that sentence. This is the
very essence of black malignity, this is mere malice itself: which crime,
that it shall be far remote from my writings, and prior to them from
my mind, I promise, if I can take upon me to promise anything sin-
cerely of myself. If I shall say anything too freely, if perhaps too
ludicrously, you must favor me by your indulgence. . . .

For my excellent father inured me to this custom, that by noting
each particular vice I might avoid it. . . . When he exhorted me that
I should live thriftily, frugally, and content with what he had provided
for me, it was a strong lesson to hinder any one from squandering away
his patrimony. [158] . . . From this method of education I am clear from
all such vices, as bring destruction along with them; by lighter foibles,
and such as you may excuse, I am possessed. . . . [So] when I have any

---

1 An ancient commentator tells us that Petillius was governor of the Capitol,
that he was accused of stealing a golden crown of Jupiter but was acquitted by the
favor of Augustus Caesar. The other names are probably fictitious. [Ed.]

leisure, I amuse myself with my papers [satires]. This is one of those lighter foibles: to which if you do not grant your indulgence, a numerous band of poets shall come, which will take my part.[159] . . .

JUVENAL

FROM *First Satire* [*c.* 110 A.D.], translated by John Dryden. In *The Works of John Dryden,* edited by Sir Walter Scott and revised by George Saintsbury. Edinburgh: William Paterson, 1882–1893. Vol. XIII, pp. 124–134.

. . . since the world with writing is possest,
I'll versify in spite; and do my best
To make as much waste paper as the rest.
But why I lift aloft the satire's rod,
And tread the path which famed Lucilius trod,
Attend the causes which my Muse have led:[126] . . .
Such fulsome objects meeting everywhere,
'Tis hard to write, but harder to forbear.
To view so lewd a town, and to refrain,
What hoops of iron could my spleen contain!
When pleading Matho, borne abroad for air,
With his fat paunch fills his new-fashioned chair,
And after him the wretch in pomp conveyed,
Whose evidence his lord and friend betrayed,
And but the wished occasion does attend
From the poor nobles the last spoils to rend,
Whom even spies dread as their superior fiend,
And bribe with presents; or, when presents fail,
They send their prostituted wives for bail:
When night-performance holds the place of merit,
And brawn and back the next of kin disinherit;
(For such good parts are in preferment's way,)
The rich old madam never fails to pay
Her legacies, by Nature's standard given,
One gains an ounce, another gains eleven:
A dear-bought bargain, all things duly weighed,
For which their thrice concocted blood is paid.[127] . . .
What indignation boils within my veins,

When perjured guardians, proud with impious gains,
Choke up the streets, too narrow for their trains!
Whose wards, by want betrayed, to crimes are led
Too foul to name, full fulsome to be read!
When he who pilled [1] his province 'scapes the laws,
And keeps his money, though he lost his cause;
His fine begged off, contemns his infamy,
Can rise at twelve, and get him drunk ere three:
Enjoys his exile, and condemned in vain,
Leaves thee, prevailing province, to complain.[128] . . .

BEN JONSON

FROM Prologue, *Every Man in His Humour* [1598]. In *The Works of Ben Jonson*, edited by Peter Whalley. London: D. Midwinter *et al.*, 1756. Vol. I, p. 19.

. . . [My play shows] deeds, and language, such as men do use,
And persons, such as Comedy would chuse,
When she would shew an image of the times,
And sport with human follies, not with crimes.
Except we make 'em such, by loving still
Our popular errors, when we know th' are ill.
I mean such errors as you'll all confess,
By laughing at them, they deserve no less:
Which when you heartily do, there's hope left then,
You, that have so grac'd monsters, may like men.[19]

FROM Opening Speech, *Every Man out of His Humour* [1599]. In *The Works of Ben Jonson*. Vol. I, pp. 141–142.

. . . Who is so patient of this impious world,
That he can check his spirit, or rein his tongue?
Or who hath such a dead unfeeling sense,
That heaven's horrid thunders cannot wake?

---

1 Pillaged. [Ed.]

To see the earth crackt with the weight of sin,
Hell gaping under us, and o'er our heads
Black rav'nous ruin, with her sail-stretch'd wings,[141]
Ready to sink us down, and cover us.
Who can behold such prodigies as these,
And have his lips seal'd up? Not I: my soul
Was never ground into such oily colours,
To flatter vice, and daub iniquity:
But (with an armed and resolved hand)
I'll strip the ragged follies of the time
Naked as at their birth: . . .
. . . and with a whip of steel
Print wounding lashes in their iron ribs.[142]

JOSEPH HALL

FROM *Virgidemiarum*, Book V,
Third Satire [1598]. Printed for R.
Clements, Oxford, 1753, pp. 92–94.

. . . The satire should be like the porcupine,
That shoots sharp quils out in each angry line,
And wounds the blushing cheeke, and fiery eye,
Of him that hears, and readeth guiltily.
Ye antique satires, how I blesse your dayes
That brook'd your bolder stile, their own dispraise,
And well near wish, yet joy my wish is vaine,
I had been then, or they been now againe!
For now our eares been of more brittle mold,
Than those dull earthen eares that were of old:
Sith theirs, like anvils, bore the hammer's head,
Our glasse can never touch unshivered.[92] . . .

DUKE OF BUCKINGHAM, JOHN DRYDEN, et al.[1]

FROM An Essay upon Satire [1680]. In The Works of John Dryden, edited by Sir Walter Scott and revised by George Saintsbury. Edinburgh: William Paterson, 1882–1893. Vol. XV, pp. 201–213.

How dull, and how insensible a beast
Is man, who yet would lord it o'er the rest!
Philosophers and poets vainly strove
In every age the lumpish mass to move;
But those were pedants when compar'd with these,
Who know not only to instruct, but please.
Poets alone found the delightful way,
Mysterious morals gently to convey
In charming numbers; so that as men grew
Pleased with their poems, they grew wiser too.
Satire has always shone among the rest,
And is the boldest way, if not the best,
To tell men freely of their foulest faults;
To laugh at their vain deeds, and vainer thoughts.
In satire, too, the wise took different ways,
To each deserving its peculiar praise.
Some did all folly with just sharpness blame,
Whilst others laughed and scorned them into shame.
But of these two, the last succeeded best,
As men aim rightest when they shoot in jest.
Yet, if we may presume to blame our guides,
And censure those, who censure all besides,
In other things they justly are preferred;
In this alone methinks the ancients erred:
Against the grossest follies they declaim;
Hard they pursue, but hunt ignoble game.[201]

---

1 The evidence concerning the authorship of this poem is inconclusive. Lord Rochester affected to believe Dryden the author and, because of an attack upon himself in the poem, had Dryden assaulted and beaten in Rose Alley. John Sheffield, the Duke of Buckingham, emphatically denied Dryden's authorship and claimed the poem as his own. So far as is known, Dryden made no claim; but Dean Lockier, who knew Dryden well, states that it was "corrected a good deal by Dryden." [Ed.]

Nothing is easier than such blots to hit,
And 'tis the talent of each vulgar wit:
Besides, 'tis labour lost; for, who would preach
Morals to Armstrong, or dull Aston teach?
'Tis being devout at play, wise at a ball,
Or bringing wit and friendship to Whitehall.
But with sharp eyes those nicer faults to find,
Which lie obscurely in the wisest mind,
That little speck which all the rest does spoil,—
To wash off that would be a noble toil;
Beyond the loose-writ libels of this age,
Or the forced scenes of our declining stage;
Above all censure, too, each little wit
Will be so glad to see the greater hit;
Who, judging better, though concerned the most,
Of such correction will have cause to boast.
In such a satire all would seek a share,
And every fool will fancy he is there.[202] . . .

JONATHAN SWIFT

FROM *The Intelligencer,* Number
III [1728]. In *The Works of Jonathan Swift,* edited by Sir Walter
Scott. Boston: Houghton Mifflin,
1883. Vol. IX, pp 86–93.

. . . a taste for humour is in some manner fixed to the very nature
of man, and generally obvious to the vulgar; except upon subjects
too refined, and superior to their understanding.

And as this taste of humour is purely natural, so is humour itself;
neither is it a talent confined to men of wit or learning; for we observe
it sometimes among common servants, and the meanest of the people,
while the very owners are often ignorant of the gift they possess. . . .

By what disposition of the mind, what influence of the stars, or
what situation of the climate, this endowment is bestowed upon mankind, may be a question fit for philosophers to discuss. It is certainly
the best ingredient toward that kind of satire which is most useful,
and gives the least offence; which, instead of lashing, laughs men out
of their follies and vices; and is the character that gives Horace the
preference to Juvenal.

And, although some things are too serious, solemn, or sacred, to be turned into ridicule, yet the abuses of them are certainly not; since it is allowed that corruptions in religion, politics, and law, may be proper topics for this kind of satire.

There are two ends that men propose in writing satire; one of them less noble than the other, as regarding nothing farther than the private satisfaction and pleasure of the writer; but without any [88] view toward personal malice; the other is a public spirit, prompting men of genius and virtue to mend the world as far as they are able. And as both these ends are innocent, so the latter is highly commendable. With regard to the former, I demand, whether I have not as good a title to laugh as men have to be ridiculous; and to expose vice, as another has to be vicious. If I ridicule the follies and corruptions of a court, a ministry, or a senate, are they not amply paid by pensions, titles, and power, while I expect and desire no other reward, than that of laughing with a few friends in a corner? Yet, if those who take offence think me in the wrong, I am ready to change the scene with them whenever they please.

But, if my design be to make mankind better, then I think it is my duty; at least, I am sure it is the interest of those very courts, and ministers, whose follies or vices I ridicule, to reward me for my good intention; for if it be reckoned a high point of wisdom to get the laughers on our side, it is much more easy, as well as wise, to get those on our side who can make millions laugh when they please.[89] . . .

EDWARD YOUNG

FROM Preface to *Love of Fame, The Universal Passion* [1728]. In *The Poetical Works of Edward Young.* London: Ward, Lock & Co., Ltd., n.d. pp. 376–378.

These Satires have been favourably received at home and abroad. I am not conscious of the least malevolence to any particular person through all the characters, though some persons may be so selfish as to engross a general application to themselves. . . .

But it is possible that satire may not do much good; men may rise in their affections to their follies, as they do to their friends, when they are abused by others. It is much to be feared, that misconduct will never be chased out of the world by satire; all, therefore, that is to be said for it is, that misconduct will certainly never be chased out of the world by satire if no satires are written. Nor is that term unapplicable to graver compositions. Ethics, Heathen and Christian, and the scriptures themselves, are, in a great measure, a satire on the weakness and iniquity of men; and some part of that satire is in verse, too. . . . Nay, historians themselves may be considered as satirists, and satirists most severe; since such are most human actions, that to relate is to expose them.

No man can converse much in the world, but, at what he meets with, he must either be insensible, or grieve, or be angry, or smile. Some passion (if we are not impassive) must be moved; for the general conduct of mankind is by no means a thing indifferent to a reasonable and virtuous man. Now, to smile at it, and turn it into ridicule, I think most eligible; as it hurts ourselves least, and gives vice and folly the greatest offence.[376]

Laughing at the misconduct of the world will, in a great measure, ease us of any more disagreeable passion about it. One passion is more effectually driven out by another than by reason, whatever some may teach.[377] . . .

HENRY FIELDING

> FROM Preface, *Joseph Andrews* [1742]. In *The Works of Henry Fielding*, edited by G. H. Maynadier. Philadelphia: John D. Morris & Co., 1902. Vol. I, pp. xxix –xxxviii.

. . . it may seem remarkable, that Aristotle, who is so fond and free of definitions, hath not thought proper to define the Ridiculous. Indeed, where he tells us it is proper to comedy, he hath remarked that villainy is not its object: but he hath not, as I remember, positively asserted what is. . . .

The only source of the true Ridiculous (as it appears to me) is affectation. But though it arises from one spring only, when we consider the infinite streams into which this one branches, we shall presently cease to admire at the copious field it affords to an observer. Now, affectation proceeds from one of these two causes, vanity or hypocrisy: for as vanity puts us on affecting false characters, in order to purchase applause; so hypocrisy sets us on an endeavour [xxxiv] to avoid censure, by concealing our vices under an appearance of their opposite virtues. . . .

From the discovery of this affectation arises the Ridiculous, which always strikes the reader with surprize and pleasure; and that in a higher and stronger degree when the affectation arises from hypocrisy, than when from vanity; for to discover any one to be the exact reverse of what he affects, is more surprizing, and consequently more ridiculous, than to find him a little deficient in the quality he desires the reputation of.[xxxv] . . . Now, from affectation only, the misfortunes and calamities of life, or the imperfections of nature, may become the objects of ridicule.[xxxvi] . . .

FROM   Dedication,   Tom   Jones
[1749]. In   The   Works   of   Henry
Fielding. Vol II, pp. xxvi–xxxi.

. . . Besides displaying that beauty of virtue which may attract the admiration of mankind, I have attempted to engage a stronger motive to human action in her favour, by convincing men, that their true interest directs them to a pursuit of her. For this purpose I have shown that no acquisitions of guilt can compensate the loss of that solid inward comfort of mind, which is the sure companion of innocence and virtue; nor can in the least balance the evil of that horror and anxiety which, in their room, guilt introduces into our bosoms. And again, that as these acquisitions are in themselves generally worthless, so are the means to attain them not only base and infamous but at best uncertain, and always full of danger. Lastly, I have endeavoured strongly to inculcate, that virtue and innocence can scarce ever be injured but by indiscretion; and that it is this alone which often betrays them into the snares that deceit and villainy spread for them. A moral which I have the more industriously laboured, as the teaching it is, of all others, the likeliest to be attended with success; since, I believe, it is much easier to make good men wise, than to make bad men good.

For these purposes I have employed all the wit and humour of which I am master in the following history; wherein I have endeavoured to laugh mankind out of their favourite follies and vices.[xxx] . . .

GEORGE MEREDITH

FROM *The Idea of Comedy and the Uses of the Comic Spirit* [1877]. New York: Charles Scribner's Sons, 1897.

. . . Generally . . . the English elect excel in satire, and they are noble humourists. The national disposition is for hard-hitting, with a moral purpose to sanction it; or for a rosy, sometimes larmoyant, geniality, not unmanly in its verging upon tenderness, and with a singular attraction for thick-headedness, to decorate it with asses' ears and the most beautiful sylvan haloes. But the Comic is a different spirit.

You may estimate your capacity for Comic perception by being able to detect the ridicule of them you love, without loving them less: and more by being able to see yourself somewhat ridiculous in dear eyes, and accepting the correction their image of you proposes.[72] . . .

If you detect the ridicule, and your kindliness is chilled by it, you are slipping into the grasp of Satire.

If instead of falling foul of the ridiculous person with a satiric rod, to make him writhe and shriek aloud, you prefer to sting him under a semi-caress, by which he shall in his anguish be rendered dubious whether indeed anything has hurt him, you are an engine of Irony.

If you laugh all round him, tumble him, roll him about, deal him a smack, and drop a tear on him, own his likeness to you and yours to[73] your neighbour, spare him as little as you shun, pity him as much as you expose, it is a spirit of Humour that is moving you.

The Comic, which is the perceptive, is the governing spirit, awakening and giving aim to these powers of laughter, but it is not to be confounded with them: it enfolds a thinner form of them, differing from satire, in not sharply driving into the quivering sensibilities, and from humour, in not comforting them and tucking them up, or indicating a broader than the range of this bustling world to them.[74] . . .

One excellent test of the civilization of a country, as I have said, I take to be the flourishing of the Comic idea and Comedy; and the test of true Comedy is that it shall awaken thoughtful laughter.

If you believe that our civilization is founded in common-sense (and it is the first condition of sanity to believe it), you will, when contemplating men, discern a Spirit overhead; not more heavenly than the light flashed upward from glassy surfaces, but luminous and watch-ful; never shooting beyond them, nor lagging in the rear; so closely attached to them that it may be taken for a slavish reflex, until its features are studied. It has the sage's brows,[82] and the sunny malice of a faun lurks at the corners of the half-closed lips drawn in an idle wariness of half tension.[83] . . .

NORTHROP FRYE

The Nature of Satire

FROM *The University of Toronto Quarterly*, XIV (October 1944), 75–89. Reprinted by permission of the author.

The word "satire" belongs to that fairly large class of words which have two meanings, one specific and technical, the other more general. In Roman literature, for instance, the study of satire is essentially the study of a specific literary form, or rather two literary forms, of that name: the poetic satire developed by Horace and Juvenal and the prose or "Menippean" satire developed by Petronius and (in Greek) Lucian. In English literature, with which we are at present concerned, the satire may also be and has been the name of a form. Juvenal and Horace are the models of Donne and Pope, and Lucian is the model of Swift. But this idea of a satire form is in English literature a Renais-sance and neo-Classical idea: it hardly existed in the Middle Ages, and it hardly exists now, though we still have our Hilaire Bellocs and Roy Campbells trying to blow up its dying fire with antique bellows. The word now means a tone or quality of art which we may find in any form: in a play by Shaw, a novel by Sinclair Lewis or a cartoon by Low. Hence in dealing with English satire we must include not only Swift and Pope, who worked with the traditional models, but all the writers who have ignored the models but have preserved the tone and attitude of satire. A distinction essential to the treatment of Roman, and perhaps also of French, satire is quite unnecessary in English literature, which has never taken kindly to strict forms.

But this, like all our cherished freedoms, was won for us by our ancestors. In the year 1597 Joseph Hall, who later became a bishop, published three books of what he called "Toothless Satires," following them with three books of "Biting Satires." Hall begins by saying that he is introducing something radically new into English literature:

I first adventure, follow me who list,
And be the second English satirist.

He does not mean that he has never heard of the *Canterbury Tales* or *Piers Plowman:* he means that from the point of view of an imitator of Juvenal and Horace they are not satires. From this point of view his claim to be first is more or less correct: that is, he was about fourth. Later in his life Bishop Hall became involved in a controversy with Milton, who did not care for bishops. Milton carefully goes over Hall's literary output to show, as the custom then was, that his adversary had been a fool from birth. When he comes to the "Toothless Satires" he says that this so-called first English satirist might have learned better from *Piers Plowman,* besides other works, and adds: "But that such a Poem should be toothless I still affirm it to be a bull, taking away the essence of that which it calls itself. For if it bite neither the persons nor the vices, how is it a Satyr, and if it bite either, how is it toothless, so that toothless Satyrs are as much as if [75] he had said toothless teeth." If there can be no toothless satires, it is the tone that makes a work of art a satire: if Langland is a great satirist because of his satiric attitude, Swift and Pope are so for the same reason, not because of their form. On this point posterity has decided for Milton against the bishop.

As a tone or attitude, then, two things are essential to satire. One is wit or humour, the other an object of attack. Attack without humour, or pure denunciation, thus forms one of the boundaries of satire; humour without attack, the humour of pure gaiety or exuberance, is the other. Now these two qualities, it is obvious, are not simply different, but opposed. For satire one needs both pleasure in conflict and determination to win; both the heat of battle and the coolness of calculation. To have too much hatred and too little gaiety will upset the balance of tone. Man is a precocious monkey, and he wins his battles by the sort of cunning that is never far from a sense of mockery. All over the world people have delighted in stories of how some strong but stupid monster was irritated by a tiny human hero into a blind, stampeding fury, and how the hero, by biding his time and keeping cool, polished off his Blunderbore or Polyphemus at leisure. In literature, too, the slugging haymaker has no more chance against an expert pen-fencer than a bull in a bullfight. Milton, a deeply serious prophet haunted by the sense that he was responsible both to God and man for making the best use of his genius, had no gift for satire, and when we see this blind giant flailing at his buzzing assailants, we can only be thankful that he never encountered a first-rate satirist. The same is true of many romantics. Lord Castlereagh, who did not kill himself before he had achieved an all-time high in unpopularity with poets, is described by Shelley, along with his confederate Sidmouth, as:

two vultures sick for battle,
Two scorpions under one wet stone,
Two bloodless wolves whose dry throats rattle,
Two crows perched on the murrained cattle,
Two vipers tangled into one.

This is very fine, but it is not fine satire. The poet is too angry and his victims too abstract. Let us try Byron:

Cold-blooded, smooth-faced, placid miscreant!
Dabbling its sleek young hands in Erin's gore,
And thus for wider carnage taught to pant,
Transferr'd to gorge upon a sister shore,
The vulgarest tool that Tyranny could want,
With just enough of talent, and no more,
To lengthen fetters of another fix'd,
And offer poison long already mix'd.

Byron wrote some great satire, but this is evidently not it. Let us turn to Tom Moore:

Why is a Pump like Viscount Castlereagh?
Because it is a slender thing of wood,[76]
That up and down its awkward arm doth sway,
And coolly spout and spout and spout away,
In one weak, washy, everlasting flood!

That does it exactly. It is rather flattering to one's ego to be called a wolf or a scorpion; there is a certain thrill in being thought a dark and terrible emissary of the demonic powers. But nobody likes to be called a pump, at any rate not with so much enthusiasm.

The satirist in whom the gift of seeing things absurdly appears most clearly as exuberance of mind is Dryden. He takes a physical pleasure in his victims; he transforms them into fantastic dinosaurs of bulging flesh and peanut brains. He is really impressed by the great bulk of his Falstaffian Og:

Round as a globe, and liquor'd every chink,
Goodly and great he sails behind his link.

He really admires the furious energy of the poet Doeg, and his heart is warmed by the spectacle of that noble Buzzard, Bishop Burnet:

A portly prince, and goodly to the sight ...
A prophet form'd to make a female proselyte.

The great effectiveness of such satire comes from the victim's realization that no one could laugh at him with such genuine pleasure unless he were genuinely amused. In other words, one cannot merely adopt satire to express a personal or moral feeling; one must be born with the sardonic vision.

Now both humour and attack depend on certain conventions which are assumed to be in existence before the satirist begins to write. The world of humour is a rigidly stylized world in which generous Scotchmen, obedient wives, beloved mothers-in-law and professors with presence of mind are not permitted to exist. All humour demands common agreement that certain things, such as a picture of a wife beating her husband in a comic strip, are funny. To introduce a comic strip in which a husband beats his wife would distress and perplex the average reader: it would mean learning a new convention. Similarly, in order to attack anything, satirist and audience must agree on its undesirability. The misery and cold of German soldiers in a Russian winter is matter for satire in our newspapers; the misery and cold of Russians is not.

Much in these conventions is only fashion, and quantities of scandal, gossip, pasquinades and lampoons have gone the way of all flashes. Even our sense of what constitutes absurdity has changed. "We laugh at deformed creatures," says Sir Philip Sidney, but he does not speak for the twentieth century. That Milton was blind, Dryden poor and Pope a cripple does not seem as amusing to us as to their contemporary enemies. When Nashe tells of the trick Jack Wilton played on a Captain, and how the best of the joke was, that the Captain was arrested as a spy, racked and flogged, we stop laughing long before Nashe does. Ben Jonson was a bricklayer's stepson, and his many enemies expected every reference to [77] bricklaying they made to be followed by knowing winks, leers and guffaws. But the whole social attitude which enabled that to be humorous has disappeared, and the satire with it. National hatreds are no longer-lived. In the Hundred Years' War, Laurence Minot vituperated the French; at the time of Flodden, Skelton poured scorn on the Scotch; when Holland was England's trade rival, Marvell persuaded himself that he disliked the Dutch; in Napoleon's time Canning's poetry of the *Anti-Jacobin* held all revolutionary ideas up to ridicule. Many of these wrote excellent satire, but it has gone stale and mouldy, and at best is something to be rescued. Now no one would claim that Chaucer or Pope or Swift had any Olympian superiority to the passions and prejudices of their times. To what, then, do they owe their amazing vitality and power of survival?

Denunciation, or humourless attack, is, we said, one of the boundaries of satire. It is a very hazy boundary, because invective is one of the most readable forms of literary art, just as panegyric is one of the dullest. It is simply an established datum of literature that we love to hear people cursed and are bored with hearing them praised; and almost any denunciation, if vigorous enough, is followed by a reader with the kind of pleasure that soon breaks into a smile. Now invective is never the expression of merely personal hatred, whatever the motivation for it may be, because the words for it simply do not exist in the language. About the only ones we have are derived from the animal world, but calling a man a swine or a skunk or even a cholera germ is merely an eructation. For effective attack we must reach some kind of impersonal level, and that commits the attacker, if only by implication, to a moral standard. As Shakespeare's Thersites says of Menelaus, "to what form, but that he is, should wit larded with malice, and malice forced with wit, turn him to? To an ass, were nothing; he is both ass and ox; to an ox, were nothing; he is both ox and ass." In the long run, then, the tone of antagonism or attack in satire must imply an assertion and a defence of a moral principle. The satirist, when attacked, takes a very high moral line. He is a prophet sent to lash the vices and follies of the time, and he will not stop until he has cleansed the foul body of the infected world. Pope says:

> Hear this, and tremble! you, who 'scape the Laws,
> Yes, while I live, no rich or noble knave
> Shall walk the World, in credit, to his grave,
> To VIRTUE ONLY and HER FRIENDS A FRIEND,
> The world beside may murmur, or commend.

That, you see, is what Pope is really doing when he is reflecting on the cleanliness of the underwear worn by the lady who had jilted him. And as far as the survival power of his satire goes, he is quite right. Hence satire based on persisting moral sentiments has a better chance for immortality than satire based on fluctuating ones, satire which strikes roots in the soil of stupidity, treachery, slovenliness, hypocrisy, and all the other things that are as evil today as in Chaucer's time.[78]

Again, we said that the humour of gaiety was the other boundary of satire. But as Juvenal truly said that whatever men do is the subject of satire, and that in consequence it is difficult not to write it, it follows that most humorous situations are at least indirectly satiric. Nonsatiric humour tends to fantasy: one finds it most clearly in the fairy worlds of Lewis Carroll, Edward Lear and Walt Disney, in Celtic romance and American tall tales. Yet even here one can never be sure, for the humour of fantasy is continually being pulled back into satire by means of that powerful undertow which we call allegory. The White Knight in Alice who felt that one should be provided for everything, and therefore put anklets around his horse's feet to guard against the bites of sharks, may pass without challenge. But what are we to make of the mob of hired revolutionaries in the same author's *Sylvie and Bruno*, who got their instructions mixed and yelled under the palace windows: "More taxes! less bread!"? Here we begin to sniff the acrid, pungent smell of satire. Those fantastic romances, *Gulliver's Travels, Utopia, Erewhon*, work on exactly the same principle.

Now just as denunciation contributes morality to satire, so exuberance or gaiety contributes to it absurdity or grotesqueness. It is absurdity of a special kind, which I should tentatively call a poetic imagination in reverse gear. The imagination of Quixote, who saw a windmill as a hundred-armed giant, was a genuinely poetic one, if over-literal in its application; but it is the business of the satirist to see giants as windmills, Castlereaghs as pumps. Poetry may deepen and intensify the imaginative impact of things; satire belittles and minimizes it. Allegory in high gear gives us a Spenser or a Bunyan; allegory in reverse gear gives us a *Tale of a Tub*. Poetry may be as primitive as you please, and may thrive on superstition or false belief: satire means civilization and a confidence in the invincibility of the intelligence. I should define satire, then, as poetry assuming a special function of analysis, that is, of breaking up the lumber of stereotypes, fossilized beliefs, superstitious terrors, crank theories, pedantic dogmatisms, oppressive fashions, and all other things that impede the free movement of society. I say free movement rather than progress: progress, besides implying a theory of history to which one may or may not subscribe, implies also that all satire is revolutionary, or at least progressive, which is nonsense. This does not explain the total effect of satire, as we shall see, but it covers its primary objectives.

For society to exist at all there must be a delegation of prestige and influence to organized groups: the church, the army, the medical and teaching professions, the government, all consist of individuals given more than individual power by the institution to which they belong. Whether they are given this power for good or for evil depends largely on them. If a satirist presents a clergyman, for instance, as a fool or a hypocrite, he is primarily attacking neither the man nor his church. The former is too petty and the latter carries him outside the range of satire. He is attacking [79] an evil man protected by the prestige of an institution. As such, he represents one of the stumbling-blocks in society which it is the satirist's business to clear out.

We have spoken of the resemblance of the giant-killing myth to the technique of satire: there is in both a victory of intelligence over stupid power. In the sort of case we are considering, the satirist's victim is a gigantic monster; monstrous because really a fool or a hypocrite while pretending to be otherwise; gigantic because protected by his position and by the prestige of the good men in it. The cowl might make the monk if it were not for the satirist. Hence, though Milton's etymology may be wrong, his principle is right: "for a Satyr as it was born out of a Tragedy, so ought to resemble his parentage, to strike high, and adventure dangerously at the most eminent vices among the greatest persons." The larger they come, the easier they fall.

When the Philistine giant comes out to battle with the children of light, he naturally expects to find someone his own size ready to meet him, someone who is head and shoulders over every man in Israel. Such a Titan would have to bear down his opponent by sheer weight of words, and hence be a master of that technique of torrential abuse which we call invective. And as invective is very close to moral denunciation, we should expect it to be a form closely allied to preaching.

Another reason for this is that the literary qualities necessary for good invective are essentially those of good swearing: a sense of rhythm, an unlimited vocabulary and a technical knowledge of the two subjects which ordinarily form the subject-matter of swearing, one of which is theology. Now if we want satire on military life and martial courage we should expect to find most of it in the army: *Don Quixote* could only have been the work of an old soldier. Similarly, we should not be surprised to find that the two greatest masters of invective, Rabelais and Swift, have been recruited from the clergy. The association between satire and preaching goes back at least to the Hebrew prophets, runs all through medieval sermons on the Seven Deadly Sins and reaches its peak with the Reformation, when controversy poured oil on the fires.

There is another reason why this last period, the sixteenth century, was the golden age of abuse. Controversy supplies the anger, but not the gaiety, of satire: for the source of the latter we must turn to the great influx of new words then coming in. The Elizabethans had a delight in words of a physical kind which we can hardly comprehend today, a kind of reversed drunkenness that comes from outpouring rather than intake. Words spawn and swarm in every corner of their writings: their expenditure of erudite technicalities, fantastically abusive epithets and dizzily inclusive compounds was as reckless as their resources were inexhaustible both in coinage and in the plunder of every language in Europe, living or dead. They could hardly touch a foreign language without gloating over their own superior resources. Thus Cotgrave's French Dictionary defines the[80] French word *lourdans* as: "a sot, dullard, grotnoll, jobernoll, blockhead; a lowt, lob, lusk, boarc, clown, churle, clusterfist; a proud, ignorant and unmannerly swaine." Rabelais tells of a man who retired to the country for quiet, and who found that the animals made such a noise that he could not sleep. Rabelais plagues him with nine sorts of animals; Urquhart of Cromarty, his Scotch translator, expands them to seventy. Urquhart, when not engaged in making Gargantua more Rabelaisian than Rabelais, was busy writing books with such titles as *Trissotetras*, *Pantochronochanon, Exkubalauron* and *Logopandecteison*. In an age when even pedantry could produce such a Holofernes, invective is not likely to die of malnutrition. Marston, Bishop Hall's chief follower, is put into a play by his enemy Ben Jonson, given a purge and made to vomit up some of his hard words. They include glibbery, lubrical, magnificate, turgidous, ventosity, oblatrant, furibund, fatuate, prorumped and obstupefact. Thomas Nashe, the greatest prose satirist of the period, calls his opponent, Gabriel Harvey, an impotent mote-catching carper, an indigested chaos of doctorship and a scholastic squitter-book. Here is one sentence from Burton's *Anatomy of Melancholy*, which, if not directly satirical in itself, certainly illustrates the method and technique of invective:

Every lover admires his mistress, though she be very deformed of herself, ill-favoured, wrinkled, pimpled, pale, red, yellow, tanned, tallow-faced, have a swollen juggler's platter face, or a thin, lean, chitty face, have clouds in her face, be crooked, dry, bald, goggle-eyed, blear-eyed, or with staring eyes, she looks like a squis'd cat, hold her head still awry, heavy, dull, hollow-eyed, black or yellow about the eyes, or squint-eyed, sparrow-mouthed, Persian hook-nosed, have a sharp fox-nose, a red nose, China flat, great nose, *nare simo patuloque*, a nose like a promontory, grubber-tushed, rotten teeth, black, uneven, brown teeth, beetle-browed, a witch's beard, her breath stink all over the room, her nose drop winter and summer, with a Bavarian poke under her chin, a sharp chin, lave-eared, with a long crane's neck, which stands awry too, *pendulis mammis*, "her dugs like two double jugs," or else no dugs, in that other extreme, bloody-fallen fingers, she have filthy, long unpared nails, scabbed hands or wrists, a tanned skin, a rotten carcass, crooked back, she stoops, is lame, splay-footed, "as slender in the middle as a cow in the waist," gouty legs, her ankles hang over her shoes, her feet stink, she breed lice, a mere changeling, a very monster, an oaf imperfect, her whole complexion savours, an harsh voice, incondite gesture, vile gait, a vast virago, or an ugly tit, a slug, a fat fustilugs, a truss, a long lean rawbone, a skeleton, a sneaker *(si qua latent meliora puta)*, and to thy judgment looks like a mard in a lanthorn, whom thou couldst not fancy for a word, but hatest, loathest, and wouldest have spit in her face, or blow thy nose in her bosom, *remedium amoris* to another man, a dowdy, a slut, a scold, a nasty, rank, rammy, filthy, beastly quean, dishonest peradventure, obscene, base, beggarly, rude, foolish, untaught, peevish, Irus' daughter, Thersites' sister, Grobian's scholar; if he love her once, he admires her for all this, he takes no notice of any such errors or imperfections of body or mind, *Ipsa haec delectant, veluti Balbinum polypus Agnae;* he had rather have her than any woman in the world.

Since Dryden, there has been little of this naïve and childlike quality in satire, which has trusted more to the rapier that stabs the heart than to the singlestick that breaks the head. Abuse of this kind is based on a solid physical laugh, an earthquake in miniature, a laugh which begins far down in the abdomen, bursts the vest buttons, rolls the stomach, shakes the [81] diaphragm, suffocates the throat, reddens the face and finally reduces the whole body to rolling and kicking in an epilepsy of joy, then, after quieting down, returns for the next few hours in a couple of dozen squalls of splutters, gasps and reminiscent chortles, and finally sinks into the subconscious to be left until called for. As Carlyle says:

How much lies in Laughter: the cipher-key, wherewith we decipher the whole man! Some men wear an everlasting barren simper; in the smile of others lies a cold glitter as of ice: the fewest are able to laugh, what can be called laughing, but only sniff and titter and snigger from the throat outwards; or at best, produce some whiffling husky cachinnation, as if they were laughing through wool: of none such comes good.

Urquhart of Cromarty, an ardent Royalist, is reputed to have laughed on King Charles' Restoration until he burst himself and died.

And anyone who has glanced at an old copy of *Punch* can see that their cartoons, with their enormous captions, elaborately festooned with garrulous explanations and parenthetic postscripts, are aimed at a John Bull or fox-hunting squire for whom a laugh was an exhausting indoor exercise. Such a fox-hunting squire might survive to hear himself described by Oscar Wilde as the unspeakable in pursuit of the uneatable. There is an entirely different kind of laughter; not the *forte* of invective but the *piano* of irony, which, like the poisoned rings of the Renaissance, distils its venom in a friendly handshake, unnoticed by its bulky victim.

For better or worse, it is the tiny David with his sudden and vicious stones who goes out to battle now, and the great Rabelaisian bellow has dropped out of literature. For that kind of satire flourishes in a world of solid assurances and unshakable values; the whole weight of a confident society is flung into the scales against limp affectation. The less sure society is of its assumptions, the more likely the satire is to take the line of irony, of the method laid down once for all in the dialogues of Plato.

It is impossible not to sympathize with the floundering red-faced brawlers in Plato, with the Thrasymachus or Callicles who is inexorably led on from one trap to another while Socrates sits quietly and smiles. Yet we know that they can never win, because they can never lay a finger on Socrates. Socrates pleads his own ignorance, convicts his opponents of equal ignorance, and there, in most of the shorter dialogues, we are. The master of irony has done nothing but sow doubt and confusion. He calls himself a midwife, but all he does is kill the mother and demonstrate that there is no child.

For irony is not simply the small man's way of fighting a bigger one: it is a kind of intellectual tear-gas that breaks the nerves and paralyses the muscles of everyone in its vicinity, an acid that will corrode healthy as well as decayed tissues. We have said that satire is primarily directed at the impediments of society; but irony has an automatically expansive and destroying force; it is a bomb dropped on an objective which, if it misses that, will at any rate hit something in an enemy's territory. Take, for example, the warfare of science against superstition. Here the satirists [82] have done famously. Chaucer and Ben Jonson riddled the alchemists with a cross-fire of their own jargon; Nashe and Swift hounded astrologers into premature graves; Browning's *Sludge the Medium* annihilated the spiritualists; and a rabble of occultists, numerologists, Pythagoreans and Rosicrucians lie dead in the wake of *Hudibras*. But when triumphant science turns to shake hands with the satirists, there is again that little prick of the poisoned ring. For all satirists are not so ready to see the sharp dividing line between alchemists and chemists, a Rosicrucian cell meeting and the Royal Society. Samuel Butler makes his scientists discover an elephant in the moon which turns out to be a mouse in the telescope. It does not matter; their scientific reputation is at stake, and an elephant in the moon it must be. Swift's Grand Academy of Lagado, in *Gulliver's Travels,* is a vast scientific laboratory in which professors are deeply engaged in such experiments as "to sow land with chaff, wherein he affirmed the true seminal virtue to be contained." In fact there seems to be as perennial a warfare between satire and all forms of science and philosophy, as between satire and superstition. What Rabelais and Erasmus thought of the scholastics, Swift thought of the Cartesians; and what Voltaire thought of the Leibnitzians, Samuel Butler II thought of the Darwinians. In every case it is not the doctrine but its application to society that is attacked; however, the satirist has a latent distrust of the adequacy of human reason that becomes most articulate in *Gulliver's Travels:*

> I was going on to more particulars, when my master commanded me to silence. He said whoever understood the nature of Yahoos might easily believe it possible for so vile an animal to be capable of every action I had named, if their strength and cunning equalled their malice. But when a creature pretending to reason could be capable of such enormities, he dreaded lest the corruption of that faculty might be worse than brutality itself. He seemed therefore confident, that instead of reason, we were only possessed of some quality fitted to increase our natural vices.

Similarly with religion. There is a great deal of hypocrisy and corruption in any church, and a great deal of superstition in popular worship. Any really devout person would welcome a satirist who cauterized such infections as an ally of true religion. But once a hypocrite who sounds exactly like a good man is sufficiently blackened, the good man himself may begin to seem a little dingier than he was. Thus Burns' Holy Willie is doubtless only a reprobate, but does not his confession make many others, who would say Amen to much of it, look a little like Holy Willies?

> When frae my mither's womb I fell,
> Thou might hae plunged me in hell,
> To gnash my gums, to weep and wail,
>   In burnin' lake,
> Where damned devils roar and yell,
>   Chain'd to a stake.
>
> Yet I am here a chosen sample,
> To show thy grace is great and ample;
> I'm here a pillar in thy temple,[83]
>   Strong as a rock,
> A guide, a buckler, an example
>   To a' thy flock.

Even the God Holy Willie is praying to begins to take on some of his features, just as the God of the Pharisee's prayer was a Pharisee. The

same thing happens to the treatment of superstition. In Lilliput, we
are told,

They bury their dead with their heads directly downwards, because they
hold an opinion, that in eleven thousand moons they are all to rise again, in
which period the earth (which they conceive to be flat) will turn upside down,
and by this means they shall, at their resurrection, be found ready standing
on their feet. The learned among them confess the absurdity of this doctrine,
but the practice still continues, in compliance to the vulgar.

But does not the satire go on quietly eating its way into the very heart
of our own views of immortality, no matter how smug or how vague?
In the same writer's *Tale of a Tub* we are much more convinced that
Jack and Peter are wrong than that Martin is right.

Or again, take that scene, one of the most powerfully ironic in all
literature, at the climax of *Huckleberry Finn,* where Huck has to decide whether he will go to heaven to the white slave-owners' God or to
hell for stealing Jim out of slavery. We know that the white slave-
owners' God is a bogey, an example, as Goya would say, of what a
tailor can do. But Huck does not know that. He is no Prometheus Unbound; it never occurs to him to doubt that the white slave-owners'
God is the only true God. And in contemplating his predicament we
can only say that the half-gods have gone: we have no evidence that
the gods have arrived.

And if we fall back from the outworks of faith and reason to the
solid and tangible realities of the senses, satire will follow us even
there. A slight shift of perspective, a different tinge in the emotional
colouring, and the same real, physical world becomes an intolerable
horror. *Gulliver's Travels* show, in rapid review, man from a large perspective as a venomous little rodent, man from a small perspective as a
noisome and clumsy pachyderm, the mind of man as a bear-pit and
the body of man as a compound of filth and ferocity. Swift shows us
everything about the human body that can be made to appear disgust-
ing and nauseating; his account of old age is the most hideous on record; and his sense of the nastiness and sordidness of ordinary life,
which oozes through his *Directions to Servants* and his more unquot-
able poems, seems not so much abnormal as merely perverse. But he
is simply following where his satiric genius leads him, and without
raising any questions about his "purpose," surely anyone who had at-
tentively read Swift could never again find complete satisfaction in
gratifying his senses. And that is an important barrier in civilization
removed.

The fact that all great satirists have been obscene suggests that
obscenity is an essential characteristic of the satirist. Swift is in the direct tradition of the medieval preachers who painted the repulsiveness
of [84] gluttony and lechery; and his account of the Struldbrugs is a
late version of the medieval dance of death. The preoccupation of

medieval satirists with the theme of death, often assigned to morbidity, is part of the same moral criticism. It is all very well to eat, drink and be merry; but one cannot always put off dying until tomorrow.

We are getting close to one of the fundamental facts about satire: that the sardonic vision is the seamy side of the tragic vision. We usually associate satire with comedy, but to the extent that a comedy is satiric it possesses a more than comic seriousness. A comedy is, or purports to be, a study of human behaviour, and in its most concentrated forms, in a play by Congreve or a novel by Jane Austen, we are superficially conscious of only an amiable and civilized prattle. The satire in such a comedy comes as a kind of backfire or recoil after it is read or seen as a whole. Once read, deserts of futile snobbery and simpering insipidity open up on all sides of it, and we begin to feel that Congreve and Jane Austen are more aware than a less able comedian would be of the importance of being earnest. Collins, in *Pride and Prejudice,* being a mere jackass, is treated as a comic relief; but if the novel's main theme had been the married life of Charlotte and Collins, how long would Collins continue to be funny? And when this chattering world of card-parties and dances comes under direct satiric fire, it turns into a racking nightmare of horror:

> As Hags hold Sabbaths, less for joy than spite,
> So these their merry, miserable Night;
> Still round and round the Ghosts of Beauty glide,
> And haunt the places where their Honour died.
>   See how the World its Veterans rewards!
> A Youth of Frolics, an old Age of Cards;
> Fair to no purpose, artful to no end,
> Young without Lovers, old without a Friend;
> A Fop their Passion, but their Prize a Sot;
> Alive, ridiculous, and dead, forgot!

It is possible for comedy on a very high plane, the plane of *The Tempest,* the *Franklin's Tale* or *The Magic Flute,* to escape altogether from satire; but tragedy can never separate itself from irony. Flights of angels sing Hamlet to his rest in the climax of a frantically muddled attempt at revenge which has taken eight lives instead of one. Cleopatra fades away with great dignity and solemn music after a careful search for the easiest way to die. And in *King Lear,* when the mad old king scampers off the stage with his flowers stuck in his hair, or Gloucester makes a noble farewell speech, throws himself from a cliff, and falls a couple of feet, tragedy and irony have completely merged in something which is neither, and yet both at once. The sublime and the ridiculous are convex and concave of the same dark lens. One may find this in the middle of one of the most terrible and bloody tragedies in English literature, Webster's *Duchess of Malfi:*

What's this flesh? A little crudded milk, fantastical puff-paste. Our bodies are weaker [85] than those paper-prisons boys use to keep flies in; more contemptible, since ours is to preserve earth-worms. Didst thou ever see a lark in a cage? Such is the soul in the body: this world is like her little turf of grass, and the heaven o'er our heads, like her looking-glass, only gives us a miserable knowledge of the small compass of our prison.

Or one may find this in a modern American ballad, of uncertain parentage:

> The old grey hearse goes rolling by,
> You don't know whether to laugh or cry,
> For you know some day it'll get you too,
> And the hearse's next load may consist of you.
>
> They'll take you out, and they'll lower you down
> While men with shovels stand all around:
> They'll throw in dirt, and they'll throw in rocks,
> And they won't give a damn if they break the box.
>
> And your eyes drop out and your teeth fall in,
> And worms crawl over your mouth and chin:
> They invite their friends and their friends' friends too,
> And you look like hell when they're through with you.

At what point does the fact of death cease to be tragic and become a grim joke? When Mr. E. J. Pratt, in his poem called "The Drag-Irons," describes the hauling up of a drowned captain, is his mood the tragic one of violent death or the satiric one of the indignity of the body?

> But with his Captain's blood he did resent,
> With livid silence and with glassy look,
> This fishy treatment when his years were spent
> To come up dead upon a grapnel hook.

The same principle is clear in Chaucer. The *Canterbury Tales* is simply a human comedy: it is not a deliberate satire. Chaucer studies his pilgrims carefully, but does not distort or caricature them. If they are fools and weaklings, they will come out as that, and we may call the result a satire if we wish; if they are decent people, like the knight or the ploughman, they will come out as such. To this larger comic aim both tragedy and satire must be subordinated. The *Knight's Tale* is pathetic rather than tragic; it is sad, but it is told to amuse the pilgrims. The *Merchant's Tale* is bitter and cynical; but, again, that is merely a contributing aspect to the human comedy. In the *Troilus* the case is very different. Here we have a full-dress tragedy, complete in itself, with all the unanswerable problems in it that tragedy raises. And when its hero dies his tragic death, he ascends into the stars and looks down upon the world:

And in hymself he lough right at the wo
Of hem that wepten for his deth so faste;
And dampned al oure werk that foloweth so
The blynde lust, the which that may nat laste.

The laugh of pure satire is the echo to his tragedy.

Satire at its most concentrated, therefore, is tragedy robbed of all its dignity and nobility, a universal negation that cheapens and belittles [86] everything. *Gulliver's Travels* destroys every standard of values except the life according to reason and nature, and then demonstrates that such a life is impossible. More makes a shambles out of Christian Europe, contrasts it with a heathen Utopia, and finally shows us that there is little hope of Utopian principles being applied to Europe and that Christianity has started to destroy the Utopia. Langland's great vision culminates in something very like a triumph of Antichrist. It is against this background that we are able to see why the most deliberate and self-conscious satire in English literature, Pope's *Dunciad,* comes to the conclusion it does. It is not only the triumph of Dullness but the triumph of satire that that great poem records, and in the complete triumph of satire the victor reigns, like Elizabeth in Ireland, only over ashes and dead carcasses:

Religion blushing veils her sacred fires,
And unawares Morality expires.
Nor public Flame, nor private, dares to shine;
Nor human Spark is left, nor Glimpse divine!
Lo! thy dread Empire, CHAOS! is restor'd;
Light dies before thy uncreating word;
Thy hand, great Anarch! lets the curtain fall,
And universal Darkness buries All.

Now, one may reasonably ask, what is the use, or, if that is too vague a question, the motive, of this art of nihilism? For the occupational hazards of satire are very considerable. "Certainly, he that hath a satirical vein," says Lord Bacon, "as he maketh others afraid of his wit, so he had need be afraid of others' memory." Satire got Nashe, Jonson, Marston and Wither into gaol; it got Defoe into both gaol and the pillory; it involved Dryden and Pope in squabbles which their worst detractors will hardly affirm they enjoyed; and it perhaps had more to do than is generally thought with the poverty and neglect of Samuel Butler. Skelton, satiric poet and thrice-crowned laureate, tutor to King Henry VIII in his youth, has put the position of the satirist as plaintively as anyone. It was only fair that he should, for the sixteenth century made him a buffoon, the seventeenth ignored him, in the eighteenth Pope called him "beastly" and in the nineteenth a female historian called him an abandoned wretch whose tutorial influence undoubtedly explained King Henry's Bluebearding tendencies:

What can it avail ...
To rhyme or to rail,
To write or to indite,
Either for delight
Or else for despight?
Or books to compile
Of divers manner style,
Vice to revile
And sin to exile?
To teach or to preach,
As reason will reach?
Say this, and say that,[87]
His head is so fat,
He wotteth never what
Nor whereof he speaketh ...
Or if he speak plain,
Then he lacketh brain,
He is but a fool;
Let him go to school ...
And if that he hit
The nail on the head,
It standeth in no stead.
The Devil, they say, is dead,
The Devil is dead!

As for the use, that is the concern of posterity. The true seminal
virtue of satire is not in the chaff, and it takes a good deal of winnow-
ing to separate the harvest from the husks of gossip and insult. The use
an age makes of satire thus depends on its own problems. In an age
such as ours, when the urgency of radical change is a main pre-occupa-
tion, the innate nihilism of satire, reactionary and wrong-headed as it
often is, can be put to a revolutionary use. Langland was doubtless
what we should now call a Tory, but his identification of Christ with
the honest workman Piers Plowman cuts through all the fat of compromise with the world down to the bare bones of an eternally subversive
and anarchic Christianity, and that is his meaning for us. Dickens's
influence also is for us completely radical, whatever he himself may
have been. When his Pickwick goes from the law court into the debt-
or's prison, it never once occurs to him that the accumulated legal
wisdom of his country, which has decided against him, is entitled to the
smallest respect whatever. That is a useful frame of mind to have in
citizens of a free democracy who are determined not to be hag-ridden
by precedent. That curious self-depreciation in respect to physical
courage which is so characteristic of the Englishman is also closer to
satire than it looks. It is founded on the profoundly satiric belief that
physical dignity can only last as far as the first banana peeling. Cock-
ney cheek and impudence have done much to save England from
swaggering and posturing tyrants; the Jorrocks of that neglected Vic-

torian genius Surtees, who is one of the best Cockneys in literature, will do for an example:

"You 'air-dresser on the chestnut 'oss," roars Mr. Jorrocks, during a check, to a gentleman with very big, ginger whiskers, "pray, 'old 'ard!"
"Hair-dresser," replies the gentleman, turning round in a fury, "I'm an officer in the ninety-first regiment."
"Then you hossifer in the ninety-fust regiment, wot looks like an 'air-dresser, 'old 'ard!"

Satire, in short, is the completion of the logical process known as the *reductio ad absurdum*, and that is not designed to hold one in perpetual captivity, but to bring one to the point at which one can escape from an incorrect procedure. Just as a mother tells a timid child afraid of the dark that there is nothing there, so the satirist presents ignorance and confusion with a negation. And when the public tells the satirist that the devil is [88] dead, the very smugness of the response proves that his work has had some effect.

I have said that the sardonic vision is the seamy side of the tragic vision, but Skelton's remark provides me with a more exact image for what I mean. At the bottom of Dante's hell, which is also the centre of the spherical earth, Dante sees Satan standing upright in the circle of ice, and as he cautiously follows Virgil over the hip and thigh of the evil giant, letting himself down by the tufts of hair on his skin, he passes the centre and finds himself no longer going down but going up, climbing out on the other side of the world to see the stars again. From this point of view, the devil is no longer upright, but standing on his head, in the same attitude in which he was hurled downward from heaven upon the other side of the earth. Both tragedy and satire take us into a hell of narrowing circles, a blasted world of repulsiveness and idiocy, a world without pity and without hope. Both culminate in some such vision as that of Dante's, of the source of all evil in a personal form. Tragedy can take us no farther; but if we persevere with the satirist, we shall pass a dead centre, and finally see the gentlemanly Prince of Darkness bottom side up.[89]

EDGAR JOHNSON

FROM *A Treasury of Satire*. New York: Simon and Schuster. Copyright 1945 by Edgar Johnson. Reprinted by permission of Simon and Schuster, Inc., New York.

. . . it cannot be too emphatically stated that satire does *not* have to arm or disguise itself with comedy. Tragic satire need no more involve laughter than the happy laughter of children or the tender laughter of lovers involves satire. A distinguished company of commentators have thus been quite wrong in declaring, as Dr. Richard Garnett, for example, does in *The Encyclopaedia Britannica*, that humor [6] must always be "a distinctly recognizable element" in satire. Dr. Garnett adds, "without humor, satire is invective"; so it may be, without ceasing to be satire. . . .

No description of satire can hold water unless it takes *all* the aspects of satire into account. Sometimes the satirist tumbles in giggling, thumbing his nose, wielding slapsticks and bladders, smacking people on their fannies, and administering electric shocks. Sometimes he bawls abuse or hisses denunciations, flays his victim and then pours burning oil or acid in the wounds. Sometimes, austere as Dante stalking through the murk of hell, he grimly describes evil fallen into its proper torments, plunged in flame or locked in thick-ribbed ice. The one ingredient common to all these activities, from satire in cap-and-bells to satire with a flaming sword, is *criticism*. Even laughing satire is laughing-at, not merely irresponsible laughing. It invites us not to let down our back hair and relax, but to lift up our eyebrows and mock. The "crack" in the wisecrack is the crack of the whip, and it is never more effective than when it cuts into someone's hide.

But criticism alone is not enough to define satire. . . . Satire's criticism must be criticism with a difference. . . . No one satirizes a child for being so contemptibly weak that it doesn't beat up a brutal father, or a man dying of cancer for being so stupid as to let himself be afflicted with the disease.[7] . . .

But satire everywhere attacks evil arrogant and triumphant, pride victorious and riding for a fall. It attacks those conventional respectabilities which are really hidden absurdities or vices blindly accepted by thoughtlessness, habit, or social custom. It attacks foolishness foolishly convinced that it makes sense, grinning and unrepentant in its folly. It attacks stuffed shirts, hypocrisies aping merit, puffed and blown-up insignificances like the frog trying to swell itself into an ox, counterfeit passing for true. The merely foolish, satire may be content to "take down a peg or two"; the dangerous and vicious it would reduce to ruin. But in both the important thing to note is a kind of unmasking. The foolishness shown up is a foolishness that usually passes for sense. The ugliness revealed in its true colors has masqueraded as merit. . . .

The essential trick of satire is a dexterous stripping away of false fronts.[8] . . .

This enables us to say . . . what satire really is. It is criticism getting around or overcoming an obstacle. Let me call this obstacle the Censor. The Censor is always insisting that we mustn't say or oughtn't to say certain things. To a lady who complained that somehow, she couldn't explain how, her fingernails were always getting dirty in London, Samuel Johnson replied, "Perhaps, madam, you scratch yourself." Now, good manners don't allow a gentleman to tell a lady that she herself is dirty, but Johnson's form of words gets around the Censor; he says it without saying it. He even extorts a certain admiration from us by being able to say it. Satire thus becomes a sort of licensed "bad form." [9] . . .

By the time we are grown up Dame Civilization gets most of us house-broken pretty well. But somewhere within us Tom Sawyer and Huck Finn still lurk, waiting to break through a thousand restrictions, bursting with wild boy-rebellion. No matter how tamed we may be, the live animal is there. The satirist enables us to kick over the traces, in thought at least, and still feel justified by the "good reasons" he gives us. He shows us Mrs. Grundy as a sham, the pillars of society as whited sepulchres, and the [11] Great and Good as stuffed shirts. This is fun because it is release; and it establishes itself as right by convincing us that it is sanity.

Even comic satire derives its significance from its truth. We laugh at seeing some overblown pretension deflated, some mounted gasbag tumbled in the common mud. There is a sort of astringent joy merely in seeing a sham, or rather seeing through it, in bursting the hot-air balloon with a wicked pinprick. The combination of hostility, sanity, and high spirits can be fun in a cockeyed world. But the revelations of tragic satire may be too dreadful for laughter. You can't laugh if the compassionate mask of Mother Church is torn off and the jowls of Moloch are revealed beneath, or if the triumphal chariot of progress is suddenly perceived as the car of Juggernaut, or if mankind is seen as a perfumed and tailored Yahoo. Only by ignoring its meaning can the fall of Man become a pratfall.

And consequently people have often felt that there is something ill-humored about satire. Its laughter hardly conceals a sneer of scorn; its tragic seriousness has an odor of bitter almonds. Isn't there, they may ask, a kind of moral jaundice in a vision so colored with ridicule or disgust? An eye blind to merit, they might say, and a nose sharp for evil are the satirist's distinguishing traits. . . .

Sometimes the accusation has a partial truth. To the sad and angry heart of Swift, to the Lucretian laughter of Anatole France, virtue was less visible than vice. But the vice they saw was real. We cannot deny it because it was almost all they saw; any more than we could call Leeuwenhoek's microbes a delusion because he saw them everywhere. Satire is the antidote to Pollyanna and Dr. Pangloss, with their rose-colored image of a best of all possible worlds. At its sanest and most penetrating it does not cancel distortion with counterdistortion. It merely focuses our gaze sharply upon the contrast between things as they should be and as they are.[12] . . .

ALVIN KERNAN

FROM *The Cankered Muse: Satire of the English Renaissance*. New Haven: Yale University Press, 1959. Reprinted by permission of the Yale University Press and the author.

. . . The necessary straightforwardness of his attacks on vice always opens the satirist to accusations of being proud. As the satirist passes a succession of absolute moral judgments on his fellow men, he inevitably becomes an egoistic monster bursting with his own righteousness and completely devoid of any sympathy for his victims or doubts about his own moral status. "Byron" in *English Bards and Scotch Reviewers* admits that,

> Every Brother Rake will smile to see
> That miracle, a Moralist in me
> (lines 699–700)

"Horace's" adversarius speaks to him about the same question (I.ii.25–27), "When you look over your own sins, your eyes are rheumy and daubed with ointment; why, when you view the failings of your friends, are you as keen of sight as an eagle?" [27]

All but a few critics of satire have unerringly sought out and concentrated on these weak spots in the satirist's character, his private personality. Thomas Love Peacock, we are told, "showed himself rather obstinately blind to many of the higher aspects of life in general." *Don Juan* consists of "the beastly utterances of a man who had lost all sense of decency," and William Blackwood was struck with horror by "the vile, heartless, and cold-blooded way in which this fiend [Byron] attempted to degrade every tender and sacred feeling of the human heart." Another critic informs us that John Marston "exhibits an insane delight in raking the cesspits of vice . . . and feels the same pleasure in drawing attention to [evil] . . . that boys experience in chalking up newly-discovered verbiage of obscenity." Speaking of the same author, Thomas Warton pontificates: "The satirist who too freely indulges himself in the display of that licentiousness which he means to proscribe, absolutely defeats his own design. He inflames those passions which he professes to suppress, gratifies the depravations of a prurient curiosity, and seduces innocent minds to an acquaintance with ideas which they might never have known." "Pope," it is argued, "finds himself unable to re-settle the equilibrium in his nervous system until he has taken out his revenge by an extra kicking administered [27] to some old mendicant or vagrant lying in a ditch."

All of the defects of character noted by these critics are unhesitatingly assigned to the authors, and while it is true that some of the greatest satiric authors have not been the most stable of men, the fact seems to have been missed that many of the characteristics confidently attributed to them derive from the very nature of satire itself. Anyone who writes vigorous satire will inevitably appear to share these traits. If, however, we accept the strange, twisted, contradictory satirist as a fictitious character created in order to achieve the satiric end, the exposure of vice and depravity, then we can direct our attention to the ways in which the authors of great satire manipulate their satirists and exploit them in a thoroughly dramatic fashion. Juvenal's stern, impoverished, decayed noble who stamps about the streets of Rome suffering indignities at the hands of the nouveaux riches, and bursting with indignation and sophistic rhetoric; Skelton's crude, rustic, straightforward, unlearned country-man whose simple piety mocks the sophisticated church-men; John Marston's biting, snarling, despairing, contradictory malcontent who noses into all the filth of Elizabethan London and becomes nearly incoherent with rage while denouncing it on the street corners; Swift's bumbling, credulous, prideful Gulliver voyaging from one misunderstood adventure to the next and finally filled with proud disdain for the human animal, the Yahoo—all these are satiric personae.

I have described in the preceding pages a basic satiric persona, and no doubt the reader has by now thought of a number of cases where some of the qualities I have called characteristic are so attenuated that they nearly cease to exist. Savagery, despair, hate, pride, intransigeance, prurience, and sadism may be innate in satire, but Horace,[28] Chaucer, Erasmus, and, to a lesser degree, Ben Jonson, all manage to soften or find out more acceptable variations of these unpleasant traits by avoiding the extreme forms of indignation and the more shocking varieties of vice. They stress the public personality of the satirist. Their kind of satire verges on the comic, and their satirists, without losing their cutting-edge, exude good humor, easy laughter, urbanity. In Jonson's words, they "sport with human follies, not with crimes," and Horace's phrase "ridentem dicere verum" characterizes their method.

On the other hand there is an even larger group of satiric writers who seem to delight in stressing every extravagant attitude and every contradiction in the satiric character. Juvenal, Swift, Pope, Byron, Marston, Rochester, Marvell, all create satirists who lash out with violence, are filled with outrage, and seek out the vilest of men. When Horace goes for a walk he encounters a bore, when Juvenal walks *he* encounters a cast-off pathic. These bitter works are characterized by Juvenal's saeva indignatio, and they seem always to be on the threshold of tragedy. The works of these authors have provided a majority of my examples for the simple reason that such writers, by carrying to the extreme the private personality of the satirist, bring into relief the tendencies of all satire, tendencies which are repressed in the gentler types.

Horace and Juvenal thus provide us with the two extremes of the satirist, and while it seems likely that the personality of the author has some connection with the type of satirist he creates, other factors are more important in molding the satiric figure. The radical characteristics are always necessarily present, but just as each age forges its own typical verse forms or its architectural style, so, allowing for minor differences resulting from the different personalities of the authors involved, each age creates its own satirist who is distinguished from the satirists of the preceding [29] age and the following. Bishop Golias, Piers Plowman, Thersites, the Pope of the *Imitations of Horace* are all related figures, but they are different in many ways, and each is a defining example of the standard satiric character of his age. Changes in satirists seem to come about in conjunction with major shifts in thought, and perhaps the best way of describing this process is to say that the satirist is always an amalgamation of the basic characteristics which develop whenever satire is written and of the ethos of a particular age. It is possible to distinguish a distinctive satiric figure in each of the major periods of our literature.[30] . . .

MEYER H. ABRAMS

FROM *A Glossary of Literary Terms,*
Revised, Copyright 1941 by Dan S.
Norton and Peters Rushton. © 1957
by M. H. Abrams. Reprinted by
permission of the publishers, Holt,
Rinehart and Winston, Inc.

Allegory. An allegory undertakes to make a doctrine or thesis interesting and persuasive by converting it into a narrative in which the agents, and sometimes the setting as well, represent general concepts, moral qualities, or other abstractions. In *The Pilgrim's Progress* Bunyan allegorizes his doctrine of Christian salvation by telling how Christian, warned by Evangelist, flees from the City of Destruction and makes his way toilsomely to the Celestial City; en route he encounters such characters as Faithful, Hopeful, and the Giant Despair, and wins through places like the Slough of Despond, the Valley of the Shadow of Death, and Vanity Fair. A paragraph from this work will give a glimpse of the allegorical process:

Now as Christian was walking solitary by himself, he espied one afar off come crossing over the field to meet him; and their hap was to meet just as they were crossing the way of each other. The Gentleman's name was Mr. Worldly-Wiseman; he dwelt in the Town of Carnal-Policy, a very great Town, and also hard by from whence Christian came.

A great variety of literary forms have been used for allegory. The medieval *Everyman* is an allegorical drama, Spenser's *Faerie Queene* an allegorical romance, *The Pilgrim's Progress* an allegorical prose narrative, and William Collins' *Ode on the Poetical Character* an allegorical lyric poem. . . . Consult C. S. Lewis, *The Allegory of Love* (1936).

A **fable** is a story, exemplifying a moral thesis, in which animals talk and act like human beings. In the fable of the fox and the grapes, the fox, after unsuccessfully exerting all his wiles to get the grapes hanging beyond his reach, concludes that they are probably sour anyway. The moral is that we tend to belittle what we can't have ourselves. The most famous collection of fables is attributed to the Greek writer, Aesop; another notable collection was written by La Fontaine, a Frenchman of the seventeenth century. John Gay and many other English authors wrote fables, and so did the American writers Joel Chandler Harris, in his Uncle Remus stories, and James Thurber, in his *Fables for Our Time*.

A **parable** also enforces a moral or other kind of doctrine, but not, like allegory, by the actions of abstract personifications, nor, like fable, by a narrative in which animals are the agents. Instead, a parable is a short [2] narrative, presented so as to bring out the analogy, or parallel, between its elements and a lesson that the speaker is trying to bring home to us. The parable was one of Christ's favorite literary devices; examples are His parables of the sower, of the Good Samaritan, and of the wise and foolish virgins. Here is the short parable of the fruit trees that Christ used in instructing His listeners how to detect false prophets (Matthew 7:16–20):

Ye shall know them by their fruits. Do men gather grapes of thorns, or figs of thistles? Even so every good tree bringeth forth good fruit; but a corrupt tree bringeth forth evil fruit. A good tree cannot bring forth evil fruit, neither can a corrupt tree bring forth good fruit. Every tree that bringeth not forth good fruit is hewn down, and cast into the fire. Wherefore by their fruits ye shall know them.

An **exemplum** was a story told by medieval preachers as a particular instance illustrating the general text of a sermon; the story was usually claimed to be true. In Chaucer's *Pardoner's Tale,* the Pardoner, preaching on the text, "Greed is the root of all evil," presents by way of exemplum the story of the three revelers who set out to find Death, but find a heap of gold instead, then kill one another in the attempt to gain sole possession of the treasure. Chaucer's Chanticleer borrows the preacher's technique in the ten exempla he tells in a vain effort to persuade his sceptical wife, Dame Pertelote the hen, that bad dreams forbode disaster.[3]

Burlesque and Parody. "Burlesque," "parody," "caricature," and "travesty" are often used interchangeably, but to equate the terms in this way is to surrender very useful critical distinctions. It is better to use **burlesque** as the generic term for all literary forms in which people, actions, or other literary works are made ridiculous by an incongruous imitation, and to reserve the other terms as names for various species of burlesque. When the laugh is raised (as it usually is), not for its own sake, but to deride some person or object existing outside the burlesque itself, burlesque in its various species serves as a vehicle of satire (see **Satire**). It should be [9] added that an extended work of burlesque is usually flexible enough to exploit a variety of the devices listed below. We name it by the device that it uses most persistently; accordingly, we say that Pope's *Rape of the Lock* is a mock epic, although it includes many more than specifically mock-epic devices.

When the incongruity arises from treating a trivial subject in an elevated and serious manner, we get "high burlesque"; when it arises from treating a serious subject in a low and comic manner, we get "low burlesque." A **mock epic** . . . employs the conventional attributes and the elaborate style of the epic genre to make a trivial and commonplace subject laughable. A **parody,** like the mock epic, is also a form of high burlesque, but it derides, not its subject, but a particular literary work or style, by imitating its features and applying them to trivial or grossly discordant materials. John Phillips' "The Splendid Shilling" (1705) was an early parody of the style of Milton's *Paradise Lost,* applied to the subject of a starveling writer composing in a garret. Henry Fielding parodied Richardson's *Pamela,* first in *Shamela* and later in *Joseph Andrews.* Compare the first stanza of Wordsworth's "She Dwelt among the Untrodden Ways" with the first stanza of Hartley Coleridge's parody:

> He lived amidst th' untrodden ways
> To Rydal Lake that lead;
> A bard whom there were none to praise,
> And very few to read.

One type of low burlesque is the **Hudibrastic,** named from Samuel Butler's *Hudibras* (1663), which describes the ridiculous adventures of a Puritan knight, not in the high style appropriate to the romance of knighthood, but in a jingly meter and ludicrously colloquial idiom. Another, the **travesty,** mocks a specific work by treating its lofty subject in grotesquely extravagant or lowly terms; as Boileau put it, in a travesty of the *Aeneid* "Dido and Aeneas are made to speak like fishwives and ruffians."

Caricature is a type of portrait which makes a person ludicrous by exaggerating or distorting prominent features without losing the likeness. The term is commonly applied to drawings or paintings, but literature has its analogues in the quick verbal sketch of the quintessential appearance. Pope in *The Rape of the Lock* described Sir Plume, "With earnest eyes, and round unthinking face," and Burns caricatured the strait-laced prudes of his day as they sat at a revival meeting "Wi' screw'd up, grace-proud faces." A **lampoon** is a full-length verbal portrait of an individual in which he is ridiculed in a biting and often scurrilous manner. Pope's satiric portrait of "Atticus" (Addison) in his "Epistle to Dr. Arbuthnot" transforms the individual too completely into a permanent type—the [10] genius lamed by a malice that is rendered impotent by timidity—to be properly called a lampoon; his caustic portrayal of Colley Cibber in *The Dunciad,* however, constitutes an indubitable lampoon.

See **Satire** and **Wit and Humor,** and refer to Richmond P. Bond, *English Burlesque Poetry* (1932), and Walter Jerrold and R. M. Leonard, editors, *A Century of Parody and Imitation* (1913).[11]

Comedy. The term "comedy" is now broadly applied to works (especially in the dramatic form) in which the characters undergo embarrassments or discomfitures which are on the whole so managed that they interest and amuse us without engaging our profoundest sympathy, and in which the action turns out well for the chief characters. . . . English comedy developed in the sixteenth century from such native materials as the farcical episodes introduced in the medieval drama . . . together with elements of character, action, and construction derived from the Roman comedy of Plautus and Terence. Nicholas Udall's *Ralph Roister Doister* (*ca.* 1533), the earliest known English comedy, exemplifies this combination. Comedy rapidly achieved a high stage of development in the Elizabethan Age. Shakespeare wrote various types, including the Roman form, such as *The Comedy of Errors* (based on a play by Plautus), and **romantic comedy** (*As You Like It, Twelfth Night*), in which the central situation is a love affair, involving a beautiful and idealized heroine, the course of which does not run smoothly but ends well. Ben Jonson's plays, such as *The Alchemist* and *Volpone,* are masterpieces of **satiric comedy,** which ridicule [13] violations of moral and social standards by one or more rascally swindlers, as well as the greed and gullibility of their victims. . . . Restoration dramatists brought to the peak of its development the **comedy of manners;** this form deals with the relations and intrigues of gentlemen and ladies living in a polished and sophisticated society, evokes laughter mainly at the violations of social conventions and decorum, and relies for its effect in great part on the wit and sparkle of the dialogue (see **Wit and Humor**). Excellent examples are Congreve's *Way of the World* and Wycherley's *The Country Wife.* A reaction against the immorality of situation and the indecency of dialogue in **Restoration comedy** resulted in the **sentimental comedy** of the eighteenth century, dealing with monumentally noble heroes and heroines of the middle class who utter sentiments of unimpeachable rectitude and suffer tribulations which, incongruously, are managed so that they evoke tears, rather than smiles, from the audience. . . . Good examples of this type are Richard Steele's *The Conscious Lovers* and Richard Cumberland's *The West Indian.* Goldsmith and Sheridan, late in the century, revived the fun and wit, though not the indecency, of the Restoration comedy of manners. After a lapse in the earlier nineteenth century, good comedy was brought back to the stage by Oscar Wilde, A. W. Pinero, and others. Our own century, the age of J. M. Synge, George Bernard Shaw, Noel Coward, and many others, has been an eminent one for this dramatic form.

Some other distinctions are often made in discussing comedy. **High comedy** was a term introduced by George Meredith in *The Idea of Comedy* (1877) to define the comedy of manners that evokes "intellectual laughter"—laughter from spectators who remain emotionally detached from the action—at the spectacle of human folly and incongruity. A peak of high comedy is to be found in the wit combats of such intelligent, sophisticated, and well-matched lovers as Benedick and Beatrice in Shakespeare's *Much Ado about Nothing*, and Millamant and Mirabell in Congreve's *Way of the World*. **Low comedy**, on the other hand, makes no intellectual appeal, but depends for its comic effect on violent and boisterous action, or **slapstick:** the Mack Sennett films and the Chaplin one-reelers were unalloyed examples of this type. **Farce** often makes use of low-comedy episodes; it is a type of comedy in which one-dimensional characters are put into ludicrous situations, while ordinary standards of probability in motivation and event are freely violated in order to evoke the maximum laughter from an audience. Examples of excellent farce range from the horseplay of Shakespeare's *Taming of the Shrew* to the polished satire of Molière's *The Imaginary Invalid* and the verbal pyrotechnics of Wilde's *The Importance of Being Earnest*. For further discussions, see . . . comic (under **Satire**), and **Wit and Humor**.[14] Refer to A. H. Thorndike, *English Comedy* (1929) and Louis Kronenberger, *The Thread of Laughter* (1952).[15]

Epigram originally meant an inscription, and was later extended to encompass any very short poem—amorous, elegiac, meditative, complimentary, anecdotal, or satiric—which is polished, terse, and pointed; usually an epigram ends with a surprising or witty turn of thought. Sir John Harington wrote a well-known example:

> Treason doth never prosper. What's the reason?
> Why, if it prosper, none dare call it treason.

Martial, the famous Roman epigrammatist, established the model for many later writers. The epigram was much cultivated in England in the late sixteenth and seventeenth centuries by such poets as Donne, Jonson, and Herrick. The form, as we might expect, flourished in the next century [31] of wit, of polish, and of Pope; many of Pope's couplets, in fact, are detachable epigrams. John Byrom proposed this toast in the eighteenth century, while the exiled Stuarts were still Pretenders to the English throne:

> God bless the King—I mean the Faith's defender!
> God bless (no harm in blessing) the Pretender!
> But who pretender is or who is king—
> God bless us all! that's quite another thing.

And here is one of Coleridge's epigrams, to show that romanticism did not preclude wit.

ON A VOLUNTEER SINGER

> Swans sing before they die—'twere no bad thing
> Should certain persons die before they sing!

In the last century or so, "epigram" has come to mean any neat and witty statement, whether in prose or verse. For prose examples, see **Wit and Humor**. . . . refer to T. K. Whipple, *Martial and the English Epigram* (1925).[32]

Irony. "Rhetorical" or "verbal irony" is a mode of speech in which the implied attitudes or evaluation are opposed to those literally expressed. Ostensible praise or approval that implies dispraise or disapproval is more frequent than the converse form. Thus in Pope's *Rape of the Lock,* after Sir Plume, egged on by the ladies, has stammered out his incoherent request for the return of the stolen lock,

> "It grieves me much," replied the Peer again,
> "Who speaks so well should ever speak in vain."

This is a simple bit of irony, because it is obvious in the circumstances that the Peer is far from grieved, and that poor Sir Plume has not spoken at all well. Sometimes, however, the use of irony by Pope and other practitioners is very complex indeed, and the clues to the ironic reversal (especially since the writer lacks a speaker's resort to such ironic indicators as facial expression and vocal intonation) are subtle and difficult. That is why the use of irony by a writer carries an implicit compliment to the intelligence of the reader, who is associated with the knowing minority not taken in by the literal meaning. That is also why so many ironists are misinterpreted and sometimes (like Defoe and Swift) get into serious trouble with the obtuse authorities. Following the intricate maneuvers of a great ironist like Swift or Henry James is an ultimate test of a student's skill in reading.

To keep up a sustainedly ironic document, the writer is apt to utilize [45] the device of a **naive hero,** or of a naive narrator or expositor, whose invincible obtuseness leads him to persist in putting an interpretation on affairs which the smiling reader just as persistently alters or reverses. Examples are Swift's well-meaning but stupid economist who makes the *Modest Proposal* to convert the children of the poverty-stricken Irish into a financial and gastronomic asset, or Swift's stubbornly credulous Gulliver, or the narrator of Fielding's *Jonathan Wild the Great,* or the chief characters of Aldous Huxley's *Antic Hay.*

Irony is related to other rhetorical modes. **Invective** is direct denunciation by the use of derogatory epithets; so Prince Hal calls the rotund Falstaff "this sanguine coward, this bed-presser, this horseback-breaker, this huge hill of flesh. . . ." (It will be noted that in this instance there is an *ironic* undertone of affection, as often when friends resort to name calling in the exuberance of their esteem.) Dryden has described the difference in efficacy between direct depreciation by invective and the indirectness of irony, in which the ironist is able to maintain the advantage of self-control and detachment by leaving it to circumstance to convert his bland compliments into insults:

How easy is it to call rogue and villain, and that wittily! But how hard to make a man appear a fool, a blockhead, or a knave, without using any of those opprobrious terms! . . . There is still a vast difference between the slovenly butchering of a man, and the fineness of a stroke that separates the head from the body, and leaves it standing in its place.

Sarcasm is a caustic and heavy use of apparent praise for actual dispraise: "Oh, you're just a great guy, a prince—I don't think"; it is the common man's usual form of irony. **Understatement,** or **meiosis,** is the kind of irony which derives from deliberately representing something as much less than it really is. Swift wrote, "Last week I saw a woman flayed, and you will hardly believe how much it altered her appearance for the worse." The effect of meiosis is often comic: "The reports of my death," Mark Twain commented, "are greatly exaggerated." See . . . Satire; and J. A. K. Thomson, *Irony: An Historical Introduction* (1926).

The word "irony" is also used in a number of extended and nonrhetorical ways. **Socratic irony** takes its name and meaning from Socrates' characteristic assumption, in his philosophical discussions, of an attitude of modesty, ignorance, and readiness to entertain points of view which differ from his own, but invariably turn out to be absurd. **Dramatic irony,** or **tragic irony,** is applied to the words and actions of characters in a play who confidently expect the opposite of what fate holds in store, or who say something that anticipates the tragic outcome, but in a sense very different from the one they intended. . . . The Greek dramatists, especially Sophocles, who based their plots on legends [46] whose outcome was already known to their audience, made frequent use of this device. A concentrated instance of dramatic irony is to be found in the Oriental story of the frightened servant who obtains permission from his master to flee to Samarrah in order to escape Death, who had looked at him strangely in the market place. The master himself encounters Death in the market place and asks him why he had looked so strangely at his servant. "Because," said Death, "I was surprised to see him here. I have an appointment with him this afternoon, in Samarrah." **Cosmic irony,** or the **irony of fate,** is attributed to literary works in which God or Destiny is represented to be manipulating events as though deliberately to frustrate and mock the protagonist. This is a favorite structural device of Thomas Hardy. In his *Tess of the D'Urbervilles* the heroine, having lost her virtue because of her innocence, then loses her happiness because of her honesty, finds it again only through murder, and having been briefly happy, is hanged. Hardy concludes: "The President of the Immortals, in Aeschylean phrase, had ended his sport with Tess." **Romantic irony** is a term used by German writers of the late eighteenth and early nineteenth century to designate a mode of dramatic or narrative writing in which the author builds up and then deliberately breaks down the illusion, by revealing himself to be the wilful creator and manipulator of his characters and their actions. . . . Byron's great narrative poem, *Don Juan*, constantly employs this device for comic or satiric effect.

In some recent critics we find "irony" used in a greatly extended sense, as a general criterion of literary value. It is claimed that only in poems of an inferior order does the poet commit himself unreservedly to any one attitude or outlook, such as love or admiration or idealism, and that superior poems always include an "ironic" awareness of the opposite and complementary attitudes as well. See . . . I. A. Richards, *Principles of Literary Criticism* (1924), Chap. 32, and Cleanth Brooks, *The Well-Wrought Urn* (1947).[47]

Satire is the literary art of diminishing a subject by making it ridiculous and evoking towards it attitudes of amusement, contempt, or scorn. It differs from comedy in that comedy evokes laughter as an end in itself, while satire "derides"; that is, it uses laughter as a weapon, and against a butt existing outside the work itself. That butt may be an individual (in "personal satire"), or a type of person, a class, a nation, or even (as in Rochester's "A Satyr against Mankind" and Swift's *Gulliver's Travels*) the whole race of man. (See **Comedy** and **Wit and Humor**.) The distinction between the **comic** and the satiric, however, is a sharp one only at its extremes. Shakespeare's Falstaff is a purely comic creation; his puritanical Malvolio is for the most part comic but has aspects of satire directed against a human type; Johnson's Volpone clearly satirizes the type of man whose cleverness is put at the service of his cupidity; and Dryden's MacFlecknoe, while representing a permanent type of the pretentious poetaster, ridicules specifically the living individual, Shadwell.

Satire has usually been justified by those who practice it as a corrective of human vice and folly. As such, its claim has been to ridicule the failing rather than the individual, and to limit its ridicule to corrigible faults, excluding those for which a man is not responsible. As Swift said, speaking of himself in his "Verses on the Death of Dr. Swift":

> Yet malice never was his aim;
> He lashed the vice, but spared the name. ...
> His satire points at no defect,
> But what all mortals may correct. ...
> He spared a hump, or crooked nose,
> Whose owners set not up for beaux.

Satire is frequently found as an incidental element in many works whose over-all form is not satiric, in a certain character, or situation, or passing reference. But in many great literary achievements satire —the attempt [85] to diminish a subject by ridicule—is the organizing principle of the whole. In discussing such writings the following distinctions will be found useful.

One common way of classifying satire is according to its aim and tone (see **Tone**), the two classes taking their names from their great Roman practitioners, Horace and Juvenal. **Horatian satire** undertakes to evoke a smile at the foibles of men; the writer speaks in the character of an urbane and tolerant man of the world who is moved to amusement rather than indignation at the spectacle of human folly—sometimes including his own. **Juvenalian satire** evokes contempt and moral indignation at the vices and corruptions of men; the satirist speaks in the character of a serious moralist denouncing aberrations which are no less dangerous because they are ridiculous. Pope's *Moral Essays* and most of his other writings are Horatian satires; Johnson's "London" and "The Vanity of Human Wishes" are Juvenalian satires.

Another system of classification distinguishes types of satire by their vehicle or form of presentation. **Formal, or direct, satire** is a commentary on people and affairs in which the satiric voice speaks out in the first person. Addison writes formal satire in some of his prose essays, and Pope in the verse essay *(Moral Essays)*, the epistle ("To Augustus"), or the dialogue ("Epistle to Dr. Arbuthnot"). **Indirect satire** is cast in the form of a plot, in which the characters make themselves ridiculous by their thought, speech, and actions, and are sometimes made even more ridiculous by the author's narrative style and commentary. The articles on **Burlesque and Parody,** . . . **Irony,** and **Wit and Humor** describe some of the many forms and stylistic devices available to indirect satire. Any narrative or dramatic vehicle can be adapted to the purposes of indirect satire. Dryden's *Absalom and Achitophel* turns Old Testament history into a satiric allegory on contemporary political maneuverings. In *Gulliver's Travels* Swift adapts to satiric uses the current narrative of travel. Byron's *Don Juan* is a versified form of the old episodic picaresque story . . . , and Evelyn Waugh's *The Loved One* is a satiric mode of the prose novel. Ben Jonson and Bernard Shaw wrote satiric comedies for the stage, and Gilbert and Sullivan's *Patience,* like John Gay's *Beggar's Opera* and its modern adaptation, *The Threepenny Opera,* are satiric operettas.

The proportioning of the examples in this article will indicate how large the Restoration and eighteenth century looms in English satiric achievement. Good satire has been written in every period beginning with the Middle Ages, and *Punch* and the *New Yorker* demonstrate that skillful satire still commands a wide audience. But the greatest age of English satire—perhaps of world satire—was the century and a half that included Dryden, Samuel Butler, Addison, Pope, Swift, Gay, Fielding, Johnson, Goldsmith, and (it should not be forgotten in this context) [86] Burns and Blake. Consult Hugh Walker, *English Satire and Satirists* (1925), and David Worcester, *The Art of Satire* (1940).[87]

Tone. In recent criticism "tone" is often employed, after the example of I. A. Richards, for the attitudes to the subject matter and to the audience implied in a discourse or literary piece. The tone of a passage might be characterized, for example, as formal or intimate, solemn or playful,[97] serious or ironic, condescending or obsequious. Compare **Irony** . . . and refer to I. A. Richards, *Practical Criticism* (1929), Part III, Chaps. 1 and 3.[98]

Wit and Humor. The word "wit" once meant "intelligence" or "knowledge," a sense it still keeps in terms like "half-wit" and "unwittingly." In the seventeenth century "wit" was often applied, in criticism, to the characteristic use of paradox and surprising combinations of ideas in the writings of metaphysical poets . . . , and in the eighteenth century there were various attempts to distinguish between the "false wit" of Cowley and other metaphysical writers and the "true wit" recommended for the expression of thought in neoclassic poetry. . . . The term has now become still more specialized. "Wit," in common usage, is applied to a brief and deftly phrased expression, intentionally contrived to produce a shock of comic surprise. The surprise is usually the result of an unexpected, but plausible, connection or distinction between ideas, or of the sudden frustration of expectation. Philip Guedalla said, "History repeats itself: historians repeat each other." The trite comment about history turns out to be comically appropriate, with an unlooked for turn of meaning, to the writers of history as well. "The only sure way to double your money," Abe Martin remarked, "is to fold it and put it in your hip pocket." The eagerly awaited advice is tendered us, but in a way which is startlingly literal and practical. The resulting laughter, in the phrase of Immanuel Kant, arises "from the sudden transformation of a strained expectation into nothing"; or perhaps it would be more accurate to say, from the sudden satisfaction of an expectation in a way we did not expect. Abe Martin's remark is what Freud called "harmless wit," evoking a laugh or smile without malice. "Tendency wit," on the other hand, is derisive, directing the laugh at a particular object, or butt. "Mr. James Payn," Oscar Wilde commented on a contemporary novelist, "hunts down the obvious with the enthusiasm of a short-sighted detective. As one turns over the pages, the suspense of the author becomes almost unbearable." Wit often approximates the form of an epigram (see **Epigram**) and utilizes a number of devices defined elsewhere, such as **Irony** . . .

Repartee is a term aptly borrowed from fencing to signify a contest of wit between two or more people, in which each tries to cap the remark of the other, or to turn it to his own purpose. The Earl of Rochester suggested as an appropriate epitaph for Charles II:

> Here lies our sovereign lord the King,
> Whose word no man relies on;
> He never says a foolish thing,
> And never does a wise one.

Although amused by the epigram, King Charles said that the paradox was easily explained: he did his own talking, but all his actions were [103] dictated by his ministers. In King Charles's own period, stage comedies usually included long episodes of sustained repartee. The classic example is the discussion of the marriage contract in Congreve's *The Way of the World*, Act IV (see **Restoration comedy** under **Comedy**).

Humor, through the Renaissance period, was a physiological term for the four primary fluids of the human body: blood, phlegm, choler (or yellow bile), and melancholy (or black bile). The "temperament," or mixture, of these humors are thought to determine both a man's physical condition and his character. A preponderance of one or another humor in a temperament was supposed to produce four types of disposition, whose names have survived the underlying theory: sanguine (from *sanguis*, blood), phlegmatic, choleric, and melancholic. Ben Jonson based on this physiology his theory of the **comedy of humors,** in which each person is regarded as motivated by a preponderant humor that gives him a characteristic bias or eccentricity of disposition. See Ben Jonson's "Induction" to his *Every Man in his Humour* (1598).

The present meaning of the word "humor" has developed from the comic attributes of this "humorous" character in the Elizabethan period. Humor, like wit, can be predicated of a comic speech, but in that case it differs from wit in one or both of two ways. Wit, as we saw, is always intentionally comic, while humor may be unintentional; and a humorous saying is not cast in the neat and startling epigrammatic form of wit. For example, the discussion of the mode of life of the goldfish in Central Park by the irascible taxi driver in J. D. Salinger's *The Catcher in the Rye* is unintentionally but superbly humorous, while the speech of Mr. Bennet in Austen's *Pride and Prejudice,* or of Mercutio in *Romeo and Juliet,* is intentionally humorous, though rarely expressed in the rhetorical shape of wit. Still more important is the difference that wit is always verbal, while humor applies to what is laughable in a person's appearance and his actions, as well as in what he says. For example, we find humor in the wordless pantomime of Charlie Chaplin and in the sometimes uncaptioned cartoons in the *New Yorker*. In a thoroughly humorous situation, the sources of the fun are more complex. In Act III, scene IV, of *Twelfth Night*, Malvolio's appearance and actions, and his speech as well, are humorous, but all despite his own intentions. One source of the greatness in a comic creation like Shakespeare's Falstaff is that he exhibits every possible kind of comedy. Falstaff is humorous in the way he looks and in what he does; what he says is always either witty or humorous; while his actions and speech are sometimes humorous against his intention, and often humorous even beyond his intention.

It will be apparent by now that humor is a species of the **comic.** We may extend the distinction Freud made between harmless and tendency wit and say that humor is pure or "harmless" comedy, in which we are made to laugh because a person is ridiculous but not because he is being [104] ridiculed. When we are made to laugh with a touch of contempt or malice, the situation is an instance, not of the humorously comic, but of "tendency" comedy, in which the laughter is derisive and is being used as a weapon. Tendency comedy, together with tendency wit, are the techniques that the satirist employs in his enterprise of diminishing and deriding his subjects. See **comic** under **Satire,** and refer to Max Eastman, *Enjoyment of Laughter* (1936).[105]

PART TWO

PRACTICE

AESOP

Town Mouse and Country Mouse

FROM *Aesop's Fables,* edited and translated by S. A. Handford. Harmondsworth, England: Penguin Books Ltd., 1954. Reprinted by permission of Penguin Books Ltd.

A field-mouse invited a friend who lived in a town house to dine with him in the country. The other accepted with alacrity; but when he found that the fare consisted only of barley and other corn, he said to his host: 'Let me tell you, my friend, you live like an ant. But I have an abundance of good things to eat, and if you will come home with me you shall share them all.' So the two of them went off at once; and when his friend showed him peas and beans, bread, dates, cheese, honey, and fruit, the astonished field-mouse congratulated him heartily and cursed his own lot. They were about to begin their meal when the door suddenly opened, and the timid creatures were so scared by the sound that they scuttled into chinks. When they had returned and were just going to take some dried figs, they saw someone else come into the room to fetch something, and once more they jumped to take cover in their holes. At this the field-mouse decided that he did not care if he had to go hungry. 'Good-bye, my friend,' he said with a groan. 'You may eat your fill and enjoy yourself. But your good cheer costs you dear in danger and fear. I would rather gnaw my poor meals of barley and corn without being afraid or having to watch anyone out of the corner of my eye.'

A simple life with peace and quiet is better than faring luxuriously and being tortured by fear.[43]

HORACE

Town Mouse and Country Mouse [*c.* 30 B.C.]

FROM *Aesop's Fables,* edited and
translated by S. A. Handford. Harmondsworth, England: Penguin
Books Ltd., 1954. Reprinted by permission of Penguin Books Ltd.

'Once upon a time, the story goes, a country mouse welcomed a
town mouse to his poor hole—an old friend whom he had entertained
before. He lived frugally and kept an anxious eye on his store of food;
yet his careful soul could unbend to [218] please a guest. You can imagine the scene. He was not the mouse to grudge a friend his hoarded
peas and long grains of oats; he brought dried berries for him in his
mouth and half-nibbled bits of bacon, hoping by this variety of fare to
tempt the other's fastidious appetite. But his guest barely condescended
to take a bit of each dainty, while the master of the house, leaving all
the best food for him, stretched himself on a couch of fresh straw and
dined off spelt and darnel. At length the townsman grew impatient.
"What pleasure do you find, my friend," he asked, "in living a hard life
on this steep wooded slope? Why not choose town and company in
preference to rough woodland? Take my advice: come right away with
me. Mortality is the lot of all earthly creatures; neither great nor small
can escape death. So, my good sir, live while you may in the enjoyment
of good things, and remember how short your life must be." The
countryman was impressed by these remarks. Out of doors he jumped
in an instant, and they did the whole journey in one stretch, hoping to
creep inside the city walls under cover of darkness. Night had just
reached the middle of its course when they set foot within a wealthy
mansion, where scarlet coverings gleamed on ivory couches and baskets
stood piled high with dishes left from yesterday's great banquet. The
country guest was made to lie at full length on a crimson coverlet,
while his host ran to and fro like a waiter with tunic girt up, serving
course upon course, and played the part of a house-slave to the very
life, taking a preliminary lick at every dish he brought. His friend lay
back, congratulating himself on the improvement in his fortune and
acting the delighted guest, when suddenly a loud slamming of the
doors made them both jump off their sofas. From end to end of the
dining-hall they scampered in alarm; then the great house echoed with
the barking of watch-dogs till they were scared out of their wits. "This

life is no use to me," said the visitor; "so I bid you good-bye. For my part, I will stay in my forest hole where I am safe from surprises, and appease my hunger with humble vetch." ' [219]

JEAN de LA FONTAINE

The Town Rat and the Country Rat [1668]

FROM *The Fables of La Fontaine,* edited and translated by Marianne Moore. New York: The Viking Press, Inc. Copyright 1954 by Marianne Moore. Reprinted by permission of The Viking Press, Inc.

In this ancient parable,
Town rat proffered country rat
A fashionable meal
As a change from this and that,

Where on a rug from Turkey,
A feast for two was ready.
Fond fancy alone could see
The pair's joint ecstasy.[20]

Fine food made each's plate replete—
More dainties there than greed could paint,
But as they were about to eat,
Noises were heard; the pair felt faint.

At the door, sniff and smell.
What was scratching steadily?
Both frightened ill, half fell,
Then fled confusedly.

When they had dared to reappear,
In seclusion with relief,
The city rat resumed, "My dear,
Come now, divide the beef."

—"I have dined," the field rat said;
"Be my guest, pray, a day hence,
Though you'll not find, I am afraid,
Similar magnificence.

Yet I'm never in danger: I've supped,
Carefree from year to year;
And so farewell. What is good cheer
Which death threats can disrupt?" [21]

JAMES THURBER

The Mouse Who Went to the Country

FROM *The New Yorker,* January 21, 1939. Reprinted by permission; Copr. © 1939 The New Yorker Magazine, Inc.

Once upon a Sunday there was a city mouse who went to visit a country mouse. He hid away on a train the country mouse had told him to take, only to find that on Sundays it did not stop at Beddington. Hence the city mouse could not get off at Beddington and catch a bus for Sibert's Junction, where he was to be met by the country mouse. The city mouse, in fact, was carried on to Middleburg, where he waited three hours for a train to take him back. When he got back to Beddington he found that the last bus for Sibert's Junction had just left, so he ran and he ran and he ran and he finally caught the bus and crept aboard, only to find that it was not the bus for Sibert's Junction at all, but was going in the opposite direction through Pell's Hollow and Grumm to a place called Wimberby. When the bus finally stopped, the city mouse got out into a heavy rain and found that there were no more buses that night going anywhere. "To the hell with it," said the city mouse, and he walked back to the city.

Moral: *Stay where you are, you're sitting pretty.*[19]

GEOFFREY CHAUCER

The Nun's Priest's Tale

FROM *The Canterbury Tales* [c. 1387]. In *Chaucer: The Canterbury Tales,* edited and translated by Nevill Coghill. Harmondsworth, England: Penguin Books Ltd., 1952. Reprinted by permission of Penguin Books Ltd.

Once, long ago, there dwelt a poor old widow
In a small cottage, by a little meadow
Beside a grove and standing in a dale.
This widow-woman of whom I tell my tale
Since the sad day when last she was a wife
Had led a very patient, simple life.
Little she had in capital or rent,
But still, by making do with what God sent,
She kept herself and her two daughters going.
Three hefty sows—no more—were all her showing,   10
Three cows as well; there was a sheep called Molly.
Sooty her hall, her kitchen melancholy,[230]
And there she ate full many a slender meal;
There was no *sauce piquante* to spice her veal,
No dainty morsel ever passed her throat,
According to her cloth she cut her coat.
Repletion never left her in disquiet
And all her physic was a temperate diet,
Hard work for exercise and heart's content.
And rich man's gout did nothing to prevent   20
Her dancing, apoplexy struck her not;
She drank no wine, nor white nor red had got.
Her board was mostly served with white and black,
Milk and brown bread, in which she found no lack;
Broiled bacon or an egg or two were common,
She was in fact a sort of dairy-woman.
She had a yard that was enclosed about
By a stockade and a dry ditch without,
In which she kept a cock called Chanticleer.
In all the land for crowing he'd no peer;   30
His voice was jollier than the organ blowing

In church on Sundays, he was great at crowing.
Far, far more regular than any clock
Or abbey bell the crowing of this cock.
The equinoctial wheel and its position
At each ascent he knew by intuition;
At every hour—fifteen degrees of movement—
He crowed so well there could be no improvement.
His comb was redder than fine coral, tall
And battlemented like a castle wall,   40
His bill was black and shone as bright as jet,
Like azure were his legs and they were set
On azure toes with nails of lily white,
Like burnished gold his feathers, flaming bright.
        This gentlecock was master in some measure
Of seven hens, all there to do his pleasure.
They were his sisters and his paramours,
Coloured like him in all particulars;
She with the loveliest dyes upon her throat
Was known as gracious Lady Pertelote.[231]   50
Courteous she was, discreet and debonair,
Companionable too, and took such care
In her deportment, since she was seven days old
She held the heart of Chanticleer controlled,
Locked up securely in her every limb;
O such happiness his love to him!
And such a joy it was to hear them sing,
As when the glorious sun began to spring,
In sweet accord *My Love is far from land*
—For in those far off days I understand   60
All birds and animals could speak and sing.
        Now it befell, as dawn began to spring,
When Chanticleer and Pertelote and all
His wives were perched in this poor widow's hall
(Fair Pertelote was next him on the perch),
This Chanticleer began to groan and lurch
Like someone sorely troubled by a dream,
And Pertelote who heard him roar and scream
Was quite aghast and said, 'O dearest heart,
What's ailing you? Why do you groan and start?   70
Fie, what a sleeper! What a noise to make!'
'Madam,' he said, 'I beg you not to take
Offence, but by the Lord I had a dream
So terrible just now I had to scream;
I still can feel my heart racing from fear.
God turn my dream to good and guard all here.
And keep my body out of durance vile!

I dreamt that roaming up and down a while
Within our yard I saw a kind of beast,
A sort of hound that tried or seemed at least   80
To try and seize me ... would have killed me dead!
His colour was a blend of yellow and red,
His ears and tail were tipped with sable fur
Unlike the rest; he was a russet cur.
Small was his snout, his eyes were glowing bright.
It was enough to make one die of fright.
That was no doubt what made me groan and swoon.'
        'For shame,' she said, 'you timorous poltroon! [232]
Alas, what cowardice! By God above,
You've forfeited my heart and lost my love.   90
I cannot love a coward, come what may.
For certainly, whatever we may say,
All women long—and O that it might be!
For husbands tough, dependable and free,
Secret, discreet, no niggard, not a fool
That boasts and then will find his courage cool
At every trifling thing. By God above,
How dare you say for shame, and to your love,
That anything at all was to be feared?
Have you no manly heart to match your beard?   100
And can a dream reduce you to such terror?
Dreams are a vanity, God knows, pure error.
Dreams are engendered in the too-replete
From vapours in the belly, which compete
With others, too abundant, swollen tight.
        'No doubt the redness in your dream to-night
Comes from the superfluity and force
Of the red choler in your blood. Of course.
That is what puts a dreamer in the dread
Of crimsoned arrows, fires flaming red,   110
Of great red monsters making as to fight him,
And big red whelps and little ones to bite him;
Just so the black and melancholy vapours
Will set a sleeper shrieking, cutting capers
And swearing that black bears, black bulls as well,
Or blackest fiends are haling him to Hell.
And there are other vapours that I know
That on a sleeping man will work their woe,
But I'll pass on as lightly as I can.
        'Take Cato now, that was so wise a man,   120
Did he not say, "Take no account of dreams"?
Now, sir,' she said, 'on flying from these beams,
For love of God do take some laxative;

Upon my soul that's the advice to give
For melancholy choler; let me urge
You free yourself from vapours with a purge.[233]
And that you may have no excuse to tarry
By saying this town has no apothecary,
I shall myself instruct you and prescribe
Herbs that will cure all vapours of that tribe,   130
Herbs from our very farmyard! You will find
Their natural property is to unbind
And purge you well beneath and well above.
Now don't forget it, dear, for God's own love!
Your face is choleric and shows distension;
Be careful lest the sun in his ascension
Should catch you full of humours, hot and many.
And if he does, my dear, I'll lay a penny
It means a bout of fever or a breath
Or tertian ague. You may catch your death.   140
    'Worms for a day or two I'll have to give
As a digestive, then your laxative.
Centaury, fumitory, caper-spurge
And hellebore will make a splendid purge;
And then there's laurel or the blackthorn berry,
Ground-ivy too that makes our yard so merry;
Peck them right up, my dear, and swallow whole.
Be happy, husband, by your father's soul!
Don't be afraid of dreams. I'll say no more.'
    'Madam,' he said, 'I thank you for your lore,   150
But with regard to Cato all the same,
His wisdom has, no doubt, a certain fame,
But though he said that we should take no heed
Of dreams, by God in ancient books I read
Of many a man of more authority
Than ever Cato was, believe you me,
Who say the very opposite is true
And prove their theories by experience too.
Dreams have quite often been significations
As well of triumphs as of tribulations   160
That people undergo in this our life.
This needs no argument at all, dear wife,
The proof is all too manifest indeed.
    'One of the greatest authors one can read [234]
Says thus: there were two comrades once who went
On pilgrimage, sincere in their intent.
And as it happened they had reached a town
Where such a throng was milling up and down
And yet so scanty the accommodation,

They could not find themselves a habitation, 170
No, not a cottage that could lodge them both.
And so they separated, very loath,
Under constraint of this necessity
And each went off to find some hostelry,
And lodge whatever way his luck might fall.
'The first of them found refuge in a stall
Down in a yard with oxen and a plough.
His friend found lodging for himself somehow
Elsewhere, by accident or destiny,
Which governs all of us and equally. 180
'Now it so happened, long ere it was day,
This fellow had a dream, and as he lay
In bed it seemed he heard his comrade call,
"Help! I am lying in an ox's stall
And shall to-night be murdered as I lie.
Help me, dear brother, help or I shall die!
Come in all haste!" Such were the words he spoke;
The dreamer, lost in terror, then awoke.
But once awake he paid it no attention,
Turned over and dismissed it as invention, 190
It was a dream, he thought, a fantasy.
And twice he dreamt this dream successively.
'Yet a third time his comrade came again,
Or seemed to come, and said, "I have been slain.
Look, look! my wounds are bleeding wide and deep.
Rise early in the morning, break your sleep
And go to the west gate. You there shall see
A cart all loaded up with dung," said he,
"And in that dung my body has been hidden.
Boldly arrest that cart as you are bidden. 200
It was my money that they killed me for."
'He told him every detail, sighing sore,[235]
And pitiful in feature, pale of hue.
This dream, believe me, Madam, turned out true;
For in the dawn, as soon as it was light,
He went to where his friend had spent the night
And when he came upon the cattle-stall
He looked about him and began to call.
'The innkeeper, appearing thereupon,
Quickly gave answer, "Sir, your friend has gone. 210
He left the town a little after dawn."
The man began to feel suspicious, drawn
By memories of his dream—the western gate,
The dung-cart—off he went, he would not wait,
Towards the western entry. There he found,

Seemingly on its way to dung some ground,
A dung-cart loaded on the very plan.
Described so closely by the murdered man.
So he began to shout courageously
For right and vengeance on the felony,   220
"My friend's been killed! There's been a foul attack,
He's in that cart and gaping on his back!
Fetch the authorities, get the sheriff down
—Whosever job it is to run the town—
Help! My companion's murdered, sent to glory!"
      'What need I add to finish off the story?
People ran out and cast the cart to ground,
And in the middle of the dung they found
The murdered man. The corpse was fresh and new.
      'O blessed God, that art so just and true,   230
Thus thou revealest murder! As we say,
"Murder will out." We see it day by day.
Murder's a foul, abominable treason,
So loathsome to God's justice, to God's reason,
He will not suffer its concealment. True,
Things may lie hidden for a year or two,
But still "Murder will out," that's my conclusion.
      'All the town officers in great confusion
Seized on the carter and they gave him hell,
And then they racked the inkeeper as well,[236]   240
And both confessed. And then they took the wrecks
And there and then they hanged them by their necks.
      'By this we see that dreams are to be dreaded.
And in the self-same book I find embedded,
Right in the very chapter after this
(I'm not inventing, as I hope for bliss)
The story of two men who started out
To cross the sea—for merchandise no doubt—
But as the winds were contrary they waited.
It was a pleasant town, I should have stated,   250
Merrily grouped about the haven-side.
A few days later with the evening tide
The wind veered round so as to suit them best;
They were delighted and they went to rest
Meaning to sail next morning early. Well,
To one of them a miracle befell.
      'This man as he lay sleeping, it would seem,
Just before dawn had an astounding dream.
He thought a man was standing by his bed
Commanding him to wait, and thus he said: 260
"If you set sail to-morrow as you intend

You will be drowned. My tale is at an end."
   'He woke and told his friend what had occurred
And begged him that the journey be deferred
At least a day, implored him not to start.
But his companion, lying there apart,
Began to laugh and treat him to derision.
"I'm not afraid," he said, "of any vision,
To let it interfere with my affairs;
A straw for all your dreamings and your scares.   270
Dreams are just empty nonsense, merest japes;
Why, people dream all day of owls and apes,
All sorts of trash that can't be understood,
Things that have never happened and never could.
But as I see you mean to stay behind
And miss the tide for wilful sloth of mind
God knows I'm sorry for it, but good day!"
And so he took his leave and went his way.[237]
   'And yet, before they'd covered half the trip
—I don't know what went wrong—there was a rip   280
And by some accident the ship went down,
Her bottom rent, all hands aboard to drown
In sight of all the vessels at her side,
That had put out upon the self-same tide.
   'So, my dear Pertelote, if you discern
The force of these examples, you may learn
One never should be careless about dreams,
For, undeniably, I say it seems
That many are a sign of trouble breeding.
   'Now, take St Kenelm's life which I've been
         reading;   290
He was Kenulphus' son, the noble King
Of Mercia. Now, St Kenelm dreamt a thing
Shortly before they murdered him one day.
He saw his murder in a dream, I say.
His nurse expounded it and gave her reasons
On every point and warned him against treasons
But as the saint was only seven years old
All that she said about it left him cold.
He was so holy how could visions hurt?
   'By God, I willingly would give my shirt   300
To have you read his legend as I've read it;
And, Madam Pertelote, upon my credit,
Macrobius wrote of dreams and can explain us
The vision of young Scipio Africanus,
And he affirms that dreams can give a due
Warnings of things that later on come true.

'And then there's the Old Testament—a manual
Well worth your study; see the *Book of Daniel.*
Did Daniel think a dream was vanity?
Read about Joseph too and you will see   310
That many dreams—I do not say that all—
Give cognizance of what is to befall
     'Look at Lord Pharaoh, king of Egypt! Look
At what befell his butler and his cook.
Did not their visions have a certain force?
But those who study history of course [238]
Meet many dreams that set them wondering.
     'What about Croesus too, the Lydian king,
Who dreamt that he was sitting in a tree,
Meaning he would be hanged? It had to be.   320
     'Or take Andromache, great Hector's wife;
The day on which he was to lose his life
She dreamt about, the very night before,
And realized that if Hector went to war
He would be lost that very day in battle.
She warned him; he dismissed it all as prattle
And sallied forth to fight, being self-willed,
And there he met Achilles and was killed.
The tale is long and somewhat overdrawn,
And anyhow it's very nearly dawn,   330
So let me say in very brief conclusion
My dream undoubtedly foretells confusion,
It bodes me ill, I say. And, furthermore,
Upon your laxatives I set no store,
For they are venomous. I've suffered by them
Often enough before and I defy them.
     'And now, let's talk of fun and stop all this.
Dear Madam, as I hope for Heaven's bliss,
Of one thing God has sent me plenteous grace,
For when I see the beauty of your face,   340
That scarlet loveliness about your eyes,
All thought of terror and confusion dies.
For it's as certain as the Creed, I know,
Mulier est hominis confusio
(A Latin tag, dear Madam, meaning this:
"Woman is man's delight and all his bliss"),
For when at night I feel your feathery side,
Although perforce I cannot take a ride
Because, alas, our perch was made too narrow,
Delight and solace fill me to the marrow   350
And I defy all visions and all dreams!'

And with that word he flew down from the beams,
For it was day, and down his hens flew all,
And with a chuck he gave the troupe a call [239]
For he had found a seed upon the floor.
Royal he was, he was afraid no more.
He feathered Pertelote in wanton play
And trod her twenty times ere prime of day.
Grim as a lion's was his manly frown
As on his toes he sauntered up and down;   360
He scarcely deigned to set his foot to ground
And every time a seed of corn was found
He gave a chuck, and up his wives ran all.
Thus royal as a prince who strides his hall
Leave we this Chanticleer engaged on feeding
And pass to the adventure that was breeding.
    Now when the month in which the world began,
March, the first month, when God created man,
Was over, and the thirty-second day
Thereafter ended, on the third of May   370
It happened that Chanticleer in all his pride,
His seven wives attendant at his side,
Cast his eyes upward to the blazing sun,
Which in the sign of *Taurus* then had run
His twenty-one degrees and somewhat more,
And knew by nature and no other lore
That it was nine o'clock. With blissful voice
He crew triumphantly and said, 'Rejoice,
Behold the sun! The sun is up, my seven.
Look, it has climbed forty degrees in heaven,   380
Forty degrees and one in fact, by this.
Dear Madam Pertelote, my earthly bliss,
Hark to those blissful birds and how they sing!
Look at those pretty flowers, how they spring!
Solace and revel fill my heart!' He laughed.
    But in that moment Fate let fly her shaft;
Ever the latter end of joy is woe,
God knows that worldly joy is swift to go.
A rhetorician with a flair for style
Could chronicle this maxim in his file   390
Of Notable Remarks with safe conviction.
Then let the wise give ear; this is no fiction [240]
My story is as true, I undertake,
As that of good Sir Lancelot du Lake
Who held all women in such high esteem.
Let me return full circle to my theme.

A coal-tipped fox of sly iniquity
That had been lurking round the grove for three
Long years, that very night burst through and passed
Stockade and hedge, as Providence forecast,   400
Into the yard where Chanticleer the Fair
Was wont, with all his ladies, to repair.
Still, in a bed of cabbages, he lay
Until about the middle of the day
Watching the cock and waiting for his cue,
As all these homicides so gladly do
That lie about in wait to murder men.
O false assassin, lurking in thy den!
O new Iscariot, new Ganelon!
And O Greek Sinon, thou whose treachery won   410
Troy town and brought it utterly to sorrow!
O Chanticleer, accursed be that morrow
That brought thee to the yard from thy high beams!
Thou hadst been warned, and truly, by thy dreams
That this would be a perilous day for thee.
But that which God's foreknowledge can foresee
Must needs occur, as certain men of learning
Have said. Ask any scholar of discerning;
He'll say the Schools are filled with altercation
On this vexed matter of predestination   420
Long bandied by a hundred thousand men.
How can I sift it to the bottom then?
The Holy Doctor St Augustine shines
In this, and there is Bishop Bradwardine's
Authority, Boethius, too, decreeing
Whether the fact of God's divine foreseeing
Constrains me to perform a certain act
—And by 'constraint' I mean the simple fact
Of mere compulsion by necessity—
Or whether a free choice is granted me [241]   430
To do a given act or not to do it
Though, ere it was accomplished, God foreknew it,
Or whether Providence is not so stringent
And merely makes necessity contingent.
But I decline discussion of the matter;
My tale is of a cock and of the clatter
That came of following his wife's advice
To walk about his yard on the precise
Morning after the dream of which I told.
O woman's counsel is so often cold!   440
A woman's counsel brought us first to woe,
Made Adam out of Paradise to go

Where he had been so merry, so well at ease.
But, for I know not whom it may displease
If I suggest that women are to blame,
Pass over that; I only speak in game.
Read the authorities to know about
What has been said of women; you'll find out.
These are the cock's words, and not mine, I'm giving;
I think no harm of any woman living.   450
    Merrily in her dust-bath in the sand
Lay Pertelote. Her sisters were at hand
Basking in sunlight. Chanticleer sang free,
More merrily than a mermaid in the sea
(For *Physiologus* reports the thing
And says how well and merrily they sing).
And so it happened as he cast his eye
Towards the cabbage at a butterfly
It fell upon the fox there, lying low.
Gone was all inclination then to crow.   460
'Cok cok,' he cried, giving a sudden start,
As one who feels a terror at his heart,
For natural instinct teaches beasts to flee
The moment they perceive an enemy,
Though they had never met with it before.
    This Chanticleer was shaken to the core
And would have fled. The fox was quick to say
However, 'Sir! Whither so fast away? [242]
Are you afraid of me, that am your friend?
A fiend, or worse, I should be, to intend   470
You harm, or practise villainy upon you;
Dear sir, I was not even spying on you!
Truly I came to do no other thing
Than just to lie and listen to you sing.
You have as merry a voice as God has given
To any angel in the courts of Heaven;
To that you add a musical sense as strong
As had Boethius who was skilled in song.
My Lord your Father (God receive his soul!),
Your mother too—how courtly, what control!—   480
Have honoured my poor house, to my great ease;
And you, sir, too, I should be glad to please.
For, when it comes to singing, I'll say this
(Else may these eyes of mine be barred from bliss),
There never was a singer I would rather
Have heard at dawn than your respected father.
All that he sang came welling from his soul
And how he put his voice under control!

The pains he took to keep his eyes tight shut
In concentration—then the tip-toe strut,   490
The slender neck stretched out, the delicate beak!
No singer could approach him in technique
Or rival him in song, still less surpass.
I've read the story in *Burnel the Ass*,
Among some other verses, of a cock
Whose leg in youth was broken by a knock
A clergyman's son had given him, and for this
He made the father lose his benefice.
But certainly there's no comparison
Between the subtlety of such an one   500
And the discretion of your father's art
And wisdom. Oh, for charity of heart,
Can you not emulate your sire and sing?'
        This Chanticleer began to beat a wing
As one incapable of smelling treason,
So wholly had this flattery ravished reason.[243]
Alas, my lords! there's many a sycophant
And flatterer that fill your courts with cant
And give more pleasure with their zeal forsooth
Than he who speaks in soberness and truth.   510
Read what *Ecclesiasticus* records
Of flatterers. 'Ware treachery, my lords!
        This Chanticleer stood high upon his toes,
He stretched his neck, his eyes began to close,
His beak to open; with his eyes shut tight
He then began to sing with all his might.
        Sir Russel Fox then leapt to the attack,
Grabbing his gorge he flung him o'er his back
And off he bore him to the woods, the brute,
And for the moment there was no pursuit.   520
        O Destiny that may not be evaded!
Alas that Chanticleer had so paraded!
Alas that he had flown down from the beams!
O that his wife took no account of dreams!
And on a Friday too to risk their necks!
O Venus, goddess of the joys of sex,
Since Chanticleer thy mysteries professed
And in thy service always did his best,
And more for pleasure than to multiply
His kind, on thine own day is he to die?   530
        O Geoffrey, thou my dear and sovereign master
Who, when they brought King Richard to disaster
And shot him dead, lamented so his death,
Would that I had thy skill, thy gracious breath,

To chide a Friday half so well as you!
(For he was killed upon a Friday too.)
Then I could fashion you a rhapsody
For Chanticleer in dread and agony.
    Sure never such a cry or lamentation
Was made by ladies of high Trojan station,   540
When Ilium fell and Pyrrhus with his sword
Grabbed Priam by the beard, their king and lord,
And slew him there as the *Aeneid* tells,
As what was uttered by those hens. Their yells [244]
Surpassed them all in palpitating fear
When they beheld the rape of Chanticleer.
Dame Pertelote emitted sovereign shrieks
That echoed up in anguish to the peaks
Louder than those extorted from the wife
Of Hasdrubal, when he had lost his life   550
And Carthage all in flame and ashes lay.
She was so full of torment and dismay
That in the very flames she chose her part
And burnt to ashes with a steadfast heart.
O woeful hens, louder your shrieks and higher
Than those of Roman matrons when the fire
Consumed their husbands, senators of Rome,
When Nero burnt their city and their home,
Beyond a doubt that Nero was their bale!
    Now let me turn again to tell my tale;   560
This blessed widow and her daughters too
Heard all these hens in clamour and halloo
And, rushing to the door at all this shrieking,
They saw the fox towards the covert streaking
And, on his shoulder, Chanticleer stretched flat.
'Look, look!' they cried, 'O mercy, look at that!
Ha! Ha! the fox!' and after him they ran,
And stick in hand ran many a serving man,
Ran Coll our dog, ran Talbot, Bran and Shaggy,
And with a distaff in her hand ran Maggie,   570
Ran cow and calf and ran the very hogs
In terror at the barking of the dogs;
The men and women shouted, ran and cursed,
They ran so hard they thought their hearts would burst,
They yelled like fiends in Hell, ducks left the water
Quacking and flapping as on point of slaughter,
Up flew the geese in terror over the trees,
Out of the hive came forth the swarm of bees;
So hideous was the noise—God bless us all,
Jack Straw and all his followers in their brawl   580

Were never half so shrill, for all their noise,
When they were murdering those Flemish boys,[245]
As that day's hue and cry upon the fox.
They grabbed up trumpets made of brass and box,
Of horn and bone, on which they blew and pooped,
And therewithal they shouted and they whooped
So that it seemed the very heavens would fall.
    And now, good people, pay attention all.
See how Dame Fortune quickly changes side
And robs her enemy of hope and pride!   590
This cock that lay upon the fox's back
In all his dread contrived to give a quack
And said, 'Sir Fox, if I were you, as God's
My witness, I would round upon these clods
And shout, "Turn back, you saucy bumpkins all!
A very pestilence upon you fall!
Now that I have in safety reached the wood
Do what you like, the cock is mine for good;
I'll eat him there in spite of every one." '
    The fox replying, 'Faith, it shall be done!'   600
Opened his mouth and spoke. The nimble bird,
Breaking away upon the uttered word,
Flew high into the tree-tops on the spot.
And when the fox perceived where he had got,
'Alas,' he cried, 'alas, my Chanticleer,
I've done you grievous wrong, indeed I fear
I must have frightened you; I grabbed too hard
When I caught hold and took you from the yard.
But, sir, I meant no harm, don't be offended,
Come down and I'll explain what I intended;   610
So help me God I'll tell the truth—on oath!
'No,' said the cock, 'and curses on us both,
And first on me if I were such a dunce
As let you fool me oftener than once.
Never again, for all your flattering lies,
You'll coax a song to make me blink my eyes;
And as for those who blink when they should look,
God blot them from his everlasting Book!'
'Nay, rather,' said the fox, 'his plagues be flung
On all who chatter that should hold their tongue.' [246]   620
    Lo, such it is not to be on your guard
Against the flatterers of the world, or yard,
And if you think my story is absurd,
A foolish trifle of a beast and bird,
A fable of a fox, a cock, a hen,
Take hold upon the moral, gentlemen.

St Paul himself, a saint of great discerning,
Says that all things are written for our learning;
So take the grain and let the chaff be still.
And, gracious Father, if it be thy will   630
As saith my Saviour, make us all good men,
And bring us to his heavenly bliss.
                                        Amen.

Words of the Host to the Nun's Priest

'Sir Priest,' our Host remarked in merry tones,
'Blest be your breeches and your precious stones,
That was a merry tale of Chanticleer!
If you had only been a secular
You would have trodden a pretty fowl, no doubt,
Had you the heart, your muscles would hold out.
You look as if you needed hens, I mean,
Yes, more than seven. Seven times seventeen!
Just look what brawn he has, this gentle priest,
And what a neck! His chest's not of the least.   10
As for his eyes, they're like a sparrow-hawk's,
And his complexion like a box of chalks;
He needs no dyes imported from the East
Or Portugal. Good luck to you, Sir Priest,
For telling a fine tale!' And saying thus
He turned, as you shall hear, to one of us.[247]

MOLIÈRE

Love Is the Best Doctor (L'Amour Médecin) [1665]

FROM *The Dramatic Works of Molière,* translated by Henri Van Laun. New York: A. W. Lovering, n.d. [c. 1878]. Vol. II.

DRAMATIS PERSONAE

IN THE PROLOGUE

COMEDY, MUSIC, THE BALLET *(dancing)*

IN THE COMEDY

SGANARELLE, *father to Lucinde*
CLITANDRE, *in love with Lucinde*
M. GUILLAUME, *dealer in hangings*
M. JOSSE, *goldsmith*
M. TOMÈS
M. DESFONANDRÈS
M. MACROTON   } *physicians*
M. BAHIS

M. FILERIN, *physician*
A NOTARY
CHAMPAGNE, *Sganarelle's servant*
LUCINDE, *daughter of Sganarelle*
AMINTA, *Sganarelle's neighbour*
LUCRETIA, *Sganarelle's niece*
LISETTE, *maid to Lucinde*

IN THE BALLET

First Entry
CHAMPAGNE, *Sganarelle's servant, dancing*
FOUR PHYSICIANS, *dancing*

Second Entry
A QUACK, *singing*
TRIVELINS *and* SCARAMOUCHES, *dancing in the suite of the quack*

Third Entry
COMEDY, MUSIC, THE BALLET
SPORTS, LAUGHTER, *and* PLEASURES, *dancing*

SCENE: *Paris, in one of the rooms of Sganarelle's house.*[146]

PROLOGUE

COMEDY, MUSIC, THE BALLET.

COMEDY. Let us our fruitless quarrels banish,
  Each other's talents not by turns dispute:
  But greater glory to attain
  This day of all let be our aim.
  Let us all three unite with matchless zeal
  The greatest King on earth with pleasure to provide.

THE THREE TOGETHER. Let us all three unite with matchless zeal
  The greatest King on earth with pleasure to provide.

COMEDY. From toils more irksome than can be imagined,
  Amongst us, now and then, he comes to unbend,
  Can greater glory, greater pleasure be our share?

THE THREE TOGETHER. Let us all three unite with matchless zeal
  The greatest King on earth with pleasure to provide.[147]

ACT I

SCENE 1   SGANARELLE, AMINTA, LUCRETIA, M. GUILLAUME, M. JOSSE

SGANARELLE. What a strange thing is life! and well may I say with a great ancient philosopher, that he who has much land has also strife, and misfortune seldom comes alone. I had but one wife, and she is dead.

M. GUILLAUME. And, pray, how many would you have?

SGANARELLE. She is dead, friend Guillaume. I take this loss very much to heart, and I cannot think of it without tears. I was not altogether satisfied with her behaviour, and we often quarrelled; but, after all, death settles everything. She is dead; I bewail her. If she were alive, we would very likely quarrel. Of all the children God sent me, He has left me but one daughter, and it is she who is the cause of all my trouble; for I see her plunged in the most dismal melancholy, the greatest sadness, of which there is no way of getting rid, and the cause of which I cannot even learn. I declare I am at my wit's end, and am very much in want of good advice about it. (To Lucretia) You are my niece; (to Aminta) you my neighbour; (to M. Guillaume and M. Josse) you my companions and friends: tell me, I pray, what I am to do.

M. JOSSE. As for me, I think that finery and dress are the things which please young girls most; and if I were you, I should buy her, this very day, a handsome set of diamonds, or rubies, or emeralds.

M. GUILLAUME. And I, if I were in your place, I would buy her a beautiful set of hangings, with a landscape, or some figures in them, and I should have them hung up in her room to cheer her spirits and to please her eyes.

AMINTA. As for me, I would not take so much trouble; I would marry her well, and as quickly as I could, to that young man who asked her hand some time ago, as I have been told.

LUCRETIA. And I, I think your daughter is not at all fit to[148] be married. She has too delicate and unhealthy a constitution, and it is almost sending her wilfully and speedily to the next world, to expose her to bear children in the state she is in. The busy world does not suit her at all, and I would advise you to put her in a convent, where she will find some amusement more to her taste.

SGANARELLE. All this advice is certainly admirable, but I think it rather interested, and I find that you are giving it very much for your own benefit. You are a goldsmith, M. Josse; and your advice savours of a man who wants to get rid of his wares. You sell hangings, M. Guillaume, and you look to me as if you had some which you would fain part with. The young man whom you are in love with, fair neighbour, is, I have been told, the very one who is somewhat favourably disposed towards my daughter; and you would not be sorry to see her the wife of another. And as for you, my dear niece, it is not my intention, as is well known, to allow my daughter to get married at all, for reasons best known to myself; but your advice to make a nun of her is that of a woman who might charitably wish to become my sole heiress. Therefore, ladies and gentlemen, although your counsels be the best in the world, with your permission, I shall not follow a single one of them. *(Alone.)* So much for those fashionable advisers.

SCENE 2   LUCINDE, SGANARELLE

SGANARELLE. Ah, here is my daughter come to take a breath of air. She does not see me. She is sighing; she looks up to the sky. *(To Lucinde)* May Heaven protect you! Good morning, my darling. Well, what is the matter? How do you feel? What! always so sad and so melancholy, and you will not tell me what ails you? Come, open your little heart to me. There, my poor pet, come and tell your little thoughts to your little fond papa. Keep your spirits up. Let me give you a kiss. Come. *(Aside)* It makes me wild to see her in that humour. *(To Lucinde)* But tell me, do you wish to kill me with displeasure; and am I not to know the reason of this great listlessness? Tell me the cause, and I promise that I shall do everything for you. Yes, if you will only tell me[149] why you are so sad, I assure you and swear on this very spot, that I shall leave nothing undone to please you; I cannot say more. Are you jealous because one of your companions is better dressed than yourself, and is it some new-fashioned stuff of which you want to dress? No. Is your room not furnished nicely enough, and do you wish for one of those cabinets from St. Laurent's Fair? It is not that. Do you feel inclined to take lessons in something, and shall I get you a master to teach you how to play upon the harpsichord? No, not that either. Are you in love with some one, and do you wish to be married? *(Lucinde gives an affirmative sign.)*

SCENE 3   SGANARELLE, LUCINDE, LISETTE

LISETTE. Well, sir, you have just been talking to your daughter. Have you found out the cause of her melancholy?

SGANARELLE. No. She is a hussy who enrages me.

LISETTE. Let me manage it, sir; I shall pump her a little.

SGANARELLE. There is no occasion; and since she prefers to be in this mood, I am inclined to let her remain in it.

LISETTE. Let me manage it, I tell you. Perhaps she will open her heart more freely to me than to you. How now! Madam, you will not tell us what ails you, and you wish to grieve everyone around you? You ought not to behave as you do, and if you have any objection to explain yourself to a father, you ought to have none to open your heart to me. Tell me, do you wish anything from him? He has told us more than once that he will spare nothing to satisfy you. Does he not allow you all the[150] freedom you could wish for? And do pleasure parties and feasts not tempt you? Say! has anyone displeased you? Say! have you not some secret liking for some one to whom you would wish your father to marry you? Ah, I begin to understand you; that is it? Why the deuce so many compliments? Sir, the secret is found out, and ...

SGANARELLE *(interrupting her).* Go, ungrateful girl; I do not wish to speak to you any more, and I leave you in your obstinacy.

LUCINDE. Dear father, since you wish me to tell you ...

SGANARELLE. Yes, I am losing all my regard for you.

LISETTE. Her sadness, sir ...

SGANARELLE. She is a hussy who wishes to drive me to my grave.

LUCINDE. But, father, I am willing ...

SGANARELLE. That is not a fit reward for having brought you up as I have done.

LISETTE. But, sir ...

SGANARELLE. No, I am in a terrible rage with her.

LUCINDE. But, father ...

SGANARELLE. I do not love you any longer.

LISETTE. But ...

SGANARELLE. She is a slut.

LUCINDE. But ...

SGANARELLE. An ungrateful girl.

LUCINDE. But ...

SGANARELLE. A hussy who will not tell me what is the matter with her.

LISETTE. It is a husband she wants.

SGANARELLE *(pretending not to hear)*. I have done with her.

LISETTE. A husband.

SGANARELLE. I hate her.

LISETTE. A husband.

SGANARELLE. And disown her as my daughter.

LISETTE. A husband.

SGANARELLE. Do not speak to me any more about her.

LISETTE. A husband.

SGANARELLE. Speak no more to me about her.

LISETTE. A husband.

SGANARELLE. Speak no more to me about her.[151]

LISETTE. A husband, a husband, a husband.

SCENE 4   LUCINDE, LISETTE

LISETTE. True enough, none so deaf as those who will not hear.

LUCINDE. Well, Lisette, I was wrong to hide my grief! I had but to speak to get all I wished from my father! You see now.

LISETTE. Upon my word, he is a disagreeable man; and I confess that it would give me the greatest pleasure to play him some trick. But how is it, Madam, that, till now, you have kept your grief from me?

LUCINDE. Alas! what would have been the use of telling you before? and would it not have been quite as well if I had kept it to myself all my life? Do you think that I have not foreseen all which you see now, that I did not thoroughly know the sentiments of my father, and that when he refused my hand to my lover's friend, who came to ask for it in his name, he had not crushed every hope in my heart?

LISETTE. What! this stranger, who asked for your hand, is the one whom you ...

LUCINDE. Perhaps it is not altogether modest in a girl to explain herself so freely; but, in short, I tell you candidly, that, were I allowed to wish for any one, it is he whom I should choose. We have never had any conversation together, and his lips have never avowed the love he has for me; but, in every spot where he had a chance of seeing me, his looks and his action have always spoken so tenderly, and his asking me in marriage seems to me so very honourable, that my heart has not been able to remain insensible to his passion; and yet, you see to what the harshness of my father is likely to bring all this tenderness.

LISETTE. Let me manage it. Whatever reason I have to blame you for the secret you kept from me, I shall not fail to serve your love; and, provided you have sufficient resolution ...

LUCINDE. But what am I to do against a father's authority? And if he will not relent ...

LISETTE. Come, come, you must not allow yourself to be led like a goose, and provided it be done honourably, we can [152] free ourselves from a father's tyranny. What does he wish you to do? Are you not of an age to be married, and does he think you are made of marble? Once more bear up, I shall take in hand your love affair, and from this very moment do all I can to favour it, and you shall see that I know some strategems ... But I see your father. Let us go in, and leave me to act.

SCENE 5   SGANARELLE (alone)

It is good sometimes to pretend not to hear things, which one hears only too well; and I have done wisely to ward off the declaration of a wish which I have no intention of satisfying. Was there ever a greater piece of tyranny than this custom to which they wish to subject all fathers; anything more preposterous and ridiculous than to amass great wealth by hard work, and to bring up a girl with the utmost tenderness and care, in order to strip one's self of the one and of the other, for the benefit of a man who is nothing to us? No, no, I laugh at that custom, and I mean to keep my wealth and my daughter to myself.

SCENE 6   SGANARELLE, LISETTE

LISETTE (running on to the stage and pretending not to see Sganarelle). Oh! what a misfortune! Oh! what a calamity! Poor Mr. Sganarelle! where can I find him?

SGANARELLE (aside). What does she say?

LISETTE (still running about). Oh! wretched father! what will you do when you hear this news?

SGANARELLE (aside). What can it be?

LISETTE. My poor mistress!

SGANARELLE. I am undone!

LISETTE. Ah!

SGANARELLE *(running after Lisette)*. Lisette!

LISETTE. What a misfortune!

SGANARELLE. Lisette!

LISETTE. What an accident!

SGANARELLE. Lisette!

LISETTE. What a calamity!

SGANARELLE. Lisette!

LISETTE. Oh, sir!

SGANARELLE. What is the matter? [153]

LISETTE. Sir!

SGANARELLE. What has happened?

LISETTE. Your daughter ...

SGANARELLE. Oh! Oh!

LISETTE. Do not cry in such a way, sir. You will make me laugh.

SGANARELLE. Tell me quickly.

LISETTE. Your daughter, overcome by your words, and seeing how dreadfully angry you were with her, went quietly up to her room, and, driven by despair, opened the window that looks out upon the river.

SGANARELLE. Well!

LISETTE. Then, casting her looks up to Heaven: No, said she, it is impossible for me to live under my father's anger, and as he disowns me for his child, I shall die.

SGANARELLE. She has thrown herself out of the window?

LISETTE. No, sir. She gently closed it, and lay down upon her bed. There she began to cry bitterly; all at once she turned pale, her eyes rolled about, her strength failed her, and she became stiff in my arms.

SGANARELLE. Oh, my child! She is dead?

LISETTE. No, sir. I pinched her till she came to herself again; but she relapses every moment, and I believe she will not live out the day.

SGANARELLE. Champagne! Champagne! Champagne!

SCENE 7   SGANARELLE, CHAMPAGNE, LISETTE

SGANARELLE. Quick, go and fetch me some doctors, and bring a lot of them. One cannot have too many in a crisis like this. Oh my daughter! my poor child!

(Champagne, servant to Sganarelle, knocks, dancing, at the doors of four Physicians.[154] *The four Physicians dance, and ceremoniously enter into Sganarelle's house.)*

ACT II

SCENE 1   SGANARELLE, LISETTE

LISETTE. What do you want with four physicians, sir? Is one not enough to kill one person?

SGANARELLE. Hold your tongue. Four heads are better than one.

LISETTE. Cannot your daughter die well enough without the assistance of those gentlemen?

SGANARELLE. Do you think people die through having physicians?

LISETTE. Undoubtedly; and I knew a man who maintained—and proved it, too, by excellent reasons—that we should never say, Such a one has died of a fever, or from inflammation of the lungs, but, Such a one has died of four physicians and two apothecaries.

SGANARELLE. Hush! do not offend those gentlemen.

LISETTE. Upon my word, sir, our cat had a narrow escape from a leap he took, a little while ago, from the top of the house into the street; he was three days without eating, and unable to wag head or foot; but it is very lucky that there are no cat doctors, else it would have been all over with him, for they would have physicked and bled him.

SGANARELLE. Will you hold your tongue when I bid you? What next! Here they are.

LISETTE. Look out; you are going to be finely edified. They will tell you in Latin that your daughter is ill.

SCENE 2   MM. TOMÈS, DESFONANDRÈS, MACROTON, BAHIS, SGANARELLE, LISETTE

SGANARELLE. Well, gentlemen?

M. TOMÈS. We have examined the patient sufficiently, and undoubtedly there is a great deal of impurity in her.

SGANARELLE. Is my daughter impure?

M. TOMÈS. I mean to say that there is a great deal of impurity in her system, and much corrupt matter.[155]

SGANARELLE. Ah! I understand you now.

M. TOMÈS. But ... We are going to consult together.

SGANARELLE. Come, hand some chairs.

LISETTE *(to M. Tomès)*. Ah! sir, are you with them?

SGANARELLE *(to Lisette)*. How do you know this gentleman?

LISETTE. From having seen him the other day at a dear friend's of your niece.

M. TOMÈS. How is her coachman?

LISETTE. Very well indeed. He is dead.

M. TOMÈS. Dead?

LISETTE. Yes.

M. TOMÈS. That cannot be.

LISETTE. I do not know whether it can be or not; but I know well enough that it is.

M. TOMÈS. He cannot be dead, I tell you.

LISETTE. And I tell you that he is dead and buried.

M. TOMÈS. You are mistaken.

LISETTE. I have seen him.

M. TOMÈS. It is impossible. Hippocrates says that these sorts of diseases end only on the fourteenth or twenty-first day; and he has been ill only six.

LISETTE. Hippocrates may say what he likes; but the coachman is dead.

SGANARELLE. Peace! chatterbox. Come, let us leave this room. Gentlemen, I pray you to consult carefully. Although it is not the custom to pay beforehand, yet, for fear I should forget it, and to have done with it, here it is . . . *(He hands them some money, and each one, on receiving it, makes a different gesture.)*

SCENE 3   MM. DESFONANDRÈS, TOMÈS, MACROTON, BAHIS *(They all sit down and begin to cough.)*

M. DESFONANDRÈS. Paris is marvellously large, and one has to take long journeys when business is a little brisk.

M. TOMÈS. I am glad to say that I have got a wonderful mule for that; and that one would hardly believe what a deal of ground he takes me over daily.

M. DESFONANDRÈS. I have got an astonishing horse, and it is an indefatigable animal.

M. TOMÈS. Do you know the ground my mule has been [156] over today? I have been, first, close by the Arsenal; from the Arsenal, to the end of the faubourg Saint Germain; from the faubourg Saint Germain, to the lower part of the Marais; from the lower part of the Marais, to the Porte Saint-Honoré; from the Porte Saint-Honoré, to the faubourg Saint-Jacques; from the faubourg Saint-Jacques, to the

Porte de Richelieu; from the Porte de Richelieu, here; and from here, I have yet to go to the Place Royale.

M. DESFONANDRÈS. My horse has done all that to-day; and, besides, I have been to see a patient at Ruel.

M. TOMÈS. But, by the bye, which side do you take in the quarrel between the two physicians Theophrastus and Artemius? for it is a matter that divides our profession.

M. DESFONANDRÈS. I? I am for Artemius.

M. TOMÈS. So am I. It is true that his advice killed the patient, as we have experienced, and that Theophrastus's was certainly much better; but the latter is wrong in the circumstances, and ought not to have been of a different opinion from his senior. What do you say?

M. DESFONANDRÈS. Certainly. We ought at all times to preserve the professional etiquette, whatever may happen.

M. TOMÈS. For my part, I am excessively strict on that subject, except among friends. The other day three of us were called in to consult with an outsider; but I stopped the whole affair, and would hold no consultation unless things were conducted according to etiquette. The people of the house did what they could and the case grew worse; but I would not give way, and the patient bravely died during the contention.

M. DESFONANDRÈS. It is highly proper to teach people how to behave, and to show them their inexperience.

M. TOMÈS. A dead man is but a dead man, and of very little consequence; but professional etiquette neglected does great harm to the whole body of physicians.[157]

SCENE 4   SGANARELLE, MM. TOMÈS, DESFONANDRÈS, MACROTON,
BAHIS

SGANARELLE. Gentlemen, my daughter is growing worse; I beg you to tell me quickly what you have decided on.

M. TOMÈS (to M. Desfonandrès). The word is with you, Sir.

M. DESFONANDRÈS. No, sir; it is for you to speak if you please.

M. TOMÈS. You are jesting.

M. DESFONANDRÈS. I shall not speak first.

M. TOMÈS. Sir.

M. DESFONANDRÈS. Sir.

SGANARELLE. For mercy's sake, gentlemen, drop these ceremonies, and consider that matters are urgent. (They all four speak at the same time.)

M. TOMÈS. Your daughter's complaint ...

M. DESFONANDRÈS. The opinion of all these gentlemen ...

M. MACROTON. After hav-ing care-fully consi-dered ...

M. BAHIS. In order to deduce ...

SGANARELLE. Ah! gentlemen, one at a time, pray ...

M. TOMES. Sir, we have duly argued upon your daughter's complaint, and my own opinion is, that it proceeds from the overheating of the blood, consequently I would have her bled as soon as possible.

M. DESFONANDRÈS. And I say that her illness arises from a putrefaction of humours, caused by too great repletion; consequently I would have her given an emetic.

M. TOMÈS. I maintain that an emetic will kill her.

M. DESFONANDRÈS. And I, that bleeding will be the death of her.

M. TOMÈS. It is like you to set up for a clever man!

M. DESFONANDRÈS. Yes, it is like me; and I can, at any rate, cope with you in all kinds of knowledge.

M. TOMÈS. Do you recollect the man you killed a few days ago?

M. DESFONANDRÈS. Do you recollect the lady you sent to the other world three days ago?

M. TOMÈS *(to Sganarelle)*. I have given you my opinion.

M. DESFONANDRÈS *(to Sganarelle)*. I have told you what I think.

M. TOMÈS. If you do not have your daughter bled directly, she is a dead woman. *(Exit.)*

M. DESFONANDRÈS. If you have her bled, she will not be alive a quarter of an hour afterwards. *(Exit.)* [158]

SCENE 5   SGANARELLE, MM. MACROTON, BAHIS

SGANARELLE. Which of the two am I to believe? And who can decide amidst such conflicting opinions? Gentlemen, I beseech you to guide me, and to tell me, dispassionately, the best means of relieving my daughter.

M. MACROTON *(drawling out his words)*. Sir, in these kind-of-ca-ses, one must pro-ceed ve-ry care-fully, and do no-thing in-con-si-der-ate-ly, as the say-ing is; the more so, as the mis-takes one may make, ac-cord-ing to our mas-ter Hip-po-cra-tes, have the most fatal con-se-quen-ces.

M. BAHIS *(jerking out his words hastily)*. That is true enough, one must take great care what one does; for this is not child's play; and, when a mistake has been made, it is not easy to rectify it, nor make good what one has spoilt: *experimentum periculosum*. It is, therefore, as well to argue beforehand, to weigh things duly, to consider the constitution of people, to examine the causes of the complaint, and to decide upon the remedies to be adopted.

SGANARELLE *(aside).* One moves like a tortoise, while the other gallops like a post-horse.

M. MACROTON. Yes, sir, to come to the fact, I find that your daugh-ter has a chro-nic dis-ease, to which she will suc-cumb if re-lief be not giv-en to her, the more as the symp-toms give in-di-ca-tions of e-mit-ting fu-li-gi-nous and mor-di-cant ex-ha-la-tions which ir-ri-tate the ce-re-bral mem-branes. And these va-pours, which in Greek we call *At-mos,* are caus-ed by pu-trid, te-na-ci-ous, and con-glu-ti-nous hu-mours, which have ag-glo-mer-at-ed in the ab-do-men.

M. BAHIS. And as these humours were engendered, there by a long suc-cession of time, they have become hardened, and have assumed those malignant fumes that rise towards the region of the brain.

M. MACROTON. Con-se-quent-ly, in or-der to with-draw, to de-tach, to loos-en, to ex-pel, to e-va-cu-ate these said [159] hu-mours, a ve-ry strong pur-ga-tive is ne-ces-sa-ry. But first of all, I think it as well, and it will not cause any in-con-ve-ni-ence, to em-ploy some lit-tle a-no-dyne me-di-ci-nes, that is to say, small e-mol-li-ent and de-ter-sive in-jec-ti-ons, re-fresh-ing ju-leps and sy-rups, which may be mix-ed with her bar-ley wa-ter.

M. BAHIS. After that, we will come to the purgatives, and to the bleed-ing, which we shall repeat, if necessary.

M. MACROTON. We do not say that your daugh-ter may not die for all this; but you will at least have the sat-is-fac-tion of hav-ing done some-thing, and the con-so-la-tion of know-ing that she died ac-cord-ing to rule.

M. BAHIS. It is better to die according to rule than to recover in viola-tion of it.

M. MACROTON. We have sin-ce-re-ly told you our o-pi-ni-ons.

M. BAHIS. And we have spoken to you as to our own brother.

SGANARELLE *(to M. Macroton, drawling out his words).* I am hum-bly o-bli-ged to you. *(To M. Bahis, sputtering)* And I am very much obliged to you for the trouble you have taken.

SCENE 6 SGANARELLE *(alone)*

Here I am, a little more in the dark than I was before. Zounds. I have got an idea! I will buy some Orvietan [160] and I will make her take it. Orvietan is a kind of remedy that has done a great deal of good to many. Soho!

SCENE 7 SGANARELLE, A QUACK

SGANARELLE. Will you, Sir, kindly give me a box of your Orvietan, for which I shall pay you?

QUACK *(sings)*. The gold of all climes which by the ocean are bound
Can e'er it repay this important secret?
My remedy cures, by its excellence rare,
More complaints than are counted up in a whole year:

The itch, the mange, the scurf, the fever, the plague,
The gout, the small-pox, ruptures, the measles,
Great power possesses my Orvietan.

SGANARELLE. Sir, I am willing to believe that all the gold in the world
could not pay for your remedy! but here is a piece of thirty sous,
which you will take, if you please.

QUACK *(sings)*. Admire how good I am. For a few paltry pence,
I dispense freely such marvellous treasure.
With this you may brave, quite devoid of all fear,
All the ills to which mortals are subject down here:

The itch, the mange, the scurf, the fever, the plague,
The gout, the small-pox, ruptures, the measles,
Great power possesses my Orvietan.

SECOND ENTRY

(Several Trivelins and Scaramouches, servants of the quack, come in dancing.) [161]

ACT III

SCENE 1   MM. FILERIN, TOMÈS, DESFONANDRÈS

M. FILERIN. Are you not ashamed, gentlemen, for men of your age to
show so little discrimination, and to quarrel like young madcaps?
Do you not plainly see the harm which these kinds of disputes do us
with the world? and is it not sufficient that the learned perceive the
dissensions and differences between our contemporaries and the old
masters of our craft, without revealing to the public, by our quarrels
and bickerings, the boasting of our art? As for me, I do not at all
understand the mischievous policy of some of our brethren; and it
must be admitted that all these controversies have somewhat
strangely disparaged us, and that, if we are not careful, we shall ruin
ourselves. I do not say so for my own interest, for, Heaven be
praised, my little affairs are already settled. Whether it blows, rains,
or hails, those who are dead are dead, and I have sufficient to be independent of the living; yet all these disputes do physic no good.
Since Heaven has done us the favour, that, for so many centuries,
people remain infatuated with us, let us not open their eyes by our
extravagant cabals, and let us take advantage of their folly as quietly
as possible. We are not the only ones, as you know full well, who
try to make the best of human foibles. The whole study of the
greatest part of mankind tends towards that; and every one en-

deavours to speculate on man's weakness, in order to derive some benefit from them. Flatterers, for example, seek to profit by men's love for praise, by giving them all the vain incense they crave; it is an art by which, as we may see, large fortunes are made. Alchemists seek to profit by the passion for wealth by promising mountains of gold to those who listen to them; the drawers of horoscopes, by their deceitful prophecies, profit by the vanity and ambition of credulous minds. But the greatest failing in men is their love of life; by our pompous speeches we benefit by it, and know how to take advantage of the veneration for our profession with which the fear of death inspires them. Let us, therefore, maintain ourselves in that esteem in [162] which their foibles have placed us, and let us agree before our patients, so as to claim for ourselves the credit of the happy issue of the complaint, and to throw on Nature all the blunders of our art. Let us not, I say, foolishly destroy the happy accident of an error, which gives bread to so many people, and which allows us to raise everywhere such beautiful estates with the money of those whom we have sent to the grave.

M. TOMÈS. You are right in all that you say; but sometimes one cannot control one's temper.

M. FILERIN. Come, gentlemen, lay aside all animosity, and make up your quarrel on the spot.

M. DESFONANDRÈS. I consent. Let him allow me to have my way with the emetic for the patient in question; and I will let him have his with the first patient he shall be concerned with.

M. FILERIN. Nothing could be better said, and that is reasonable.

M. DESFONANDRÈS. Very well, that is settled.

M. FILERIN. Shake hands then. Farewell. Another time, show more tact.

SCENE 2   M. TOMÈS, M. DESFONANDRÈS, LISETTE

LISETTE. What! gentlemen, you are here, and you do not think of repairing the wrong done to the medical profession?

M. TOMÈS. What now? What is the matter?

LISETTE. Some insolent fellow has had the impudence to encroach upon your trade, and, without your prescription, has killed a man by running a sword clean through his body.

M. TOMÈS. Look you here, you may laugh at us now; but you shall fall into our hands one of these days.

LISETTE. If ever I have recourse to you, I give you leave to kill me. [163]

SCENE 3   CLITANDRE (disguised as a physician), LISETTE

CLITANDRE. Well, Lisette, what do you think of my disguise? Do you believe that I can trick the good man in these clothes? Do I look all right thus.

LISETTE. It could not be better; and I have been waiting impatiently for you. Heaven has given me the most humane disposition in the world, and I cannot bear to see two lovers sigh for one another, without entertaining a charitable tenderness towards them, and an ardent wish to relieve the ills which they are suffering. I mean, no matter at what cost, to free Lucinde from the tyranny to which she is subjected, and to confide her to your care. I liked you at first sight: I am a good judge of people, and she could not have made a better choice. Love risks extraordinary things, and we have concocted a little scheme, which may perhaps be successful. All our measures are already taken: the man we have to deal with is not one of the sharpest; and if this trick fail, we shall find a thousand other ways to encompass our end. Just wait here a little, I shall come back to fetch you. (*Clitandre retires to the far end of the stage.*)

SCENE 4   SGANARELLE, LISETTE

LISETTE. Hurrah! hurrah! Sir.

SGANARELLE. What is the matter?

LISETTE. Rejoice.

SGANARELLE. At what?

LISETTE. Rejoice, I say.

SGANARELLE. Tell me what it is about, and then I shall rejoice, perhaps.

LISETTE. No. I wish you to rejoice first, I wish you to sing, to dance.

SGANARELLE. On what grounds?

LISETTE. On my bare word.

SGANARELLE. Be it so. (*He sings and dances.*) La, lera, la, la, la, lera, la. What the deuce!

LISETTE. Your daughter is cured, Sir.

SGANARELLE. My daughter is cured?

LISETTE. Yes. I have brought you a doctor, but a doctor [164] of importance, who works wonderful cures, and who laughs at the other physicians.

SGANARELLE. Where is he?

LISETTE. I shall bring him in.

SGANARELLE (*alone*). It remains to be seen if he will do more than the others.

SCENE 5   CLITANDRE (*disguised as a physician*), SGANARELLE, LISETTE

LISETTE *(leading Clitandre)*. Here he is.

SGANARELLE. That doctor has not much beard, as yet.

LISETTE. Knowledge is not measured by the beard, and his skill does not lie in his chin.

SGANARELLE. Sir, they tell me that you have some capital recipes for relieving the bowels.

CLITANDRE. My remedies, sir, are different from those of other physicians. They use emetics, bleeding, drugs, and injections; but I cure by words, sounds, letters, talismans, and rings.

LISETTE. Did I not tell you so?

SGANARELLE. A great man this!

LISETTE. Sir, as your daughter is yonder, ready dressed, in her chair, I shall bring her here.

SGANARELLE. Yes, do.

CLITANDRE *(feeling Sganarelle's pulse)*. Your daughter is very ill, Sir.

SGANARELLE. You can tell that here?

CLITANDRE. Yes, by the sympathy which exists between father and daughter.

SCENE 6   SGANARELLE, LUCINDE, CLITANDRE, LISETTE

LISETTE *(to Clitandre)*. Sir, here is a chair near her. *(To Sganarelle)* Come, let us leave them to themselves.

SGANARELLE. Why so? I wish to remain here.

LISETTE. Are you jesting? We must leave them. A doctor has a hundred things to ask, which is not decent for a man to hear. *(Sganarelle and Lisette retire.)*

CLITANDRE *(softly to Lucinde)*. Ah! lady, how great is my delight! and how little do I know how to begin my discourse! As long as I spoke to you only with my eyes, it seemed to me that I had a hundred things to say; and [165] now that I have the opportunity of speaking to you, as I wished, I remain silent, and my great joy prevents my utterance.

LUCINDE. I may say the same; and I feel, like you, thrills of joy which prevent me from speaking.

CLITANDRE. Ah! madam, how happy should I be, if it were true that you feel all I do, and that I were allowed to judge of your heart by mine. But, may I at least believe, dear lady, that I owe to you the idea of this happy scheme which enables me to enjoy your presence.

LUCINDE. If you do not altogether owe the thought to me, you are, at any rate, my debtor for having gladly approved of the proposal.

SGANARELLE *(to Lisette)*. It seems to me that he talks very close to her.

LISETTE. He is studying her physiognomy, and all the features of her face.

CLITANDRE *(to Lucinde)*. Will you be constant, dear lady, in these favours which you are bestowing upon me?

LUCINDE. But you, will you be firm in the resolutions which you have taken?

CLITANDRE. Ah! madam, till death. I desire nothing so much as to be yours; and I shall prove it to you.

SGANARELLE *(to Clitandre)*. Well! how does our patient? She seems a little more cheerful.

CLITANDRE. That is because I have already tried upon her one of the remedies which my art teaches me. As the mind has a great influence on the body, and as it is from the first that diseases most generally arise, my custom is to cure the mind before dealing with the body. I have therefore studied this young lady's looks, her features, and the lines of both her hands; and by the knowledge which Heaven has bestowed upon me, I have discovered she is ill in mind, and that the whole of her complaint arises only from a disordered imagination, from an inordinate desire of being married. As for myself, I think nothing more extravagant and ridiculous than this hankering after marriage.

SGANARELLE *(aside)*. A clever fellow this!

CLITANDRE. And I have and always shall have, a frightful dislike to it.[166]

SGANARELLE *(aside)*. A great doctor this!

CLITANDRE. But as we must humour the imagination of patients, and as I have perceived in her a wandering of the mind, and even that there was great danger in not giving her prompt relief, I have taken her at her foible, and told her that I came here to solicit her hand from you. Suddenly her countenance changed, her complexion cleared, her eyes became animated; and if you will leave her for a few days in this error, you will see that we shall cure her.

SGANARELLE. Indeed, I do not mind.

CLITANDRE. After that, we shall apply other means to cure her of this fancy.

SGANARELLE. Yes, that will do very well. Listen! my girl, this gentleman wishes to marry you, and I have told him that I give my consent.

LUCINDE. Alas! can it be possible?

SGANARELLE. Of course.

LUCINDE. But really, in earnest?

SGANARELLE. Certainly.

LUCINDE *(to Clitandre)*. What! You wish to be my husband?

CLITANDRE. Yes, madam.

LUCINDE. And my father consents to it?

SGANARELLE. Yes, my child.

LUCINDE. Ah how happy I am! if that is true.

CLITANDRE. Doubt it not, madam. My love for you, and my ardent wish to be your husband, do not date from to-day, I came only for this; and, if you wish me to tell you the plain truth, this dress is nothing but a mere disguise; I acted the physician only to get near to you, and the more easily to obtain what I desire.

LUCINDE. These are signs of a very tender love, and I am fully sensible of them.

SGANARELLE *(aside)*. Oh, poor silly girl! silly girl! silly girl!

LUCINDE. You do consent then, father, to give me this gentleman for a husband?

SGANARELLE. Yes, certainly. Come, give me your hand. Give me yours also, Sir, for a moment.

CLITANDRE. But, Sir ... [167]

SGANARELLE *(with suppressed laughter)*. No, no, it is ... to satisfy her mind. Take it. That is over.

CLITANDRE. Accept, as a pledge of my faith, this ring which I give you. *(Softly to Sganarelle)* It is a constellated ring, which cures aberrations of the mind.

LUCINDE. Let us draw up the contract, so that nothing may be wanting.

CLITANDRE. I have no objections, Madam. *(Softly to Sganarelle)* I will bring the fellow who writes my prescriptions, and will make her believe that he is a notary.

SGANARELLE. Just so.

CLITANDRE. Hulloo! send up the notary I have brought with me.

LUCINDE. What! you brought a notary with you?

CLITANDRE. Yes, Madam.

LUCINDE. I am glad of that.

SGANARELLE. Oh the poor silly girl! the silly girl!

SCENE 7 THE NOTARY, CLITANDRE, SGANARELLE, LUCINDE, LISETTE
(Clitandre speaks softly to the Notary.)

SGANARELLE *(to the Notary)*. Yes, Sir, you are to draw up a contract for these two people. Write. *(To Lucinde)* We are making the contract.

(To the Notary) I give her twenty thousand crowns as a portion. Write that down.

LUCINDE. I am very much obliged to you, dear father.

NOTARY. That is done. You have only to sign it.

SGANARELLE. That is a quickly drawn contract.

CLITANDRE *(to Sganarelle)*. But at least, Sir ... [168]

SGANARELLE. No, no, I tell you. Do we not all know ... *(To the Notary)* Come, hand him the pen to sign. *(To Lucinde)* Come you, sign now, sign, sign. Well, I shall sign presently.

LUCINDE. No, no, I will have the contract in my own hands.

SGANARELLE. Well! there then. *(After having signed)* Are you satisfied?

LUCINDE. Better than you can imagine.

SGANARELLE. That is all right, then, that is all right.

CLITANDRE. I have not only had the precaution to bring a notary; I have also brought singers, musicians, and dancers to celebrate the feast, and for our enjoyment. Let them come in. They are people I always have with me, and whom I daily make use of to calm, by their harmony and dancing, the troubles of the mind.

SCENE 8   COMEDY, THE BALLET, MUSIC

TOGETHER. Without our aid, all humankind
Would soon become unhealthy.
We are indeed the best of all physicians.
COMEDY. Would you dispel by easy means
Splenetic fumes that man is heir to.
Avoid Hippocrates, and come to us.
TOGETHER. Without our aid, all humankind
Would soon become unhealthy.
We are indeed the best of all physicians.

(While the Sports, Laughter, and Pleasures are dancing together, Clitandre leads Lucinde away.)

SCENE 9   SGANARELLE, LISETTE, MUSIC, THE BALLET, SPORTS, LAUGHTER, PLEASURES.

SGANARELLE. A pleasant way of curing people this! But where are my daughter and the doctor?

LISETTE. They are gone to finish the remaining part of the marriage.

SGANARELLE. What do you mean by the marriage? [169]

LISETTE. The fact is, Sir, you have been cleverly done; and the joke you thought to play remains a truth.

SGANARELLE. The devil it does! *(He wishes to rush after Clitandre and Lucinde, the dancers restrain him.)* Let me go, let me go, I tell you. *(The dancers still keep hold of him.)* Again! *(They wish to make him dance by force.)* Plague take you all! [170]

JONATHAN SWIFT

A Modest Proposal [1729]

FROM *The Portable Swift,* edited by Carl Van Doren. New York: The Viking Press, Inc., 1948.

It is a melancholy object to those who walk through this great town, or travel in the country, when they see the streets, the roads, and cabin-doors crowded with beggars of the female sex, followed by three, four, or six children, *all in rags,* and importuning every passenger for an alms. These mothers, instead of being able to work for their honest livelihood, are forced to employ all their time in strolling, to beg sustenance for their helpless infants, who, as they grow up, either turn thieves for want of work, or leave their dear Native Country to fight for the Pretender in Spain, or sell themselves to the Barbadoes.

I think it is agreed by all parties that this prodigious number of children, in the arms, or on the backs, or at the heels of their mothers, and frequently of their fathers, is in the present deplorable state of the kingdom a very great additional grievance; and therefore whoever could find out a fair, cheap, and easy method of making these children sound useful members of the commonwealth would deserve so well of the public as to have his statue set up for a preserver of the nation.

But my intention is very far from being confined to provide only for the children of professed beggars; it is [549] of a much greater extent, and shall take in the whole number of infants at a certain age who are born of parents in effect as little able to support them as those who demand our charity in the streets.

As to my own part, having turned my thoughts, for many years, upon this important subject, and maturely weighed the several schemes of other projectors, I have always found them grossly mistaken in their computation. It is true a child, just dropped from its dam, may be supported by her milk for a solar year with little other nourishment, at most not above the value of two shillings, which the mother may certainly get, or the value in scraps, by her lawful occupation of begging, and it is exactly at one year old that I propose to provide for them, in such a manner as, instead of being a charge upon their parents, or the parish, or wanting food and raiment for the rest of their lives, they shall, on the contrary, contribute to the feeding and partly to the clothing of many thousands.

There is likewise another great advantage in my scheme, that it will prevent those voluntary abortions, and that horrid practice of women murdering their bastard children, alas, too frequent among us, sacrificing the poor innocent babes, I doubt, more to avoid the expense than the shame, which would move tears and pity in the most savage and inhuman breast.

The number of souls in this kingdom being usually reckoned one million and a half, of these I calculate there may be about two hundred thousand couple whose wives are breeders, from which number I subtract thirty thousand couples who are able to maintain their own children, although I apprehend there cannot be so many under the present distresses of the kingdom, but this being granted, there will remain an hundred and seventy [550] thousand breeders. I again subtract fifty thousand for those women who miscarry, or whose children die by accident or disease within the year. There only remain an hundred and twenty thousand children of poor parents annually born: The question therefore is, how this number shall be reared, and provided for, which, as I have already said, under the present situation of affairs, is utterly impossible by all the methods hitherto proposed, for we can neither employ them in handicraft, or agriculture; we neither build houses (I mean in the country), nor cultivate land: they can very seldom pick up a livelihood by stealing till they arrive at six years old, except where they are of towardly parts, although, I confess they learn the rudiments much earlier, during which time they can however be properly looked upon only as *probationers,* as I have been informed by a principal gentleman in the County of Cavan, who protested to me that he never knew above one or two instances under the age of six, even in a part of the kingdom so renowned for the quickest proficiency in that art.

I am assured by our merchants that a boy or a girl, before twelve years old, is no saleable commodity, and even when they come to this age, they will not yield above three pounds, or three pounds and half-a-crown at most on the Exchange, which cannot turn to account either to the parents or the kingdom, the charge of nutriment and rags having been at least four times that value.

I shall now therefore humbly propose my own thoughts, which I hope will not be liable to the least objection.

I have been assured by a very knowing American of my acquaintance in London, that a young healthy child well nursed is at a year old a most delicious, nourishing,[551] and wholesome food, whether stewed, roasted, baked, or boiled, and I make no doubt that it will equally serve in a fricassee, or a ragout.

I do therefore humbly offer it to public consideration, that of the hundred and twenty thousand children already computed, twenty thousand may be reserved for breed, whereof only one fourth part to be males, which is more than we allow to sheep, black-cattle, or swine, and my reason is that these children are seldom the fruits of marriage, a circumstance not much regarded by our savages, therefore one male will be sufficient to serve four females. That the remaining hundred thousand may at a year old be offered in sale to the persons of quality, and fortune, through the kingdom, always advising the mother to let them suck plentifully in the last month, so as to render them plump, and fat for a good table. A child will make two dishes at an entertainment for friends, and when the family dines alone, the fore or hind quarter will make a reasonable dish, and seasoned with a little pepper or salt will be very good boiled on the fourth day, especially in winter.

I have reckoned upon a medium, that a child just born will weigh 12 pounds, and in a solar year if tolerably nursed increaseth to 28 pounds.

I grant this food will be somewhat dear, and therefore very proper for landlords, who, as they have already devoured most of the parents, seem to have the best title to the children.

Infants' flesh will be in season throughout the year, but more plentiful in March, and a little before and after, for we are told by a grave author, an eminent French physician, that fish being a prolific diet, there are more children born in Roman Catholic countries about nine months after Lent than at any other season; therefore reckoning a year after Lent, the markets will [552] be more glutted than usual, because the number of Popish infants is at least three to one in this kingdom, and therefore it will have one other collateral advantage by lessening the number of Papists among us.

I have already computed the charge of nursing a beggar's child (in which list I reckon all cottagers, labourers, and four-fifths of the farmers) to be about two shillings *per annum*, rags included, and I believe no gentleman would repine to give ten shillings for the carcass of a good fat child, which, as I have said, will make four dishes of excellent nutritive meat, when he hath only some particular friend or his own family to dine with him. Thus the Squire will learn to be a good landlord, and grow popular among his tenants, the mother will have eight shillings net profit, and be fit for work till she produces another child.

Those who are more thrifty (as I must confess the times require) may flay the carcass; the skin of which, artificially dressed, will make admirable gloves for ladies, and summer boots for fine gentlemen.

As to our City of Dublin, shambles may be appointed for this purpose, in the most convenient parts of it, and butchers we may be assured will not be wanting, although I rather recommend buying the children alive, and dressing them hot from the knife, as we do roasting pigs.

A very worthy person, a true lover of this country, and whose virtues I highly esteem, was lately pleased, in discoursing on this matter, to offer a refinement upon my scheme. He said that many gentlemen of this kingdom, having of late destroyed their deer, he conceived that the want of venison might be well supplied by the bodies of young lads and maidens, not exceeding fourteen years of age, nor under twelve, so great a number of both sexes in every country being now ready to starve,[553] for want of work and service: and these to be disposed of by their parents if alive, or otherwise by their nearest relations. But with due deference to so excellent a friend, and so deserving a patriot, I cannot be altogether in his sentiments; for as to the males, my American acquaintance assured me from frequent experience that their flesh was generally tough and lean, like that of our schoolboys, by continual exercise, and their taste disagreeable, and to fatten them would not answer the charge. Then as to the females, it would, I think with humble submission, be a loss to the public, because they soon would become breeders themselves: And besides, it is not improbable that some scrupulous people might be apt to censure such a practice (although indeed very unjustly) as a little bordering upon cruelty, which, I confess, hath always been with me the strongest objection against any project, however so well intended.

But in order to justify my friend, he confessed that this expedient was put into his head by the famous Psalmanazar, a native of the island Formosa, who came from thence to London, about twenty years ago, and in conversation told my friend that in his country when any young person happened to be put to death, the executioner sold the carcass to persons of quality, as a prime dainty, and that, in his time, the body of a plump girl of fifteen, who was crucified for an attempt to poison the emperor, was sold to his Imperial Majesty's Prime Minister of State, and other great Mandarins of the Court, in joints from the gibbet, at four hundred crowns. Neither indeed can I deny that if the same use were made of several plump young girls in this town, who, without one single groat to their fortunes, cannot stir abroad without a chair, and appear at the playhouse, and assemblies in foreign fineries, which they never will pay for, the kingdom would not be the worse.[554]

Some persons of a desponding spirit are in great concern about that vast number of poor people, who are aged, diseased, or maimed, and I have been desired to employ my thoughts what course may be taken to ease the nation of so grievous an encumbrance. But I am not in the least pain upon that matter, because it is very well known that they are every day dying, and rotting, by cold, and famine, and filth, and vermin, as fast as can be reasonably expected. And as to the younger labourers they are now in almost as hopeful a condition. They cannot get work, and consequently pine away for want of nourishment, to a degree, that if at any time they are accidentally hired to common labour, they have not strength to perform it; and thus the country and themselves are happily delivered from the evils to come.

I have too long digressed, and therefore shall return to my subject. I think the advantages by the proposal which I have made are obvious and many, as well as of the highest importance.

For first, as I have already observed, it would greatly lessen the number of Papists, with whom we are yearly over-run, being the principal breeders of the nation, as well as our most dangerous enemies, and who stay at home on purpose with a design to deliver the kingdom to the Pretender, hoping to take their advantage by the absence of so many good Protestants, who have chosen rather to leave their country than stay at home, and pay tithes against their conscience to an Episcopal curate.

Secondly, The poorer tenants will have something valuable of their own, which by law may be made liable to distress, and help to pay their landlord's rent, their corn and cattle being already seized, and *money a thing unknown.*

Thirdly, Whereas the maintenance of an hundred thousand children, from two years old, and upwards,[555] cannot be computed at less than ten shillings a piece *per annum,* the nation's stock will be thereby increased fifty thousand pounds *per annum,* besides the profit of a new dish, introduced to the tables of all gentlemen of fortune in the kingdom, who have any refinement in taste, and the money will circulate among ourselves, the goods being entirely of our own growth and manufacture.

Fourthly, The constant breeders, besides the gain of eight shillings sterling *per annum,* by the sale of their children, will be rid of the charge of maintaining them after the first year.

Fifthly, This food would likewise bring great custom to taverns, where the vintners will certainly be so prudent as to procure the best receipts for dressing it to perfection, and consequently have their houses frequented by all the fine gentlemen, who justly value themselves upon their knowledge in good eating; and a skilful cook, who understands how to oblige his guests, will contrive to make it as expensive as they please.

Sixthly, This would be a great inducement to marriage, which all wise nations have either encouraged by rewards, or enforced by laws and penalties. It would increase the care and tenderness of mothers toward their children, when they were sure of a settlement for life, to the poor babes, provided in some sort by the public to their annual profit instead of expense. We should see an honest emulation among the married women, which of them could bring the fattest child to the market, men would become fond of their wives, during the time of their pregnancy, as they are now of their mares in foal, their cows in calf, or sows when they are ready to farrow, nor offer to beat or kick them (as it is too frequent a practice) for fear of a miscarriage.

Many other advantages might be enumerated: For instance,[556] the addition of some thousand carcasses in our exportation of barrelled beef; the propagation of swine's flesh, and improvement in the art of making good bacon, so much wanted among us by the great destruction of pigs, too frequent at our tables, which are no way comparable in taste or magnificence to a well-grown, fat yearling child, which roasted whole will make a considerable figure at a Lord Mayor's feast, or any other public entertainment. But this and many others I omit, being studious of brevity.

Supposing that one thousand families in this city would be constant customers for infants' flesh, besides others who might have it at merry-meetings, particularly weddings and christenings, I compute that Dublin would take off annually about twenty thousand carcasses, and the rest of the kingdom (where probably they will be sold somewhat cheaper) the remaining eighty thousand.

I can think of no one objection that will possibly be raised against this proposal, unless it should be urged that the number of people will be thereby much lessened in the kingdom. This I freely own, and was indeed one principal design in offering it to the world. I desire the reader will observe, that I calculate my remedy for this one individual *Kingdom of Ireland, and for no other that ever was, is, or, I think, ever can be upon earth.* Therefore let no man talk to me of other expedients: *Of taxing our absentees at five shillings a pound: Of using neither clothes, nor household furniture, except what is of our own growth and manufacture: Of utterly rejecting the materials and instruments that promote foreign luxury: Of curing the expensiveness of pride, vanity, idleness, and gaming in our women: Of introducing a vein of parsimony, prudence, and temperance: Of learning to love our Country, wherein we differ even from* LAPLANDERS, *and the inhabitants of* TOPINAMBOO: [557] *Of quitting our animosities and factions, nor act any longer like the Jews, who were murdering one another at the very moment their city was taken: Of being a little cautious not to sell our country and consciences for nothing: Of teaching landlords to have at least one degree of mercy toward their tenants. Lastly, of putting a spirit of honesty, industry, and skill into our shopkeepers, who, if a resolution could now be taken to buy only our native goods, would immediately unite to cheat and exact upon us in the price, the measure, and the goodness, nor could ever yet be brought to make one fair proposal of just dealing, though often and earnestly invited to it.*

Therefore I repeat, let no man talk to me of these and the like expedients, till he hath at least some glimpse of hope that there will ever be some hearty and sincere attempt to put them in practice.

But as to myself, having been wearied out for many years with offering vain, idle, visionary thoughts, and at length utterly despairing of success, I fortunately fell upon this proposal, which as it is wholly new, so it hath something solid and real, of no expense and little trouble, full in our own power, and whereby we can incur no danger in *disobliging* ENGLAND. For this kind of commodity will not bear exportation, the flesh being of too tender a consistence to admit a long continuance in salt, *although perhaps I could name a country which would be glad to eat up our whole nation without it.*

After all I am not so violently bent upon my own opinion as to reject any offer, proposed by wise men, which shall be found equally innocent, cheap, easy, and effectual. But before something of that kind shall be advanced in contradiction to my scheme, and offering a better, I desire the author, or authors, will be pleased maturely to consider two points. First, as things now [558] stand, how they will be able to find food and raiment for an hundred thousand useless mouths and backs. And secondly, there being a round million of creatures in human figure, throughout this kingdom, whose whole subsistence put into a common stock would leave them in debt two millions of pounds sterling; adding those, who are beggars by profession, to the bulk of farmers, cottagers, and labourers with their wives and children, who are beggars in effect. I desire those politicians, who dislike my overture, and may perhaps be so bold to attempt an answer, that they will first ask the parents of these mortals whether they would not at this day think it a great happiness to have been sold for food at a year old, in the manner I prescribe, and thereby have avoided such a perpetual scene of misfortunes as they have since gone through, by the oppression of landlords, the impossibility of paying rent without money or trade, the want of common sustenance, with neither house nor clothes to cover them from the inclemencies of the weather, and the most inevitable prospect of entailing the like, or greater miseries upon their breed for ever.

I profess in the sincerity of my heart that I have not the least personal interest in endeavouring to promote this necessary work, having no other motive than the *public good of my country, by advancing our trade, providing for infants, relieving the poor, and giving some pleasure to the rich.* I have no children by which I can propose to get a single penny; the youngest being nine years old, and my wife past child-bearing.[559]

ALEXANDER POPE

The Rape of the Lock [1712-1714]

FROM Alexander Pope: *The Poetry of Pope, A Selection,* edited by M. H. Abrams. Copyright, 1954, Appleton-Century-Crofts, Inc. Reprinted by permission of the publisher.

CANTO I

What dire offense from amorous causes springs,
What mighty contests rise from trivial things,
I sing—This verse to CARYLL, Muse! is due:
This, even Belinda may vouchsafe to view:
Slight is the subject, but not so the praise,
If she inspire, and he approve my lays.
    Say what strange motive, goddess! could compel
A well-bred lord t'assault a gentle belle?
O say what stranger cause, yet unexplored,
Could make a gentle belle reject a lord?   10
In tasks so bold, can little men engage,
And in soft bosoms dwells such mighty rage?
    Sol through white curtains shot a timorous ray,
And oped those eyes that must eclipse the day:
Now lap-dogs give themselves the rousing shake,
And sleepless lovers, just at twelve, awake:
Thrice rung the bell, the slipper knocked the ground,
And the pressed watch returned a silver sound.
Belinda still her downy pillow pressed,
Her guardian sylph prolonged the balmy rest: 20
'Twas he had summoned to her silent bed
The morning dream that hovered o'er her head;
A youth more glittering than a birth-night beau,
(That even in slumber caused her cheek to glow)
Seemed to her ear his winning lips to lay,
And thus in whispers said, or seemed to say.
    "Fairest of mortals, thou distinguished care
Of thousand bright inhabitants of air! [28]
If e'er one vision touched thy infant thought,
Of all the nurse and all the priest have taught;   30

Of airy elves by moonlight shadows seen,
The silver token, and the circled green,
Or virgins visited by angel powers,
With golden crowns and wreaths of heavenly flowers;
Hear and believe! thy own importance know,
Nor bound thy narrow views to things below.
Some secret truths, from learnèd pride concealed,
To maids alone and children are revealed:
What though no credit doubting wits may give?
The fair and innocent shall still believe.   40
Know, then, unnumbered spirits round thee fly,
The light militia of the lower sky:
These, though unseen, are ever on the wing,
Hang o'er the box, and hover round the ring.
Think what an equipage thou hast in air.
And view with scorn two pages and a chair.
As now your own, our beings were of old,
And once enclosed in woman's beauteous mold;
Thence, by a soft transition, we repair
From earthly vehicles to these of air,   50
Think not, when woman's transient breath is fled,
That all her vanities at once are dead;
Succeeding vanities she still regards,
And though she plays no more, o'erlooks the cards.
Her joy in gilded chariots, when alive,
And love of ombre, after death survive.
For when the fair in all their pride expire,
To their first elements their souls retire:
The sprites of fiery termagants in flame
Mount up, and take a salamander's name.   60
Soft yielding minds to water glide away,
And sip, with nymphs, their elemental tea.
The graver prude sinks downward to a gnome,
In search of mischief still on earth to roam.
The light coquettes in sylphs aloft repair,
And sport and flutter in the fields of air.
    "Know farther yet; whoever fair and chaste
Rejects mankind, is by some sylph embraced:
For spirits, freed from mortal laws, with ease
Assume what sexes and what shapes they please.   70
What guards the purity of melting maids,
In courtly balls, and midnight masquerades,
Safe from the treacherous friend, the daring spark,[29]
The glance by day, the whisper in the dark,
When kind occasion prompts their warm desires,
When music softens, and when dancing fires?

'Tis but their sylph, the wise celestials know,
Though honor is the word with men below.
  "Some nymphs there are, too conscious of their face,
For life predestined to the gnomes' embrace.   80
These swell their prospects and exalt their pride,
When offers are disdained, and love denied:
Then gay ideas crowd the vacant brain,
While peers, and dukes, and all their sweeping train,
And garters, stars, and coronets appear,
And in soft sounds, 'Your Grace' salutes their ear.
'Tis these that early taint the female soul,
Instruct the eyes of young coquettes to roll,
Teach infant cheeks a bidden blush to know,
And little hearts to flutter at a beau.   90
  "Oft, when the world imagine women stray,
The sylphs through mystic mazes guide their way,
Through all the giddy circle they pursue,
And old impertinence expel by new.
What tender maid but must a victim fall
To one man's treat, but for another's ball?
When Florio speaks, what virgin could withstand,
If gentle Damon did not squeeze her hand?
With varying vanities, from every part,
They shift the moving toyshop of their heart;   100
Where wigs with wigs, with sword-knots sword-knots strive,
Beaux banish beaux, and coaches coaches drive.
This erring mortals levity may call,
Oh blind to truth! the sylphs contrive it all.
  "Of these am I, who thy protection claim,
A watchful sprite, and Ariel is my name.
Late, as I ranged the crystal wilds of air,
In the clear mirror of thy ruling star
I saw, alas! some dread event impend,
Ere to the main this morning sun descend,   110
But heaven reveals not what, or how, or where:
Warned by the sylph, oh pious maid, beware!
This to disclose is all thy guardian can:
Beware of all, but most beware of man!"
  He said; when Shock, who thought she slept too long,
Leaped up, and waked his mistress with his tongue.
'Twas then, Belinda, if report say true,[30]
Thy eyes first opened on a billet-doux;
Wounds, charms, and ardors were no sooner read,
But all the vision vanished from thy head.   120
  And now, unveiled, the toilet stands displayed,
Each silver vase in mystic order laid.

First, robed in white, the nymph intent adores,
With head uncovered, the cosmetic powers.
A heavenly image in the glass appears,
To that she bends, to that her eyes she rears;
Th' inferior priestess, at her altar's side,
Trembling, begins the sacred rites of pride.
Unnumbered treasures ope at once, and here
The various offerings of the world appear;   130
From each she nicely culls with curious toil,
And decks the goddess with the glittering spoil.
This casket India's glowing gems unlocks,
And all Arabia breathes from yonder box.
The tortoise here and elephant unite,
Transformed to combs, the speckled, and the white.
Here files of pins extend their shining rows,
Puffs, powders, patches, Bibles, billets-doux.
Now awful beauty puts on all its arms;
The fair each moment rises in her charms,   140
Repairs her smiles, awakens every grace,
And calls forth all the wonders of her face;
Sees by degrees a purer blush arise,
And keener lightnings quicken in her eyes.
The busy sylphs surround their darling care,
These set the head, and those divide the hair,
Some fold the sleeve, while others plait the gown;
And Betty's praised for labors not her own.

CANTO II

Not with more glories, in th' ethereal plain,
The sun first rises o'er the purpled main,
Than, issuing forth, the rival of his beams
Launched on the bosom of the silver Thames.
Fair nymphs, and well-dressed youths around her shone,
But every eye was fixed on her alone.
On her white breast a sparkling cross she wore,
Which Jews might kiss, and infidels adore.
Her lively looks a sprightly mind disclose,
Quick as her eyes, and as unfixed as those: 10
Favors to none, to all she smiles extends;
Oft she rejects, but never once offends.[31]
Bright as the sun, her eyes the gazers strike,
And, like the sun, they shine on all alike.
Yet graceful ease, and sweetness void of pride,
Might hide her faults, if belles had faults to hide:
If to her share some female errors fall,
Look on her face, and you'll forget 'em all.

This nymph, to the destruction of mankind,
Nourished two locks, which graceful hung behind   20
In equal curls, and well conspired to deck
With shining ringlets the smooth ivory neck.
Love in these labyrinths his slaves detains,
And mighty hearts are held in slender chains.
With hairy springes we the birds betray,
Slight lines of hair surprise the finny prey,
Fair tresses man's imperial race ensnare,
And beauty draws us with a single hair.
Th' adventurous Baron the bright locks admired;
He saw, he wished, and to the prize aspired,   30
Resolved to win, he meditates the way,
By force to ravish, or by fraud betray;
For when success a lover's toil attends,
Few ask, if fraud or force attained his ends.
For this, ere Phoebus rose, he had implored
Propitious Heaven, and every power adored,
But chiefly Love—to Love an altar built,
Of twelve vast French romances, neatly gilt.
There lay three garters, half a pair of gloves;
And all the trophies of his former loves;   40
With tender billets-doux he lights the pyre,
And breathes three amorous sighs to raise the fire.
Then prostrate falls, and begs with ardent eyes
Soon to obtain, and long possess the prize:
The powers gave ear, and granted half his prayer,
The rest, the winds dispersed in empty air.
But now secure the painted vessel glides,
The sunbeams trembling on the floating tides:
While melting music steals upon the sky,
And softened sounds along the waters die;   50
Smooth flow the waves, the zephyrs gently play,
Belinda smiled, and all the world was gay.
All but the sylph—with careful thoughts oppressed,
Th' impending woe sat heavy on his breast.
He summons strait his denizens of air;
The lucid squadrons round the sails repair: [32]
Soft o'er the shrouds aërial whispers breathe,
That seemed but zephyrs to the train beneath.
Some to the sun their insect-wings unfold,
Waft on the breeze, or sink in clouds of gold;   60
Transparent forms, too fine for mortal sight,
Their fluid bodies half dissolved in light.
Loose to the wind their airy garments flew,
Thin glittering textures of the filmy dew,

Dipped in the richest tincture of the skies,
Where light disports in ever-mingling dyes,
While every beam new transient colors flings,
Colors that change whene'er they wave their wings.
Amid the circle, on the gilded mast,
Superior by the head, was Ariel placed;   70
His purple pinions opening to the sun,
He raised his azure wand, and thus begun.
    "Ye sylphs and sylphids, to your chief give ear!
Fays, fairies, genii, elves, and daemons, hear!
Ye know the spheres and various tasks assigned
By laws eternal to th' aërial kind.
Some in the fields of purest ether play,
And bask and whiten in the blaze of day.
Some guide the course of wandering orbs on high,
Or roll the planets through the boundless sky.   80
Some less refined, beneath the moon's pale light,
Pursue the stars that shoot athwart the night,
Or suck the mists in grosser air below,
Or dip their pinions in the painted bow,
Or brew fierce tempests on the wintry main,
Or o'er the glebe distill the kindly rain.
Others on earth o'er human race preside,
Watch all their ways, and all their actions guide:
Of these the chief the care of nations own,
And guard with arms divine the British throne.   90
    "Our humbler province is to tend the fair,
Not a less pleasing, though less glorious care;
To save the powder from too rude a gale,
Nor let the imprisoned essences exhale;
To draw fresh colors from the vernal flowers;
To steal from rainbows e'er they drop in showers
A brighter wash; to curl their waving hairs,
Assist their blushes, and inspire their airs;
Nay oft, in dreams, invention we bestow,
To change a flounce, or add a furbelow.[33]   100
    "This day, black omens threat the brightest fair
That e'er deserved a watchful spirit's care;
Some dire disaster, or by force, or slight;
But what, or where, the fates have wrapped in night.
Whether the nymph shall break Diana's law,
Or some frail china jar received a flaw;
Or stain her honor, or her new brocade;
Forget her prayers, or miss a masquerade;
Or lose her heart, or necklace, at a ball;
Or whether Heaven has doomed that Shock must fall.   110

Haste, then, ye spirits! to your charge repair:
The fluttering fan be Zephyretta's care;
The drops to thee, Brillante, we consign;
And, Momentilla, let the watch be thine;
Do thou, Crispissa, tend her favorite lock;
Ariel himself shall be the guard of Shock.
    "To fifty chosen sylphs, of special note,
We trust th' important charge, the petticoat:
Oft have we known that sevenfold fence to fail,
Though stiff with hoops, and armed with ribs of whale.   120
Form a strong line about the silver bound,
And guard the wide circumference around.
    "Whatever spirit, careless of his charge,
His post neglects, or leaves their fair at large,
Shall feel sharp vengeance soon o'ertake his sins,
Be stopped in vials, or transfixed with pins;
Or plunged in lakes of bitter washes lie,
Or wedged whole ages in a bodkin's eye:
Gums and pomatums shall his flight restrain,
While clogged he beats his silken wings in vain;   130
Or alum styptics with contracting power
Shrink his thin essence like a riveled flower:
Or, as Ixion fixed, the wretch shall feel
The giddy motion of the whirling mill,
In fumes of burning chocolate shall glow,
And tremble at the sea that froths below!"
    He spoke; the spirits from the sails descend;
Some, orb in orb, around the nymph extend;
Some thrid the mazy ringlets of her hair;
Some hang upon the pendants of her ear;   140
With beating hearts the dire event they wait,
Anxious, and trembling for the birth of Fate.[34]

CANTO III

Close by those meads, for ever crowned with flowers,
Where Thames with pride surveys his rising towers,
There stands a structure of majestic frame,
Which from the neighboring Hampton takes its name.
Here Britain's statesmen oft the fall foredoom
Of foreign tyrants, and of nymphs at home;
Here thou, great ANNA! whom three realms obey,
Dost sometimes counsel take—and sometimes tea.
    Hither the heroes and the nymphs resort,
To taste awhile the pleasures of a court;   10
In various talk th' instructive hours they passed,

Who gave the ball, or paid the visit last;
One speaks the glory of the British Queen,
And one describes a charming Indian screen;
A third interprets motions, looks, and eyes;
At every word a reputation dies.
Snuff, or the fan, supply each pause of chat,
With singing, laughing, ogling, and all that.
    Meanwhile, declining from the noon of day,
The sun obliquely shoots his burning ray;   20
The hungry judges soon the sentence sign,
And wretches hang that jurymen may dine;
The merchant from th' exchange returns in peace,
And the long labors of the toilet cease.
Belinda now, whom thirst of fame invites,
Burns to encounter two adventurous knights,
At omber singly to decide their doom;
And swells her breast with conquests yet to come.
Straight the three bands prepare in arms to join,
Each band the number of the sacred nine.   30
Soon as she spreads her hand, th' aërial guard
Descend, and sit on each important card:
First Ariel perched upon a Matadore,
Then each, according to the rank they bore;
For sylphs, yet mindful of their ancient race,
Are, as when women, wondrous fond of place.
    Behold, four Kings in majesty revered,
With hoary whiskers and a forky beard;
And four fair Queens whose hands sustain a flower,[35]
Th' expressive emblem of their softer power;   40
Four Knaves in garbs succinct, a trusty band,
Caps on their heads, and halberds in their hand;
And particolored troops, a shining train,
Draw forth to combat on the velvet plain.
    The skillful nymph reviews her force with care:
"Let Spades be trumps!" she said, and trumps they were.
    Now move to war her sable Matadores,
In show like leaders of the swarthy Moors.
Spadillio first, unconquerable lord!
Led off two captive trumps, and swept the board.   50
As many more Manillio forced to yield,
And marched a victor from the verdant field.
Him Basto followed, but his fate more hard
Gained but one trump and one plebeian card.
With his broad saber next, a chief in years,
The hoary Majesty of Spades appears,
Puts forth one manly leg, to sight revealed,

The rest, his many-colored robe concealed.
The rebel Knave, who dares his prince engage,
Proves the just victim of his royal rage.   60
Even mighty Pam, that kings and queens o'erthrew
And mowed down armies in the fights of Lu,
Sad chance of war! now destitute of aid,
Falls undistinguished by the victor Spade!
   Thus far both armies to Belinda yield;
Now to the baron fate inclines the field.
His warlike Amazon her host invades,
Th' imperial consort of the crown of Spades.
The Club's black tyrant first her victim died,
Spite of his haughty mien, and barbarous pride: 70
What boots the regal circle on his head,
His giant limbs, in state unwieldy spread;
That long behind he trails his pompous robe,
And, of all monarchs, only grasps the globe?
   The baron now his Diamonds pours apace;
Th' embroidered King who shows but half his face,
And his refulgent Queen, with powers combined,
Of broken troops an easy conquest find.
Clubs, Diamonds, Hearts, in wild disorder seen,
With throngs promiscuous strow the level green.   80
Thus when dispersed a routed army runs,
Of Asia's troops, and Afric's sable sons,[36]
With like confusion different nations fly,
Of various habit, and of various dye,
The pierced battalions disunited fall,
In heaps on heaps; one fate o'erwhelms them all.
   The Knave of Diamonds tries his wily arts,
And wins (oh shameful chance!) the Queen of Hearts.
At this, the blood of virgin's cheek forsook,
A livid paleness spreads o'er all her look;   90
She sees, and trembles at th' approaching ill,
Just in the jaws of ruin, and codille.
And now (as oft in some distempered state)
On one nice trick depends the general fate.
An Ace of Hearts steps forth: The King unseen
Lurked in her hand, and mourned his captive Queen:
He springs to vengeance with an eager pace,
And falls like thunder on the prostrate Ace.
The nymph exulting fills with shouts the sky;
The walls, the woods, and long canals reply.   100
   Oh thoughtless mortals! ever blind to fate,
Too soon dejected, and too soon elate.

Sudden, these honors shall be snatched away,
And cursed for ever this victorious day.
    For lo! the board with cups and spoons is crowned,
The berries crackle, and the mill turns round;
On shining altars of Japan they raise
The silver lamp; the fiery spirits blaze:
From silver spouts the grateful liquors glide,
While China's earth receives the smoking tide: 110
At once they gratify their scent and taste,
And frequent cups prolong the rich repast.
Straight hover round the fair her airy band;
Some, as she sipped, the fuming liquor fanned,
Some o'er her lap their careful plumes displayed,
Trembling, and conscious of the rich brocade.
Coffee (which makes the politician wise,
And see through all things with his half-shut eyes)
Sent up in vapors to the baron's brain
New stratagems, the radiant lock to gain.   120
Ah cease, rash youth! desist ere 'tis too late,
Fear the just gods, and think of Scylla's fate!
Changed to a bird, and sent to flit in air,[37]
She dearly pays for Nisus' injured hair!
    But when to mischief mortals bend their will,
How soon they find fit instruments of ill!
Just then, Clarissa drew with tempting grace
A two-edged weapon from her shining case:
So ladies in romance assist their knight,
Present the spear, and arm him for the fight.   130
He takes the gift with reverence and extends
The little engine on his fingers' ends;
This just behind Belinda's neck he spread,
As o'er the fragrant steams she bends her head.
Swift to the lock a thousand sprites repair,
A thousand wings, by turns, blow back the hair;
And thrice they twitched the diamond in her ear;
Thrice she looked back, and thrice the foe drew near.
Just in that instant, anxious Ariel sought
The close recesses of the virgin's thought;   140
As on the nosegay in her breast reclined,
He watched th' ideas rising in her mind,
Sudden he viewed, in spite of all her art,
An earthly lover lurking at her heart.
Amazed, confused, he found his power expired,
Resigned to fate, and with a sigh retired.
    The peer now spreads the glittering forfex wide,
T' enclose the lock; now joins it, to divide.

Even then, before the fatal engine closed,
A wretched sylph too fondly interposed;   150
Fate urged the shears, and cut the sylph in twain,
(But airy substance soon unites again)
The meeting points the sacred hair dissever
From the fair head, for ever, and for ever!
    Then flashed the living lightning from her eyes,
And screams of horror rend th' affrighted skies.
Not louder shrieks to pitying Heaven are cast,
When husbands, or when lap-dogs breathe their last;
Or when rich China vessels fallen from high,
In glittering dust, and painted fragments lie!   160
    "Let wreaths of triumph now my temples twine,"
(The victor cried) "the glorious prize is mine!
While fish in streams, or birds delight in air,
Or in a coach and six the British fair,
As long as Atalantis shall be read,
Or the small pillow grace a lady's bed,[38]
While visits shall be paid on solemn days,
When numerous wax lights in bright order blaze,
While nymphs take treats, or assignations give,
So long my honor, name, and praise shall live!   170
What time would spare, from steel receives its date,
And monuments, like men, submit to fate!
Steel could the labor of the gods destroy,
And strike to dust th' imperial towers of Troy;
Steel could the works of mortal pride confound,
And hew triumphal arches to the ground.
What wonder then, fair nymph! thy hairs should feel
The conquering force of unresisted steel?"

CANTO IV

But anxious cares the pensive nymph oppressed,
And secret passions labored in her breast.
Not youthful kings in battle seized alive,
Not scornful virgins who their charms survive,
Not ardent lovers robbed of all their bliss,
Not ancient ladies when refused a kiss,
Not tyrants fierce that unrepenting die,
Not Cynthia when her manteau's pinned awry,
E'er felt such rage, resentment, and despair,
As thou, sad virgin! for thy ravished hair.   10
    For, that sad moment, when the sylphs withdrew,
And Ariel weeping from Belinda flew,
Umbriel, a dusky, melancholy sprite,

As ever sullied the fair face of light,
Down to the central earth, his proper scene,
Repaired to search the gloomy Cave of Spleen.
 Swift on his sooty pinions flits the gnome,
And in a vapor reached the dismal dome.
No cheerful breeze this sullen region knows,
The dreaded east is all the wind that blows.   20
Here in a grotto, sheltered close from air,
And screened in shades from day's detested glare,
She sighs for ever on her pensive bed,
Pain at her side, and Megrim at her head.
 Two handmaids wait the throne: alike in place,
But differing far in figure and in face.
Here stood Ill-nature like an ancient maid,
Her wrinkled form in black and white arrayed;
With store of prayers, for mornings, nights, and noons, [39]
Her hand is filled; her bosom with lampoons.   30
 There Affectation, with a sickly mien,
Shows in her cheek the roses of eighteen,
Practiced to lisp, and hang the head aside,
Faints into airs, and languishes with pride,
On the rich quilt sinks with becoming woe,
Wrapped in a gown, for sickness, and for show.
The fair ones feel such maladies as these,
When each new nightdress gives a new disease.
 A constant vapor o'er the palace flies;
Strange phantoms rising as the mists arise;   40
Dreadful, as hermit's dreams in haunted shades,
Or bright, as visions of expiring maids.
Now glaring fiends, and snakes on rolling spires,
Pale specters, gaping tombs, and purple fires:
Now lakes of liquid gold, Elysian scenes,
And crystal domes, and angels in machines.
 Unnumbered throngs on every side are seen
Of bodies changed to various forms by Spleen.
Here living teapots stand, one arm held out,
One bent; the handle this, and that the spout: 50
A pipkin there, like Homer's tripod walks;
Here sighs a jar, and there a goose pie talks;
Men prove with child, as powerful fancy works,
And maids turned bottles, call aloud for corks.
 Safe passed the gnome through this fantastic band,
A branch of healing spleenwort in his hand.
Then thus addressed the power: "Hail, wayward Queen!
Who rule the sex to fifty from fifteen:
Parent of vapors and of female wit,

Who give th' hysteric or poetic fit,   60
On various tempers act by various ways,
Make some take physic, others scribble plays;
Who cause the proud their visits to delay,
And send the godly in a pet to pray.
A nymph there is, that all thy power disdains,
And thousands more in equal mirth maintains.
But oh! if e'er thy gnome could spoil a grace,
Or raise a pimple on a beauteous face,
Like citron waters matrons' cheeks inflame,
Or change complexions at a losing game;   70
If e'er with airy horns I planted heads,
Or rumpled petticoats, or tumbled beds,
Or caused suspicion when no soul was rude,
Or discomposed the headdress of a prude,[40]
Or e'er to costive lap dog gave disease,
Which not the tears of brightest eyes could ease:
Hear me, and touch Belinda with chagrin;
That single act gives half the world the spleen."
    Thy Goddess with a discontented air
Seems to reject him, though she grants his prayer.   80
A wondrous bag with both her hands she binds,
Like that where once Ulysses held the winds;
There she collects the force of female lungs,
Sighs, sobs, and passions, and the war of tongues.
A vial next she fills with fainting fears,
Soft sorrows, melting griefs, and flowing tears.
The gnome rejoicing bears her gifts away,
Spreads his black wings, and slowly mounts to day.
    Sunk in Thalestris' arms the nymph he found,
Her eyes dejected and her hair unbound.   90
Full o'er their heads the swelling bag he rent,
And all the furies issued at the vent.
Belinda burns with more than mortal ire,
And fierce Thalestris fans the rising fire.
"O wretched maid!" she spread her hands, and cried,
(While Hampton's echoes, "Wretched maid!" replied)
"Was it for this you took such constant care
The bodkin, comb, and essence to prepare?
For this your locks in paper durance bound,
For this with torturing irons wreathed around?   100
For this with fillets strained your tender head,
And bravely bore the double loads of lead?
Gods! shall the ravisher display your hair,
While the fops envy and the ladies stare!
Honor forbid! at whose unrivaled shrine

Ease, pleasure, virtue, all our sex resign.
Methinks already I your tears survey,
Already hear the horrid things they say,
Already see you a degraded toast,
And all your honor in a whisper lost!   110
How shall I, then, your helpless fame defend?
'Twill then be infamy to seem your friend!
And shall this prize, th' inestimable prize,
Exposed through crystal to the gazing eyes,
And heightened by the diamond's circling rays,
On that rapacious hand for ever blaze?
Sooner shall grass in Hyde Park Circus grow,[41]
And wits take lodgings in the sound of Bow;
Sooner let earth, air, sea, to chaos fall,
Men, monkeys, lap dogs, parrots, perish all!"   120
    She said; then raging to Sir Plume repairs
And bids her beau demand the precious hairs:
(Sir Plume of amber snuffbox justly vain,
And the nice conduct of a clouded cane)
With earnest eyes, and round unthinking face,
He first snuffbox opened, then the case,
And thus broke out—"My Lord, why, what the devil?
Z——ds! damn the lock! 'fore Gad, you must be civil!
Plague on't! 'tis past a jest—nay prithee, pox!
Give her the hair"—he spoke, and rapped his box.   130
"It grieves me much" (replied the peer again)
"Who speaks so well should ever speak in vain,
But by this lock, this sacred lock I swear,
(Which never more shall join its parted hair;
Which never more its honors shall renew,
Clipped from the lovely head where late it grew)
That while my nostrils draw the vital air,
This hand, which won it, shall for ever wear."
He spoke, and speaking, in proud triumph spread
The long-contended honors of her head.   140
    But Umbriel, hateful gnome! forbears not so;
He breaks the vial whence the sorrows flow.
Then see! the nymph in beauteous grief appears,
Her eyes half languishing, half drowned in tears;
On her heaved bosom hung her drooping head,
Which, with a sigh, she raised; and thus she said:
    "For ever cursed be this detested day,
Which snatched my best, my favorite curl away!
Happy! ah ten times happy had I been,
If Hampton Court these eyes had never seen!   150
Yet am I not the first mistaken maid,

By love of courts to numerous ills betrayed.
Or had I rather unadmired remained
In some lone isle, or distant northern land;
Where the gilt chariot never marks the way,
Where none learn omber, none e'er taste bohea!
There kept my charms concealed from mortal eye,[42]
Like roses that in deserts bloom and die.
What moved my mind with youthful lords to roam?
Oh had I stayed, and said my prayers at home!   160
'Twas this, the morning omens seemed to tell:
Thrice from my trembling hand the patchbox fell;
The tottering china shook without a wind,
Nay, Poll sat mute, and Shock was most unkind!
A sylph too warned me of the threats of fate,
In mystic visions, now believed too late!
See the poor remnants of these slighted hairs!
My hands shall rend what even thy rapine spares:
These in two sable ringlets taught to break,
Once gave new beauties to the snowy neck;   170
The sister lock now sits uncouth, alone,
And in its fellow's fate foresees its own;
Uncurled it hangs, the fatal shears demands,
And tempts, once more, thy sacrilegious hands.
Oh hadst thou, cruel! been content to seize
Hairs less in sight, or any hairs but these!"

CANTO V

She said: the pitying audience melt in tears.
But fate and love had stopped the baron's ears.
In vain Thalestris with reproach assails,
For who can move when fair Belinda fails?
Not half so fixed the Trojan could remain,
While Anna begged and Dido raged in vain.
Then grave Clarissa graceful waved her fan;
Silence ensued, and thus the nymph began.
    "Say why are beauties praised and honored most,
The wise man's passion, and the vain man's toast?   10
Why decked with all that land and sea afford,
Why angels called, and angel-like adored?
Why round our coaches crowd the white-gloved beaux,
Why bows the side-box from its inmost rows?
How vain are all these glories, all our pains,
Unless good sense preserve what beauty gains:
That men may say, when we the front-box grace,
'Behold the first in virtue as in face!'

Oh! if to dance all night, and dress all day,
Charmed the smallpox, or chased old age away;   20
Who would not scorn what housewife's care produce,
Or who would learn one earthly thing of use?
To patch, nay ogle, might become a saint,[43]
Nor could it sure be such a sin to paint.
But since, alas! frail beauty must decay,
Curled or uncurled, since locks will turn to gray;
Since painted, or not painted, all shall fade,
And she who scorns a man, must die a maid;
What then remains, but well our power to use,
And keep good-humor still whate'er we lose?   30
And trust me, dear! good-humor can prevail,
When airs, and flights, and screams, and scolding fail.
Beauties in vain their pretty eyes may roll;
Charms strike the sight, but merit wins the soul."
    So spoke the dame, but no applause ensued;
Belinda frowned, Thalestris called her prude.
"To arms, to arms!" the fierce virago cries,
And swift as lightning to the combat flies.
All side in parties, and begin th' attack;
Fans clap, silks rustle, and tough whalebones crack;   40
Heroes' and heroines' shouts confusedly rise,
And bass, and treble voices strike the skies.
No common weapons in their hands are found,
Like gods they fight, nor dread a mortal wound.
    So when bold Homer makes the gods engage,
And heavenly breasts with human passions rage;
'Gainst Pallas, Mars; Latona, Hermes arms;
And all Olympus rings with loud alarms:
Jove's thunder roars, Heaven trembles all around,
Blue Neptune storms, the bellowing deeps resound: 50
Earth shakes her nodding towers, the ground gives way,
And the pale ghosts start at the flash of day!
    Triumphant Umbriel on a sconce's height
Clapped his glad wings, and sate to view the fight:
Propped on their bodkin spears, the sprites survey
The growing combat, or assist the fray.
    While through the press enraged Thalestris flies,
And scatters death around from both her eyes,
A beau and witling perished in the throng,
One died in metaphor, and one in song.   60
"O cruel nymph! a living death I bear,"
Cried Dapperwit, and sunk beside his chair.
A mournful glance Sir Fopling upwards cast,
"Those eyes are made so killing"—was his last.

Thus on Maeander's flowery margin lies
Th' expiring swan, and as he sings he dies.
When bold Sir Plume had drawn Clarissa down,
Chloe stepped in, and killed him with a frown; [44]
She smiled to see the doughty hero slain,
But, at her smile, the beau revived again.   70
Now Jove suspends his golden scales in air,
Weighs the men's wits against the lady's hair;
The doubtful beam long nods from side to side;
At length the wits mount up, the hairs subside.
See fierce Belinda on the baron flies,
With more than usual lightning in her eyes:
Nor feared the chief th' unequal fight to try,
Who sought no more than on his foe to die.
But this bold lord with manly strength endued,
She with one finger and thumb subdued: 80
Just where the breath of life his nostrils drew,
A charge of snuff the wily virgin threw;
The gnomes direct, to every atom just,
The pungent grains of titillating dust.
Sudden with starting tears each eye o'erflows,
And the high dome re-echoes to his nose.
"Now meet thy fate," incensed Belinda cried,
And drew a deadly bodkin from her side.
(The same, his ancient personage to deck,
Her great-great-grandsire wore about his neck,   90
In three seal rings; which after, melted down,
Formed a vast buckle for his widow's gown:
Her infant grandame's whistle next it grew,
The bells she jingled, and the whistle blew;
Then in a bodkin graced her mother's hairs,
Which long she wore, and now Belinda wears.)
"Boast not my fall" (he cried) "insulting foe!
Thou by some other shalt be laid as low.
Nor think, to die dejects my lofty mind:
All that I dread is leaving you behind!   100
Rather than so, ah let me still survive,
And burn in Cupid's flames—but burn alive."
"Restore the lock!" she cries; and all around
"Restore the lock!" the vaulted roofs rebound.
Not fierce Othello in so loud a strain
Roared for the handkerchief that caused his pain.
But see how oft ambitious aims are crossed,
And chiefs contend till all the prize is lost!
The lock, obtained with guilt, and kept with pain,
In every place is sought, but sought in vain: 110

With such a prize no mortal must be blessed,
So Heaven decrees! with Heaven who can contest?
   Some thought it mounted to the lunar sphere,[45]
Since all things lost on earth are treasured there.
There heroes' wits are kept in ponderous vases,
And beaux' in snuff-boxes and tweezer-cases.
There broken vows, and deathbed alms are found,
And lovers' hearts with ends of riband bound,
The courtier's promises, and sick man's prayers,
The smiles of harlots, and the tears of heirs,   120
Cages for gnats, and chains to yoke a flea,
Dried butterflies, and tomes of casuistry.
   But trust the Muse—she saw it upward rise,
Though marked by none but quick, poetic eyes:
(So Rome's great founder to the heavens withdrew,
To Proculus alone confessed in view)
A sudden star, it shot through liquid air,
And drew behind a radiant trail of hair.
Not Berenice's locks first rose so bright,
The heavens bespangling with disheveled light.   130
The sylphs behold it kindling as it flies,
And pleased pursue its progress through the skies.
   This the beau monde shall from the Mall survey,
And hail with music its propitious ray.
This the blest lover shall for Venus take,
And send up vows from Rosamonda's lake.
This Partridge soon shall view in cloudless skies,
When next he looks through Galileo's eyes;
And hence th' egregious wizard shall foredoom
The fate of Louis, and the fall of Rome.   140
   Then cease, bright nymph! to mourn thy ravished hair,
Which adds new glory to the shining sphere!
Not all the tresses that fair head can boast,
Shall draw such envy as the lock you lost.
For, after all the murders of your eye,
When, after millions slain, yourself shall die;
When those fair suns shall set, as set they must,
And all those tresses shall be laid in dust; [46]
This lock, the Muse shall consecrate to fame,
And 'midst the stars inscribe Belinda's name.[47]   150

VOLTAIRE

Memnon the Philosopher [1750]

FROM *The Works of Voltaire,* edited
by John Morley. Paris: E. R. Du-
Mont, 1901. Vol. IV.

Memnon one day took it into his head to become a great philosopher. "To be perfectly happy," said he to himself, "I have nothing
to do but to divest myself entirely of passions, and nothing is more
easy, as everybody knows. In the first place, I will never be in love, for
when I see a beautiful woman I will say to myself, These cheeks will
one day grow sallow and wrinkled, these eyes be encircled with vermil-
ion, that bosom become lean and emaciated, that head bald and palsied.
Now, I have only to consider her at present in imagination as she will
afterwards appear in reality, and certainly a fair face will never turn
my head.

"In the second place, I shall always be temperate. It will be in vain
to tempt me with good cheer, with delicious wines, or the charms of
society. I will have only to figure to myself the consequences of excess
—an aching head, a loathing stomach, the loss of reason, of health, and
of time; I will then only eat to supply the waste of nature; my health
will be always equal, my ideas pure and luminous. All this is so easy
that there is no merit in accomplishing it.

"But," says Memnon, "I must think a little of how I am to regu-
late my fortune; why, my desires [33] are moderate, my wealth is
securely placed with the receiver-general of the finances of Nineveh. I
have wherewithal to live independent, and that is the greatest of bless-
ings. I shall never be under the cruel necessity of dancing attendance
at court. I will never envy any one, and nobody will envy me. Still all
this is easy. I have friends, and I will preserve them, for we shall never
have any difference. I will never take amiss anything they may say or
do; and they will behave in the same way to me. There is no diffi-
culty in all this."

Having thus laid this little plan of philosophy in his closet, Memnon put his head out of the window. He saw two women walking
under the plane trees near his house. The one was old and appeared
quite at her ease. The other was young, handsome, and seemingly
much agitated. She sighed, she wept, and seemed on that account still
more beautiful. Our philosopher was touched, not, to be sure, with the
lady (he was too much determined not to feel any uneasiness of that

kind), but with the distress which he saw in her. He came downstairs and accosted the young Ninevite, designing to console her with philosophy. That lovely person related to him, with an air of the greatest simplicity and in the most affecting manner, the injuries she sustained from an imaginary uncle—with what art he had deprived her of some imaginary property, and of the violence which she pretended to dread from him.

"You appear to me," said she, "a man of such wisdom [34] that if you will come to my house and examine into my affairs, I am persuaded you will be able to relieve me from the cruel embarrassment I am at present involved in."

Memnon did not hesitate to follow her, to examine her affairs philosophically, and to give her sound counsel.

The afflicted lady led him into a perfumed chamber and politely made him sit down with her on a large sofa, where they both placed themselves opposite to each other, in the attitude of conversation, the one eager in telling her story, the other listening with devout attention. The lady spoke with downcast eyes, whence there sometimes fell a tear, and which, as she now and then ventured to raise them, always met those of the sage Memnon. Their discourse was full of tenderness, which redoubled as often as their eyes met. Memnon took her affairs exceedingly to heart and felt himself every instant more and more inclined to oblige a person so virtuous and so unhappy. By degrees, in the warmth of conversation, they drew nearer. Memnon counselled her with great wisdom, and gave her most tender advice.

At this interesting moment, as may easily be imagined, who should come in but the uncle? He was armed from head to foot, and the first thing he said was that he would immediately sacrifice, as was just, both Memnon and his niece. The latter, who made her escape, knew that he was disposed to pardon, provided a good round sum were offered to him.[35] Memnon was obliged to purchase his safety with all he had about him. In those days people were happy in getting so easily quit. America was not then discovered, and distressed ladies were not then so dangerous as they are now.

Memnon, covered with shame and confusion, got home to his own house. He there found a card inviting him to attend dinner with some of his intimate friends.

"If I remain at home alone," said he, "I shall have my mind so occupied with this vexatious adventure that I shall not be able to eat a bit and I shall bring upon myself some disease. It will therefore be prudent in me to go to my intimate friends and partake with them of a frugal repast. I shall forget in the sweets of their society the folly I have this morning been guilty of."

Accordingly he attends the meeting; he is discovered to be uneasy at something, and he is urged to drink and banish care.

"A little wine, drunk in moderation, comforts the heart of God and man"—so reasoned Memnon the philosopher, and he became intoxicated. After the repast, play is proposed.

"A little play with one's intimate friends is a harmless pastime." He plays and loses all in his purse and four times as much on his word. A dispute arises on some circumstance in the game and the disputants grow warm. One of his intimate friends [36] throws a dice-box at his head and strikes out one of his eyes. The philosopher Memnon is carried home drunk and penniless, with the loss of an eye.

He sleeps out his debauch and when his head becomes clear he sends his servant to the receiver-general of the finances of Nineveh to draw a little money to pay his debt of honor to his intimate friends. The servant returns and informs him that the receiver-general had that morning been declared a fraudulent bankrupt, and that by this means a hundred families are reduced to poverty and despair. Memnon, almost beside himself, puts a plaster on his eye and a petition in his pocket, and goes to court to solicit justice from the king against the bankrupt. In the saloon he meets a number of ladies, all in the highest spirits and sailing along with hoops four-and-twenty feet in circumference. One of them, slightly acquainted with him, eyed him askance, and cried aloud: "Ah! what a horrid monster!"

Another, who was better acquainted with him, thus accosts him: "Good-morrow, Mr. Memnon; I hope you are well, Mr. Memnon. La! Mr. Memnon, how did you lose your eye?" and, turning upon her heel, she tripped unconcernedly away.

Memnon hid himself in a corner and waited for the moment when he could throw himself at the feet of the monarch. That moment at last arrived. Three times he kissed the earth and presented his petition. His gracious majesty received him very favorably [37] and referred the paper to one of his satraps. The satrap takes Memnon aside and says to him, with a haughty air and satirical grin:

"Hark ye, you fellow with the one eye; you must be a comical dog indeed to address yourself to the king rather than to me, and still more so to dare to demand justice against an honest bankrupt, whom I honor with my protection, and who is also a nephew to the waiting-maid of my mistress. Proceed no further in this business, my good friend, if you wish to preserve the eye you have left."

Memnon, having thus in his closet resolved to renounce women, the excess of the table, play, and quarrelling, but especially having determined never to go to court, had been, in the short space of four-and-twenty hours, duped and robbed by a gentle dame, had got drunk, had gamed, had been engaged in a quarrel, had got his eye knocked out, and had been at court, where he was sneered at and also insulted.

Petrified with astonishment, and his heart broken with grief, Memnon returns homeward in despair. As he was about to enter his house, he is repulsed by a number of officers who are carrying off his furniture for the benefit of his creditors. He falls down almost lifeless under a plane tree. There he finds the fair dame of the morning, who was walking with her dear uncle, and both set up a loud laugh on seeing Memnon with his plaster. The night approached, and Memnon made his bed on some straw near the [38] walls of his house. Here the ague seized him and he fell asleep in one of the fits, when a celestial spirit appeared to him in a dream.

It was all resplendent with light; it had six beautiful wings, but neither feet, nor head, and could be likened to nothing.

"What art thou?" said Memnon.

"Thy good genius," replied the spirit.

"Restore me, then, my eye, my health, my fortune, my reason," said Memnon, and he related how he had lost them all in one day.

"These are adventures which never happen to us in the world we inhabit," said the spirit.

"And what world do you inhabit?" said the man of affliction.

"My native country," replied the other, "is five hundred millions of leagues distant from the sun, in a little star near Sirius."

"Charming country!" said Memnon. "And are there indeed with you no jades to dupe a poor devil, no intimate friends that win his money and knock out an eye for him, no fraudulent bankrupts, no satraps that make a jest of you while they refuse you justice?"

"No," said the inhabitant of the star, "we have nothing of the kind. We are never duped by women because we have none among us; we never commit excesses at table because we neither eat nor drink; we have no bankrupts because with us there is neither silver nor gold; our eyes cannot be knocked out because [39] we have not bodies in the form of yours, and satraps never do us injustice, because in our world we are all equal."

"Pray, my lord," said Memnon, "without women and without eating, how do you spend your time?"

"In watching over the other worlds that are entrusted to us, and I am now come to give you consolation."

"Alas!" replied Memnon, "why did you not come yesterday to hinder me from committing so many indiscretions?"

"I was with your elder brother Hassan," said the celestial being. "He is still more to be pitied than you are. His most gracious majesty, the sultan of the Indies, in whose court he has the honor to serve, has caused both his eyes to be put out for some small indiscretion, and he is now in a dungeon, his hands and feet loaded with chains."

" 'Tis a happy thing, truly," said Memnon, "to have a good genius in one's family, when out of two brothers, one is blind of an eye, the other blind of both; one stretched upon straw, the other in a dungeon."

"Your fate will soon change," said the spirit of the star. "It is true you will never recover your eye, but, except that, you may be sufficiently happy if you never again take it into your head to be a perfect philosopher."

"Is it, then, impossible?" said Memnon.

"As impossible as to be perfectly wise, perfectly [40] strong, perfectly powerful, perfectly happy. We ourselves are very far from it. There is a world, indeed, where all this takes place; but, in the hundred thousand millions of worlds dispersed over the regions of space, everything goes on by degrees. There is less philosophy and less enjoyment in the second than in the first, less in the third than in the second, and so forth till the last in the scale, where all are completely fools."

"I am afraid," said Memnon, "that our little terraqueous globe here is the madhouse of those hundred thousand millions of worlds of which your lordship does me the honor to speak."

"Not quite," said the spirit, "but very nearly; everything must be in its proper place."

"But are those poets and philosophers wrong, then, who tell us that everything is for the best?"

"No, they are right, when we consider things in relation to the gradation of the whole universe."

"Oh! I shall never believe it till I recover my eye again," said the unfortunate Memnon.[41]

SAMUEL LANGHORNE CLEMENS

FROM *The Adventures of Huckleberry Finn* [1884], Uniform Edition. New York and London: Harper & Brothers, 1904.

. . . One morning, when we was pretty well down [185] the state of Arkansaw, we come in sight of a little one-horse town in a big bend; so we tied up about three-quarters of a mile above it, in the mouth of a crick which was shut in like a tunnel by the cypress trees, and all of us but Jim took the canoe and went down there to see if there was any chance in that place for our show.

We struck it mighty lucky; there was going to be a circus there that afternoon, and the country-people was already beginning to come in, in all kinds of old shackly wagons, and on horses. The circus would leave before night, so our show would have a pretty good chance. The duke he hired the court-house, and we went around and stuck up our bills. They read like this:

Shaksperean Revival ! ! !
Wonderful Attraction!
For One Night Only!
The world renowned tragedians,
David Garrick the younger, of Drury Lane Theatre,
London,
and
Edmund Kean the elder, of the Royal Haymarket
Theatre, Whitechapel, Pudding Lane, Piccadilly,
London, and the Royal Continental
Theatres, in their sublime
Shakesperean Spectacle entitled
The Balcony Scene
in
Romeo and Juliet ! ! !

Romeo .... Mr. Garrick
Juliet .... Mr. Kean [186]

Assisted by the whole strength of the company!
New costumes, new scenery, new appointments!

Also:

The thrilling, masterly, and blood-curdling
Broad-sword conflict
In Richard III. ! ! !

Richard III .... Mr. Garrick
Richmond .... Mr. Kean

Also:

(by special request)
Hamlet's Immortal Soliloquy ! !
By the Illustrious Kean!
Done by him 300 consecutive nights in Paris!
For One Night Only,
On account of imperative European engagements!
Admission 25 cents; children and servants, 10 cents.

Then we went loafing around town. The stores and houses was
most all old, shackly, dried-up frame concerns that hadn't ever been
painted; they was set up three or four feet above ground on stilts, so as
to be out of reach of the water when the river was overflowed. The
houses had little gardens around them, but they didn't seem to raise
hardly anything in them but jimpson-weeds, and sunflowers, and ash-
piles, and old curled-up boots and shoes, and pieces of bottles, and rags,
and played-out tinware. The fences was made of different kinds of
boards, nailed on at different times; and they leaned every which way,
and had gates that didn't generly have but one hinge—a leather one.
Some of the fences had been whitewashed some time or another, but

the duke said it was in Columbus's time, like enough. There was generly hogs in the garden, and people driving them out.

All the stores was along one street. They had white domestic
awnings in front, and the country-people hitched their horses to the
awning-posts. There was empty dry-goods boxes under the awnings,
and loafers roosting on them all day long, whittling them with their
Barlow knives; and chawing tobacco, and gaping and yawning and
stretching—a mighty ornery lot. They generly [187] had on yellow straw
hats most as wide as an umbrella, but didn't wear no coats nor waist-
coats; they called one another Bill, and Buck, and Hank, and Joe, and
Andy, and talked lazy and drawly, and used considerable many cuss-
words. There was as many as one loafer leaning up against every awn-
ing-post, and he most always had his hands in his britches pockets,
except when he fetched them out to lend a chaw of tobacco or scratch.
What a body was hearing amongst them all the time was:

"Gimme a chaw 'v tobacker, Hank."

"Cain't; I hain't got but one chaw left. Ask Bill."

Maybe Bill he gives him a chaw; maybe he lies and says he ain't
got none. Some of them kinds of loafers never has a cent in the world,
nor a chaw of tobacco of their own. They get all their chawing by bor-
rowing; they say to a fellow, "I wisht you'd len' me a chaw, Jack, I jist
this minute give Ben Thompson the last chaw I had"—which is a lie
pretty much every time; it don't fool nobody but a stranger; but Jack
ain't no stranger, so he says:

"*You* give him a chaw, did you? So did your sister's cat's grand-
mother. You pay me back the chaws you've awready borry'd off'n me,
Lafe Buckner, then I'll loan you one or two ton of it, and won't charge
you no back intrust, nuther."

"Well, I *did* pay you back some of it wunst."

"Yes, you did—'bout six chaws. You borry'd store tobacker and
paid back nigger-head."

Store tobacco is flat black plug, but these fellows mostly chaws
the natural leaf twisted. When they borrow a chaw they don't generly
cut it off with a knife, but set the plug in between their teeth, and
gnaw with [188] their teeth and tug at the plug with their hands till
they get it in two; then sometimes the one that owns the tobacco looks
mournful at it when it's handed back, and says, sarcastic:

"Here, gimme the *chaw*, and you take the *plug*."

All the streets and lanes was just mud; they warn't nothing else
but mud—mud as black as tar and nigh about a foot deep in some
places, and two or three inches deep in *all* the places. The hogs loafed
and grunted around everywheres. You'd see a muddy sow and a litter
of pigs come lazying along the street and whollop herself right down
in the way, where folks had to walk around her, and she'd stretch out
and shut her eyes and wave her ears whilst the pigs was milking her,
and look as happy as if she was on salary. And pretty soon you'd hear

a loafer sing out, "Hi! *so* boy; sick him, Tige!" and away the sow would go, squealing most horrible, with a dog or two swinging to each ear, and three or four dozen more a-coming; and then you would see all the loafers get up and watch the thing out of sight, and laugh at the fun and look grateful for the noise. Then they'd settle back again till there was a dog-fight. There couldn't anything wake them up all over, and make them happy all over, like a dog-fight—unless it might be putting turpentine on a stray dog and setting fire to him, or tying a tin pan to his tail and see him run himself to death.

On the river-front some of the houses was sticking out over the bank, and they was bowed and bent, and about ready to tumble in. The people had moved out of them. The bank was caved away under one corner of some others, and that corner was hanging over. People lived in them yet, but it was dangersome, because sometimes [189] a strip of land as wide as a house caves in at a time. Sometimes a belt of land a quarter of a mile deep will start in and cave along and cave along till it all caves into the river in one summer. Such a town as that has to be always moving back, and back, and back, because the river's always gnawing at it.

The nearer it got to noon that day the thicker and thicker was the wagons and horses in the streets, and more coming all the time. Families fetched their dinners with them from the country, and eat them in the wagons. There was considerable whisky-drinking going on, and I seen three fights. By and by somebody sings out:

"Here comes old Boggs!—in from the country for his little old monthly drunk; here he comes, boys!"

All the loafers looked glad; I reckoned they was used to having fun out of Boggs. One of them says:

"Wonder who he's a-gwyne to chaw up this time. If he'd a-chawed up all the men he's ben a-gywne to chaw up in the last twenty year he'd have considerable ruputation now."

Another one says, "I wisht old Boggs 'd threaten me, 'cuz then I'd know I warn't gwyne to die for a thousan' year."

Boggs comes a-tearing along on his horse, whooping and yelling like an Injun, and singing out:

"Cler the track, thar. I'm on the waw-path, and the price uv coffins is a-gwyne to raise."

He was drunk, and weaving about in his saddle; he was over fifty year old, and had a very red face. Everybody yelled at him and laughed at him and sassed him, and he sassed back, and said he'd attend to them and lay them out in their regular turns, but he couldn't wait [190] now because he'd come to town to kill old Colonel Sherburn, and his motto was, "Meat first, and spoon vittles to top off on."

He see me, and rode up and says:

"Whar'd you come f'm, boy? You prepared to die?"

Then he rode on. I was scared, but a man says:

"He don't mean nothing; he's always a-carryin' on like that when he's drunk. He's the best-naturedest old fool in Arkansaw—never hurt nobody, drunk nor sober."

Boggs rode up before the biggest store in town, and bent his head down so he could see under the curtain of the awning and yells:

"Come out here, Sherburn! Come out and meet the man you've swindled. You're the houn' I'm after, and I'm a-gwyne to have you, too!"

And so he went on, calling Sherburn everything he could lay his tongue to, and the whole street packed with people listening and laughing and going on. By and by a proud-looking man about fifty-five —and he was a heap the best-dressed man in that town, too—steps out of the store, and the crowd drops back on each side to let him come. He says to Boggs, mighty ca'm and slow—he says:

"I'm tired of this, but I'll endure it till one o'clock. Till one o'clock, mind—no longer. If you open your mouth against me only once after that time you can't travel so far but I will find you."

Then he turns and goes in. The crowd looked mighty sober; nobody stirred, and there warn't no more laughing. Boggs rode off black-guarding Sherburn as loud as he could yell, all down the street; and pretty soon back he comes and stops before the store, still keeping it up.[191] Some men crowded around him and tried to get him to shut up, but he wouldn't; they told him it would be one o'clock in about fifteen minutes, and so he *must* go home—he must go right away. But it didn't do no good. He cussed away with all his might, and throwed his hat down in the mud and rode over it, and pretty soon he went a-raging down the street again, with his hair a-flying. Everybody that could get a chance at him tried their best to coax him off of his horse so they could lock him up and get him sober; but it warn't no use—up the street he would tear again, and give Sherburn another cussing. By and by somebody says:

"Go for his daughter!—quick, go for his daughter; sometimes he'll listen to her. If anybody can persuade him, she can."

So somebody started on a run. I walked down street a ways and stopped. In about five or ten minutes here comes Boggs again, but not on his horse. He was a-reeling across the street towards me, bareheaded, with a friend on both sides of him a-holt of his arms and hurrying him along. He was quiet, and looked uneasy; and he warn't hanging back any, but was doing some of the hurrying himself. Somebody sings out:

"Boggs!"

I looked over there to see who said it, and it was that Colonel Sherburn. He was standing perfectly still in the street, and had a pistol raised in his right hand—not aiming it, but holding it out with the barrel tilted up towards the sky. The same second I see a young girl coming on the run, and two men with her. Boggs and the men turned round to see who called him, and when they see the pistol the men

jumped to one side, and the pistol-barrel come down slow and steady
to a [192] level—both barrels cocked. Boggs throws up both of his
hands and says, "O Lord, don't shoot!" Bang! goes the first shot, and
he staggers back, clawing at the air—bang! goes the second one, and
he tumbles backwards onto the ground, heavy and solid, with his arms
spread out. That young girl screamed out and comes rushing, and
down she throws herself on her father, crying, and saying, "Oh, he's
killed him, he's killed him!" The crowd closed up around them, and
shouldered and jammed one another, with their necks stretched, trying
to see, and people on the inside trying to shove them back and shout-
ing, "Back, back! give him air, give him air!"

Colonel Sherburn he tossed his pistol onto the ground, and turned
around on his heels and walked off.

They took Boggs to a little drug store, the crowd pressing around
just the same, and the whole town following, and I rushed and got a
good place at the window, where I was close to him and could see in.
They laid him on the floor and put one large Bible under his head,
and opened another one and spread it on his breast; but they tore open
his shirt first, and I seen where one of the bullets went in. He made
about a dozen long gasps, his breast lifting the Bible up when he
drawed his breath, and letting it down again when he breathed it out
—and after that he laid still; he was dead. Then they pulled his daughter away from him, screaming and crying, and took her off. She was
about sixteen, and very sweet and gentle looking, but awful pale and
scared.

Well, pretty soon the whole town was there, squirming and scroug-
ing and pushing and shoving to get at the window and have a look, but
people that had the [193] places wouldn't give them up, and folks behind them was saying all the time, "Say, now, you've looked enough,
you fellows; 'tain't right and 'tain't fair for you to stay thar all the
time, and never give nobody a chance; other folks has their rights as
well as you."

There was considerable jawing back, so I slid out, thinking maybe
there was going to be trouble. The streets was full, and everybody was
excited. Everybody that seen the shooting was telling how it happened,
and there was a big crowd packed around each one of these fellows,
stretching their necks and listening. One long, lanky man, with long
hair and a big white fur stovepipe hat on the back of his head, and a
crooked-handled cane, marked out the places on the ground where
Boggs stood and where Sherburn stood, and the people following him
around from one place to t'other and watching everything he done,
and bobbing their heads to show they understood, and stooping a little and resting their hands on their thighs to watch him mark the
places on the ground with his cane; and then he stood up straight and
stiff where Sherburn had stood, frowning and having his hat-brim
down over his eyes, and sung out, "Boggs!" and then fetched his cane

down slow to a level, and says "Bang!" staggered backwards, says "Bang!" again, and fell down flat on his back. The people that had seen the thing said he done it perfect; said it was just exactly the way it all happened. Then as much as a dozen people got out their bottles and treated him.

Well, by and by somebody said Sherburn ought to be lynched. In about a minute everybody was saying it; so away they went, mad and yelling, and snatching down every clothes-line they come to to do the hanging with.[194]

They swarmed up towards Sherburn's house, a-whooping and raging like Injuns, and everything had to clear the way or get run over and tromped to mush, and it was awful to see. Children was heel-ing it ahead of the mob, screaming and trying to get out of the way; and every window along the road was full of women's heads, and there was nigger boys in every tree, and bucks and wenches looking over every fence; and as soon as the mob would get nearly to them they would break and skaddle back out of reach. Lots of the women and girls was crying and taking on, scared most to death.

They swarmed up in front of Sherburn's palings as thick as they could jam together, and you couldn't hear yourself think for the noise. It was a little twenty-foot yard. Some sung out "Tear down the fence! tear down the fence!" Then there was a racket of ripping and tearing and smashing, and down she goes, and the front wall of the crowd begins to roll in like a wave.

Just then Sherburn steps out onto the roof of his little front porch, with a double-barrel gun in his hand, and takes his stand, perfectly ca'm and deliberate, not saying [195] a word. The racket stopped, and the waved sucked back.

Sherburn never said a word—just stood there, looking down. The stillness was awful creepy and uncomfortable. Sherburn run his eye slow along the crowd; and wherever it struck the people tried a little to outgaze him, but they couldn't; they dropped their eyes and looked sneaky. Then pretty soon Sherburn sort of laughed; not the pleasant kind, but the kind that makes you feel like you're eating bread with sand in it.

Then he says, slow and scornful:

"The idea of *you* lynching anybody! It's amusing. The idea of you thinking you had pluck enough to lynch a *man!* Because you're brave enough to tar and feather poor friendless cast-out women that come along here, did that make you think you had grit enough to lay your hands on a *man?* Why, a *man's* safe in the hands of ten thousand of your kind—as long as it's daytime and you're not behind him.

"Do I know you? I know you clear through. I was born and raised in the South, and I've lived in the North; so I know the average all around. The average man's a coward. In the North he lets anybody walk over him that wants to, and goes home and prays for a humble spirit to bear it. In the South one man, all by himself, has stopped a stage full of men in the daytime, and robbed the lot. Your newspapers call you a brave people so much that you think you *are* braver than any other people—whereas you're just *as* brave, and no braver. Why don't your juries hang murderers? Because they're afraid the man's friends will shoot them in the back, in the dark—and it's just what they *would* do.

"So they always acquit; and then a *man* goes in the [196] night, with a hundred masked cowards at his back, and lynches the rascal. Your mistake is, that you didn't bring a man with you; that's one mistake, and the other is that you didn't come in the dark and fetch your masks. You brought *part* of a man—Buck Harkness, there—and if you hadn't had him to start you, you'd 'a' taken it out in blowing.

"You didn't want to come. The average man don't like trouble and danger. *You* don't like trouble and danger. But if only *half* a man —like Buck Harkness, there—shouts 'Lynch him! lynch him!' you're afraid to back down—afraid you'll be found out to be what you are— *cowards*—and so you raise a yell, and hang yourselves onto that half-a-man's coat-tail, and come raging up here, swearing what big things you're going to do. The pitifulest thing out is a mob; that's what an army is—a mob; they don' fight with courage that's born in them, but with courage that's borrowed from their mass, and from their officers. But a mob without any *man* at the head of it is *beneath* pitifulness. Now the thing for *you* to do is to droop your tails and go home and crawl in a hole. If any real lynching's going to be done it will be done in the dark, Southern fashion; and when they come they'll bring their masks, and fetch a *man* along. Now *leave*—and take your half-a-man with you"—tossing his gun up across his left arm and cocking it when he says this.

The crowd washed back sudden, and then broke all apart, and went tearing off every which way, and Buck Harkness he heeled it after them, looking tolerable cheap. I could 'a' stayed if I wanted to, but I didn't want to.[197]

IVAN BUNIN

The Gentleman from San Francisco [1915]

FROM *The Gentleman from San Francisco,* translated by Bernard Guilbert Guerney. Reprinted by permission of Alfred A. Knopf, Inc. New York: Alfred A. Knopf, Inc., 1934. Copyright 1923 by Alfred A. Knopf, Inc.

> *Alas, alas that great city Babylon,*
> *that mighty city!*
>
> THE APOCALYPSE

The gentleman from San Francisco—neither at Naples nor at Capri had any one remembered his name—was going to the Old World for two whole years, with wife and daughter, solely for the sake of pleasure.

He was firmly convinced that he was fully entitled to rest, to pleasure, to prolonged and comfortable travel, and to not a little else besides. For such a conviction he had his reasons,—that, in the first place, he was rich, and, in the second, that he was only now beginning to live, despite his eight and fifty years. Until now he had not lived, but had merely existed,—not at all badly, it is true, but, never the less, putting all his hopes on the future. He had laboured with never a pause for rest,—the coolies, whom he had imported by whole thousands, well knew what this meant!—and finally he saw that much had already been accomplished, that he had almost come abreast of those whom he had at one time set out to emulate, and he decided to enjoy breathing space. It was a custom among the class of people to which he belonged to commence their enjoyment of life with a journey to Europe, to India, to Egypt. He, too, proposed to do the same.[280] Of course he desired, first of all, to reward himself for his years of toil; however, he rejoiced on account of his wife and daughter as well. His wife had never been distinguished for any special sensitiveness to new impressions,—but then, all elderly American women are fervid travellers. As for his daughter,—a girl no longer in her first youth, and somewhat sickly,—travel was a downright necessity for her: to say nothing of the benefit to her health, were there no fortuitous encounters during travels? It is while travelling that one may at times sit at table with a *milliardaire,* or scrutinize frescoes by his side.

The itinerary worked out by the gentleman from San Francisco was an extensive one. In December and January he hoped to enjoy the sun of Southern Italy, the monuments of antiquity, the *tarantella*, the serenades of strolling singers, and that which men of his age relish with the utmost *finesse:* the love of little, youthful Neapolitaines, even though it be given not entirely without ulterior motives; he contemplated spending the Carnival in Nice, in Monte Carlo, whither the very pick of society gravitates at that time,—that very society upon which all the benefits of civilization depend: not merely the cut of tuxedos, but, as well, the stability of thrones, and the declaration of wars, and the prosperity of hotels,—Monte Carlo, where some give themselves up with passion to automobile and sail races; others to roulette; a third group to that which it is the custom to call flirting; a fourth, to trap-shooting, in which the pigeons, released from their cotes, soar up most gracefully above emerald-green swards, against the background of a sea that is the colour of forget-me-nots,—only, in the same minute, to strike against the ground as little, crumpled clods of white.[281] ... The beginning of March he wanted to devote to Florence; about the time of the Passion of Our Lord to arrive at Rome, in order to hear the *Miserere* there; his plans also embraced Venice, and Paris, and bull-fighting in Seville, and sea-bathing in the British Islands, and Athens, and Constantinople, and Palestine, and Egypt, and even Japan,—of course, be it understood, already on the return trip. ... And everything went very well at first.

It was the end of November; almost as far as Gibraltar it was necessary to navigate now through an icy murk, now amidst a blizzard of wet snow; but the ship sailed in all safety and even without rolling; the passengers the steamer was carrying proved to be many, and all of them people of note; the ship—the famous *Atlantida*—resembled the most expensive of European hotels, with all conveniences: an all-night bar, Turkish baths, a newspaper of its own,—and life upon it flowed in accordance with a most complicated system of regulations: people got up early, to the sounds of bugles, stridently resounding through the corridors at that dark hour when day was so slowly and inimically dawning over the grayish-green desert of waters, ponderously turbulent in the midst. Putting on their flannel pyjamas, the passengers drank coffee, chocolate, cocoa; then they got into marble baths, did their exercises, inducing an appetite and a sense of well-being, performed their toilet for the day, and went to breakfast. Until eleven one was supposed to promenade the decks vigorously, inhaling the fresh coolness of the ocean, or to play at shuffle-board and other games for the sake of arousing the appetite anew, and, at eleven, to seek sustenance in bouillon and sandwiches; having refreshed [282] themselves, the passengers perused their newspaper with gusto and calmly awaited lunch, a meal still more nourishing and varied than the breakfast. The next two hours were sacred to repose,—the decks were then encumbered with *chaises longues,* upon which the travellers reclined, covered up with plaids, contemplating the cloud-flecked sky and the foaming hummocks flashing by over the side, or else pleasantly dozing off; at five o'clock, refreshed and put in good spirits, they were drenched with strong fragrant tea, served with cookies; at seven they were apprized by bugle signals of a dinner of nine courses. ... And thereupon the gentleman from San Francisco, in an access of animal spirits, would hurry to his resplendent *cabine de luxe,* to dress.

In the evening the tiers of the *Atlantida* gaped through the dusk as though they were fiery, countless eyes, and a great multitude of servants worked with special feverishness in the kitchens, sculleries, and wine vaults. The ocean, heaving on the other side of the walls, was awesome; but none gave it a thought, firmly believing it under the sway of the captain,—a red-haired man of monstrous bulk and ponderousness, always seeming sleepy, resembling, in his uniform frock-coat, with its golden chevrons, an enormous idol; it was only very rarely that he left his mysterious quarters to appear in public. A siren on the forecastle howled every minute in hellish sullenness and whined in frenzied malice, but not many of the diners heard the siren,—it was drowned by the strains of a splendid stringed orchestra, playing exquisitely and ceaselessly in the two-tiered hall, decorated with marble, its floors covered with velvet rugs; festively flooded with the lights of crystal lustres and gilded *girandoles,* filled [283] to overflowing with diamond-bedecked ladies in *décolleté* and men in tuxedos, graceful waiters and deferent *maitres d'hôtel,*—among whom one, who took orders for wines exclusively, even walked about with a chain around his neck, like a lord mayor. A tuxedo and perfect linen made the gentleman from San Francisco appear very much younger. Spare, not tall, clumsily but strongly built, groomed until he shone and moderately animated, he sat in the aureate-pearly refulgence of this palatial room, at a table with a bottle of amber Johannesberg, with countless goblets, small and large, of the thinnest glass, with a curly bouquet of curly hyacinths. There was something of the Mongol about his yellowish face with clipped silvery moustache; his large teeth gleamed with gold fillings; his stalwart, bald head glistened like old ivory. Rich, yet in keeping with her years, was the dress of his wife,—a big woman, expansive and calm; elaborate, yet light and diaphanous, with an innocent frankness, was that of his daughter,— tall, slender, with magnificent hair, exquisitely dressed, with breath aromatic from violet cachous and with the tenderest of tiny, rosy pimples about her lips and between her shoulder blades, just the least bit powdered. ... The dinner lasted for two whole hours, while after dinner there was dancing in the ball room, during which the men,— the gentleman from San Francisco among their number, of course,— with their feet cocked up, determined, upon the basis of the latest political and stock-exchange news, the destinies of nations, smoking Habana cigars and drinking *liqueurs* until they were crimson in the face, seated in the bar, where the waiters were negroes in red jackets, the whites of their eyes resembling hard boiled eggs with the shell off. The [284] ocean, with a dull roar, was moiling in black mountains on the other side of the wall; the snow-gale whistled mightily through the sodden rigging; the whole steamer quivered as it mastered both the gale and the mountains, sundering to either side, as though with a plough, their shifting masses, that again and again boiled up and reared high, with tails of foam; the siren, stifled by the fog, was moaning with a deathly anguish; the lookouts up in their crow's-nest froze from the cold and grew dazed from straining their attention beyond their strength. Like to the grim and sultry depths of the infernal regions, like to their ultimate, their ninth circle, was the womb of the steamer, below the water line,—that womb where dully gurgled the gigantic furnaces, devouring with their incandescent maws mountains of hard coal, cast into them by men stripped to the waist, purple from the flames, and with smarting, filthy sweat pouring over them; whereas here, in the bar, men threw their legs over the arms of their chairs with never a care, sipping cognac and *liqueurs,* and were wafted among clouds of spicy smoke as they indulged in well-turned conversation; in the ball room everything was radiant with light and warmth and joy; the dancing couples were now awhirl in waltzes, now twisting in the tango,—and the music insistently, in some delectably-shameless melancholy, was suppliant always of the one, always of the same thing. ... There was an ambassador among this brilliant throng,—a lean, modest little old man; there was a great man of riches,—cleanshaven, lanky, of indeterminate years, and with the appearance of a prelate, in his dress-coat of an old-fashioned cut; there was a well-known Spanish writer; there was a world-celebrated beauty, already just the very least trifle [285] faded and of an unenviable morality; there was an exquisite couple in love with each other, whom all watched with curiosity and whose happiness was unconcealed: *he* danced only with *her;* sang—and with great ability—only to *her* accompaniment; and everything they did was carried out so charmingly, that the captain was the only one who knew that this pair was hired by Lloyd's to play at love for a good figure, and that they had been sailing for a long time, now on one ship, now on another.

At Gibraltar everybody was gladdened by the sun,—it seemed to be early spring; a new passenger, whose person aroused the general interest, made his appearance on board the *Atlantida,*—he was the hereditary prince of a certain Asiatic kingdom, travelling incognito; a little man who somehow seemed to be all made of wood, even though he was alert in his movements; broad of face, with narrow eyes, in gold-rimmed spectacles; a trifle unpleasant through the fact that his skin showed through his coarse black moustache like that of a cadaver;

on the whole, however, he was charming, unpretentious, and modest. On the Mediterranean Sea there was a wiff of winter again; the billows ran high, and were as multi-coloured as the tail of a peacock; they had snowy-white crests, lashed up—although the sun was sparkling brightly and the sky was perfectly clear—by a *tramontana*, a chill northern wind from beyond the mountains, that was joyously and madly rushing to meet the ship. ... Then, on the second day, the sky began to pale, the horizon became covered with mist, land was nearing; Ischia, Capri appeared; through the binoculars Naples—lumps of sugar strewn at the foot of some dove-coloured mass—could be seen; while over it and this dove-coloured thing were visible [286] the ridges of distant mountains, vaguely glimmering with the dead whiteness of snows. There was a great number of people on deck; many of the ladies and gentlemen had already put on short, light fur coats, with the fur outside; Chinese boys, never contradictory and never speaking above a whisper, bow-legged striplings with pitch-black queues reaching to their heels and with eye-lashes as long and thick as those of young girls, were already dragging, little by little, sundry plaids, canes, and portmanteaux and grips of alligator hide toward the companion-ways. ... The daughter of the gentleman from San Francisco was standing beside the prince, who had been, through a fortuitous circumstance, presented to her yesterday evening, and she pretended to be looking intently into the distance, in a direction he was pointing out to her, telling, explaining something or other to her, hurriedly and quietly. On account of his height he seemed a boy by contrast with others,—he was queer and not at all prepossessing of person, with his spectacles, his derby, his English great coat, while his scanty moustache looked just as if it were of horse-hair, and the swarthy, thin skin seemed to be drawn tightly over his face, and somehow had the appearance of being lacquered,—but the young girl was listening to him, without understanding, in her agitation, what he was saying; her heart was thumping from an incomprehensible rapture before his presence and from pride that he was speaking with her, and not some other; everything about him that was different from others,—his lean hands, his clear skin, under which flowed the ancient blood of kings, even his altogether unpretentious, yet somehow distinctively neat, European dress,—everything held a secret, inexplicable charm, evoked a [287] feeling of amorousness. As for the gentleman from San Francisco himself,—he, in a high silk hat, in gray spats over patent-leather shoes, kept on glancing at the famous beauty, who was standing beside him,—a tall blonde of striking figure, her eyes were painted in the latest Parisian fashion; she was holding a diminutive, hunched-up, mangy lap dog on a silver chain and was chattering to it without cease. And the daughter, in some vague embarrassment, tried not to notice her father.

Like all Americans of means he was very generous on his travels,

and, like all of them, believed in the full sincerity and good-will of those who brought him food and drink with such solicitude, who served him from morn till night, forestalling his least wish; of those who guarded his cleanliness and rest, lugged his things around, summoned porters for him, delivered his trunks to hotels. Thus had it been everywhere, thus had it been on the ship, and thus was it to be in Naples as well. Naples grew, and drew nearer; the musicians, the brass of their instruments flashing, had already clustered upon the deck, and suddenly deafened everybody with the triumphant strains of a march; the gigantic captain, in his full dress uniform, appeared upon his stage, and, like a condescending heathen god, waved his hand amiably to the passengers,—and to the gentleman from San Francisco it seemed that it was for him alone that the march so beloved by proud America was thundering, that it was he whom the captain was felicitating upon a safe arrival. And every other passenger felt similarly about himself—or herself. And when the *Atlantida* did finally enter the harbour, had heaved to at the wharf with her many-tiered mass, black with people, and the gang-planks clattered down,— what [288] a multitude of porters and their helpers in caps with gold braid, what a multitude of different *commissionaires*, whistling gamins, and strapping ragamuffins with packets of coloured postal cards in their hands, made a rush toward the gentleman from San Francisco, with offers of their services! And he smiled, with a kindly contemptuousness, at these ragamuffins, as he went toward the automobile of precisely that hotel where there was a possibility of the prince's stopping as well, and drawled through his teeth, now in English, now in Italian:
"Go away! * *Via!*"

Life at Naples at once assumed its wonted, ordered current: in the early morning, breakfast in the sombre dining room with its damp draught from windows opening on some sort of a stony little garden; the sky was usually overcast, holding out but little promise, and there was the usual crowd of guides at the door of the vestibule; then came the first smiles of a warm, rosy sun; there was, from the high hanging balcony, a view of Vesuvius, enveloped to its foot by radiant morning mists, and of silver-and-pearl eddies on the surface of the Bay, and of the delicate contour of Capri against the horizon; one could see tiny burros, harnessed in twos to little carts, running down below over the quay, sticky with mire, and detachments of diminutive soldiers, marching off to somewhere or other to lively and exhilarating music. Next came the procession to the waiting automobile and the slow progress through populous, narrow, and damp corridors of streets, between tall, many-windowed houses; the inspection of lifelessly-clean museums, evenly and [289] pleasantly, yet bleakly, lit, seemingly illuminated by

---

* English in the original. The same applies to the other phrases in this story marked with asterisks. *Trans.*

snow; or of cool churches, smelling of wax, which everywhere and always contain the same things: a majestic portal, screened by a heavy curtain of leather, and inside,—silence, empty vastness, unobtrusive little flames of a seven-branched candle-stick glowing redly in the distant depths, on an altar bedecked with laces; a solitary old woman among the dark wooden pews; slippery tombstones underfoot; and somebody's *Descent from the Cross,*—inevitably a celebrated one. At one o'clock there was luncheon upon the mountain of San Martino, where, toward noon, gathered not a few people of the very first quality, and where the daughter of the gentleman from San Francisco had once almost fainted away for joy, because she thought she saw the prince sitting in the hall, although she already knew through the newspapers that he had left for a temporary stay at Rome. At five came tea at the hotel, in the showy salon, so cosy with its rugs and flaming fireplaces; and after that it was already time to get ready for dinner,—and once more came the mighty, compelling reverberation of the gong through all the stories; once more the processions in Indian file of ladies in *décolleté,* rustling in their silks upon the staircases and reflected in all the mirrors; once more the palatial dining room, widely and hospitably opened, and the red jackets of the musicians upon their platform, and the black cluster of waiters about the *maitre d'hôtel,* who, with a skill out of the ordinary, was ladling some sort of a thick, roseate soup into plates. ... The dinners, as everywhere else, were the crowning glory of each day; the guests dressed for them as for a rout, and these dinners were so abundant in edibles, and wines, and mineral [290] waters, and sweets, and fruits, that toward eleven o'clock at night the chambermaids were distributing through all the corridors rubber bags with hot water to warm sundry stomachs.

However, the December of that year proved to be not altogether a successful one for Naples; the porters grew confused when one talked with them of the weather, and merely shrugged their shoulders guiltily, muttering that they could not recall such another year,—although it was not the first year that they had been forced to mutter this, and to urge in extenuation that "something terrible is happening everywhere"; there were unheard of storms and torrents of rain on the Riviera; there was snow in Athens; Etna was also all snowed over and was aglow of nights; tourists were fleeing from Palermo in all directions, escaping from the cold. The morning sun deceived the Neapolitans every day that winter: toward noon the sky became gray and a fine rain began falling, but growing heavier and colder all the time; at such times the palms near the entrance of the hotel glistened as though they were of tin, the town seemed especially dirty and cramped, the museums exceedingly alike; the cigar stumps of the corpulent cabmen, whose rubber-coats flapped in the wind like wings, seemed to have an insufferable stench, while the energetic snapping of their whips over their scrawny-necked nags was patently false; the footgear of the *signori* sweeping the rails of the tramways seemed horrible; the women, splashing through the mud, their black-haired heads bared to the rain, appeared hideously short-legged; as for the dampness, and the stench of putrid fish from the sea foaming at the quay,—they were a matter of course. The gentleman and the [291] lady from San Francisco began quarreling in the morning; their daughter either walked about pale, with a headache, or, coming to life again, went into raptures over everything, and was, at such times both charming and beautiful: beautiful were those tender and complex emotions which had been awakened within her by meeting that homely man through whose veins flowed uncommon blood; for, after all is said and done, perhaps it is of no real importance just what it is, precisely, that awakens a maiden's soul,—whether it be money, or fame, or illustrious ancestry. ...

Everybody affirmed that things were entirely different in Sorrento, in Capri,—there it was both warmer and sunnier, and the lemons were in blossom, and the customs were more honest, and the wine was more natural. And so the family from San Francisco determined to set out with all its trunks to Capri, and, after seeing it all, after treading the stones where the palace of Tiberius had once stood, after visiting the faery-like caverns of the Azure Grotto, and hearing the bag-pipers of Abruzzi, who for a whole month preceding Christmas wander over the island and sing the praises of the Virgin Mary, they meant to settle in Sorrento.

On the day of departure,—a most memorable one for the family from San Francisco!—there was no sun from the early morning. A heavy fog hid Vesuvius to the very base; this gray fog spread low over the leaden heaving of the sea that was lost to the eye at a distance of a half a mile. Capri was entirely invisible,—as though there had never been such a thing in the world. And the little steamer that set out for it was so tossed from side to side that the family from San Francisco was laid prostrate [292] upon the divans in the sorry general cabin of this tub, their feet wrapped up in plaids, and their eyes closed from nausea. Mrs. suffered,—so she thought,—more than anybody; she was overcome by sea-sickness several times; it seemed to her that she was dying, whereas the stewardess, who always ran up to her with a small basin,—she had been, for many years, day in and day out, rolling on these waves, in freezing weather and in torrid, and yet was still tireless and kind to everybody,—merely laughed. Miss was dreadfully pale and held a slice of lemon between her teeth; now she could not have been cheered even by the hope of a chance encounter with the prince at Sorrento, where he intended to be about Christmas. Mr., who was lying on his back, in roomy overcoat and large cap, never unlocked his jaws all the way over; his face had grown darker and his moustache whiter, and his head ached dreadfully: during the last days, thanks to the bad weather, he had been drinking too heavily of evenings, and had too much admired the "living pictures" in dives of *recherché* libertinage. But the rain kept on lashing against the jarring windows, the water from them running down on the divans; the wind, howling, bent the masts, and at times, aided by the onslaught of a wave, careened the little steamer entirely to one side, and then something in the hold would roll with a rumble. During the stops, at Castellamare, at Sorrento, things were a trifle more bearable, but even then the rocking was fearful,—the shore, with all its cliffs, gardens, *pigin,*[1] its pink and white hotels and hazy mountains clad in curly greenery, swayed up and down as if on a swing; boats bumped up against the sides of the ship;[293] sailors and steerage passengers were yelling vehemently; somewhere, as though it had been crushed, a baby was wailing and smothering; a raw wind was blowing in at the door; and, from a swaying boat with a flag of the Hotel Royal, a lisping gamin was screaming, luring travellers: "Kgoya-al! Hôtel Kgoya-al! ..." And the gentleman from San Francisco, feeling that he was an old man,—which was but proper,— was already thinking with sadness and melancholy of all these Royals, Splendids, Excelsiors, and of these greedy, insignificant mannikins, reeking of garlic, that are called Italians. Once, having opened his eyes and raised himself from the divan, he saw, underneath the craggy steep of the shore, a cluster of stone hovels, mouldy through and through, stuck one on top of another near the very edge of the water, near boats, near all sorts of rags, tins, and brown nets,—hovels so miserable, that, at the recollection that this was that very Italy he had come hither to enjoy, he felt despair. ... Finally, at twilight, the dark mass of the island began to draw near, seemingly bored through and through by little red lights near its base; the wind became softer, warmer, more fragrant; over the abating waves, as opalescent as black oil, golden pythons flowed from the lanterns on the wharf. ... Then came the sudden rumble of the anchor, and it fell with a splash into the water; the ferocious yells of the boatmen, vying with one another, floated in from all quarters,—and at once the heart grew lighter, the lights in the general cabin shone more brightly, a desire arose to eat, to drink, to smoke, to be stirring. ... Ten minutes later the family from San Francisco had descended into a large boat; within fifteen minutes it had set foot upon the stones of the wharf, and [294] had then got into a bright little railway car and to its buzzing started the ascent of the slope, amid the stakes of the vineyards, half-crumbled stone enclosures, and wet, gnarled orange trees, some of them under coverings of straw,—trees with thick, glossy foliage, and aglimmer with the orange fruits; all these objects were sliding downward, past the open windows of the little car, toward the base of the mountain. ...

---

[1] Pino-groves. *Trans.*

Sweetly smells the earth of Italy after rain, and her every island has its own, its especial aroma! The island of Capri was damp and dark on this evening. But now it came into life for an instant; lights sprang up here and there, as always on the steamer's arrival. At the top of the mountain, where stood the station of the *funicular*, there was another throng of those whose duty lay in receiving fittingly the gentleman from San Francisco. There were other arrivals also, but they merited no attention,—several Russians, who had taken up their abode in Capri,—absent-minded because of their bookish meditations, unkempt, bearded, spectacled, the collars of their old drab overcoats turned up; and a group of long-legged, long-necked, round-headed German youths in Tyrolean costumes, with canvas knapsacks slung over their shoulders,—these latter stood in need of nobody's services, feeling themselves at home everywhere, and were not at all generous in their expenditures. The gentleman from San Francisco, on the other hand, who was calmly keeping aloof from both the one group and the other, was immediately noticed. He and his ladies were bustlingly assisted to get out, some men running ahead of him to show him the way: he was surrounded anew by urchins, and by those robust Caprian wives who carry on their [295] heads the portmanteaux and trunks of respectable travellers. The wooden patterns of these women clattered over a *piazetta*, that seemed to belong to some opera, an electric globe swaying above it in the damp wind; the rabble of urchins burst into sharp, bird-like whistles,—and, as though on a stage, the gentleman from San Francisco proceeded in their midst toward some mediæval arch, underneath houses that had become welded into one mass, beyond which a little echoing street,— with the tuft of a palm above flat roofs on its left, and with blue stars in the black sky overhead,—led slopingly to the grand entrance of the hotel glittering ahead. ... And again it seemed that it was in honour of the guests from San Francisco that this damp little town of stone on a craggy little island of the Mediterranean Sea had come to life, that it was they who had made so happy and affable the proprietor of the hotel, that it was they only who had been waited for by the Chinese gong, that now began wailing the summons to dinner through all the stories of the hotel, the instant they had set foot in the vestibule.

The proprietor, a young man of haughty elegance, who had met them with a polite and exquisite bow, for a minute dumbfounded the gentleman from San Francisco: having glanced at him, the gentleman from San Francisco suddenly recalled that just the night before, among the rest of the confusion of images that had beset him in his sleep, he had seen precisely this gentleman,—just like him, down to the least detail: in the same sort of frock with rounded skirts, and with the same pomaded and painstakingly combed head. Startled, he was almost taken aback; but since, from long, long before, there was not even a mustard seed of any sort of so-called mystical [296] emotions left in his soul, his astonishment was dimmed the same instant, passing through a corridor of the hotel, he spoke jestingly to his wife and daughter of this strange coincidence of dream and reality. And only his daughter glanced at him with alarm at that moment: her heart suddenly contracted from sadness, from a feeling of their loneliness upon this foreign, dark island,—a feeling so strong that she almost burst into tears. But still she said nothing of her feelings to her father,—as always.

An exalted personage—Rais XVII,— who had been visiting Capri, had just taken his departure, and the guests from San Francisco were given the same apartments that he had occupied. To them was assigned the handsomest and most expert chambermaid, a Belgian, whose waist was slenderly and firmly corseted, and who wore a little starched cap that looked like a pronged crown; also, the stateliest and most dignified of flunkies, a fiery-eyed Sicilian, swarthy as coal; and the nimblest of bell-boys, the short and stout Luigi,—a fellow who was very fond of a joke, and who had changed many places in his time. And a minute later there was a slight tap at the door of the room of the gentleman from San Francisco,—the French *maitre d'hôtel* had come to find out if the newly arrived guests would dine, and, in the event of an answer in the affirmative,—of which, however, there was no doubt,—to inform them that the *carte de jour* consisted of crawfish, roast beef, asparagus, pheasants, and so forth. The floor was still rocking under the gentleman from San Francisco,—so badly had the atrocious little Italian steamer tossed him about,—but, without hurrying, with his own hands, although somewhat clumsily from being unaccustomed to such things, he shut a window that had banged upon the [297] entrance of the *maitre d'hôtel* and had let in the odours of the distant kitchen and of the wet flowers in the garden, and with a leisurely precision replied that they would dine, that their table must be placed at a distance from the door, at the farthest end of the dining room, that they would drink local wine and champagne,—moderately dry and only slightly chilled. The *maitre d'hôtel concurred* in every word of his, in intonations most varied, having, however, but one significance,—that there was never a doubt, nor could there possibly be any, about the correctness of the wishes of the gentleman from San Francisco, and that everything would be carried out punctiliously. In conclusion he inclined his head, and asked deferentially:

"Will that be all, sir?"

And, having received a long-drawn-out "Yes" * in answer, he added that the *tarantella* would be danced in the vestibule to-day,— the dancers would be Carmella and Giuseppe, known to all Italy, and to "the entire world of tourists."

"I have seen her on post cards," said the gentleman from San Francisco in a voice devoid of all expression. "About this Giuseppe, now,—is he her husband?"

"Her cousin, sir," answered the *maitre d'hôtel*.

And, after a little wait, after considering something, the gentleman from San Francisco dismissed him with a nod.

And then he began his preparations anew, as though for a wedding ceremony: he turned on all the electric lights, filling all the mirrors with reflections of light and glitter, of furniture and opened trunks; he began shaving and [298] washing, ringing the bell every minute, while other impatient rings from his wife's and daughter's rooms floated through the entire corridor and interrupted his. And Luigi, in his red apron, was rushing headlong to answer the bell, with an ease peculiar to many stout men, the while he made grimaces of horror that made the chambermaids, running by with glazed porcelain pails in their hands, laugh till they cried. Having knocked on the door with his knuckles, he asked with an assumed timidity, with a respectfulness that verged on idiocy:

"*Ha sonato, signore?* (Did you ring, sir?)"

And from the other side of the door came an unhurried, grating voice, insultingly polite:

"Yes, come in. ..." *

What were the thoughts, what were the emotions of the gentleman from San Francisco on this evening, that was of such portent to him? He felt nothing exceptional,—for the trouble in this world is just that everything is apparently all too simple! And even if he had sensed within his soul that something was impending, he would, never the less, have thought that this thing would not occur for some time to come,—in any case, not immediately. Besides that, like everyone who has gone through the rocking of a ship, he wanted very much to eat, was anticipating with enjoyment the first spoonful of soup, the first mouthful of wine, and performed the usual routine of dressing even with a certain degree of exhilaration that left no time for reflections.

Having shaved and washed himself, having inserted several artificial teeth properly, he, standing before a mirror, wetted the remnants of his thick, pearly-gray [299] hair and plastered it down around his swarthy-yellow skull, with brushes set in silver; drew a suit of cream-coloured silk underwear over his strong old body, beginning to be full at the waist from excesses in food, and put on silk socks and dancing slippers on his shrivelled, splayed feet; sitting down, he put in order his black trousers, drawn high by black silk braces, as well as his snowy-white shirt, with the bosom bulging out; put the links through the glossy cuffs, and began the torturous pursuit of the collar-button underneath the stiffly starched collar. The floor was still swaying beneath him, the tips of his fingers pained him greatly, the collar-button at times nipped hard the flabby skin in the hollow under his Adam's-apple, but he was persistent and finally, his eyes glittering from the exertion, his face all livid from the collar that was choking his throat,—a collar far too tight,—he did contrive to accomplish his task, and sat down in exhaustion in front of the pier glass, reflected in it from head to foot, a reflection that was repeated in all the other mirrors.

"Oh, this is dreadful!" he muttered, letting his strong bald head drop, and without trying to understand, without reflecting, just what, precisely, was dreadful; then, with an accustomed and attentive glance, he inspected his stubby fingers, with gouty hardenings at the joints, and his convex nails of an almond colour, repeating, with conviction: "This is dreadful. ..."

But at this point the second gong, sonorously, as in some heathen temple, reverberated through the entire house. And, getting up quickly from his seat, the gentleman from San Francisco drew his collar still tighter with the necktie and his stomach by means of the low-cut vest, put on his [300] tuxedo, drew out his cuffs, scrutinized himself once more in the mirror. ... This Carmella, swarthy, with eyes which she knew well how to use most effectively, resembling a mulatto woman, clad in a dress of many colours, with the colour of orange predominant, must dance exceptionally, he reflected. And, stepping briskly out of his room and walking over the carpet to the next one,—his wife's—he asked, loudly, if they would be ready soon?

"In five minutes, Dad!" a girl's voice, ringing and by now gay, responded from the other side of the door.

"Very well," said the gentleman from San Francisco.

And, leisurely, he walked down red-carpeted corridors and stair-cases, descending in search of the reading room. The servants he met stood aside and hugged the wall to let him pass, but he kept on his way as though he had never even noticed them. An old woman who was late for dinner, already stooping, with milky hair but décolleté in a light-gray gown of silk, was hurrying with all her might, but drolly, in a hen-like manner, and he easily outstripped her. Near the glass doors of the dining room, where all the guests had already assembled, and were beginning their dinner, he stopped before a little table piled with boxes of cigars and Egyptian cigarettes, took a large Manila cigar, and tossed three *lire* upon the little table; upon the closed veranda he glanced, in passing, through the open window: out of the darkness he felt a breath of the balmy air upon him, thought he saw the tip of an ancient palm, that had flung wide across the stars its fronds, which seemed gigantic, heard the distant, even noise of the sea floating in to him. ... In the reading room,—snug, quiet, and illuminated only above the tables,[301] some gray-haired German was standing, rustling the newspapers,—unkempt, resembling Ibsen, in round silver spectacles and with the astonished eyes of a madman. Having scrutinized him coldly, the gentleman from San Francisco sat down in a deep leather chair in a corner near a green-shaded lamp, put on his *pince nez*, twitching his head because his collar was choking him, and hid himself completely behind the newspaper sheet. He rapidly ran through the headlines of certain items, read a few lines about the never-ceasing Balkan war, with an accustomed gesture turned the newspaper over,—when suddenly the lines flared up before him with a glassy glare, his neck became taut, his eyes bulged out, the *pince nez* flew off his nose. ... He lunged forward, tried to swallow some air,—and gasped wildly; his lower jaw sank, lighting up his entire mouth with the reflection of the gold fillings; his head dropped back on his shoulder and began to sway; the bosom of his shirt bulged out like a basket,—and his whole body, squirming, his heels catching the carpet, slid downward to the floor, desperately struggling with someone.

Had the German not been in the reading room, the personnel of the hotel would have managed, quickly and adroitly, to hush up this dreadful occurrence; instantly, through back passages, seizing him by the head and feet, they would have rushed off the gentleman from San Francisco as far away as possible,—and never a soul among the guests would have found out what he had been up to. But the German had dashed out of the reading room with a scream,—he had aroused the entire house, the entire dining room. And many jumped up from their meal, overturning their chairs; many, paling, ran toward [302] the reading room. "What—what has happened?" was heard in all languages,—and no one gave a sensible answer, no one comprehended anything, since even up to now men are amazed most of all by death, and will not, under any circumstances, believe in it. The proprietor dashed from one guest to another, trying to detain those who were running away and to pacify them with hasty assurances that this was just a trifling occurrence, a slight fainting spell of a certain gentleman from San Francisco. ... But no one listened to him; many had seen the waiters and bell-boys tearing off the necktie, the vest, and the rumpled tuxedo off this gentleman, and even, for some reason or other, the dancing slippers off his splayed feet, clad in black silk. But he was still struggling. He was still obdurately wrestling with death; he absolutely refused to yield to her, who had so unexpectedly and churlishly fallen upon him. His head was swaying, he rattled hoarsely, like one with his throat cut; his eyes had rolled up, like a drunkard's. ... When he was hurriedly carried in and laid upon a bed in room number forty-three,—the smallest, the poorest, the dampest and the coldest, situated at the end of the bottom corridor,—his daughter ran in, with her hair down, in a little dressing gown that had flown open, her bosom, raised up by the corset, uncovered; then his wife, big and ponderous, already dressed for dinner,—her mouth rounded in terror. ... But by now he had ceased even to bob his head.

A quarter of an hour later everything in the hotel had assumed some semblance of order. But the evening was irreparably spoiled. Some guests, returning to the dining room, finished their dinner, but in silence, with aggrieved [303] countenances, while the proprietor would approach now one group, now another, shrugging his shoulders in polite yet impotent irritation, feeling himself guilty without guilt, assuring everybody that he understood very well "how unpleasant all this was," and pledging his word that he would take "all measures within his power" to remove this unpleasantness. It was necessary to call off the *tarantella*, all unnecessary electric lights were switched off, the majority of the guests withdrew into the bar, and it became so quiet that one heard distinctly the ticking of the clock in the vestibule, whose sole occupant was a parrot, dully muttering something, fussing in his cage before going to sleep, contriving to doze off at last with one claw ludicrously stretched up to the upper perch. ... The gentleman from San Francisco was lying upon a cheap iron bed, under coarse woolen blankets, upon which the dull light of a single bulb beat down from the ceiling. An ice-bag hung down to his moist and cold forehead. The livid face, already dead, was gradually growing cold; the hoarse rattling, expelled from the open mouth, illuminated by the reflection of gold, was growing fainter. This was no longer the gentleman from San Francisco rattling,—he no longer existed,—but some other. His wife, his daughter, the doctor and the servants were standing, gazing at him dully. Suddenly, that which they awaited and feared was consummated,—the rattling ceased abruptly. And slowly, slowly, before the eyes of all, a pallor flowed over the face of the man who had died, and his features seemed to grow finer, to become irradiated, with a beauty which had been rightfully his in the long ago. ...

The proprietor entered. "*Già è morto*," said the doctor [304] to him in a whisper. The proprietor, his face dispassionate, shrugged his shoulders. The wife, down whose cheeks the tears were quietly coursing, walked up to him and timidly said that the deceased ought now to be carried to his own room.

"Oh, no, madam," hastily, correctly, but now without any amiability and not in English, but in French, retorted the proprietor, who was not at all interested now in such trifling sums as the arrivals from San Francisco might leave in his coffers. "That is absolutely impossible, madam," said he, and added in explanation that he valued the apartments occupied by them very much; that, were he to carry out her wishes, everybody in Capri would know it and the tourists would shun those apartments.

The young lady, who had been gazing at him strangely, sat down on a chair, and, stuffing her mouth with a handkerchief, burst into sobs. The wife dried her tears immediately, her face flaring up. She adopted a louder tone, making demands in her own language, and still incredulous of the fact that all respect for them had been completely lost. The proprietor, with a polite dignity, cut her short: if madam was not pleased with the customs of the hotel, he would not venture to detain her; and he firmly announced that the body must be gotten away this very day, at dawn, that the police had already been notified, and one of the police officers would be here very soon and would carry out all the necessary formalities. Was it possible to secure even a common coffin in Capri, madam asks? Regrettably, no,—it was beyond possibility, and no one would be able to make one in time. It would be necessary to have recourse to something else. ... For instance, —English soda water came in large and long [305] boxes. ... It was possible to knock the partitions out of such a box. ...

At night the whole hotel slept. The window in room number forty-three was opened,—it gave out upon a corner of the garden where, near a high stone wall with broken glass upon its crest, a phthisic banana tree was growing; the electric light was switched off; the key was turned in the door, and everybody went away. The dead man remained in the darkness,—the blue stars looked down upon him from the sky, a cricket with a pensive insouciance began his song in the wall. ... In the dimly lit corridor two chambermaids were seated on a window sill, at some darning. Luigi, in slippers, entered with a pile of clothing in his arms.

"Pronto? (All ready?)" he asked solicitously, in a ringing whisper, indicating with his eyes the fearsome door at the end of the corridor. And, he waved his hand airily in that direction. ... "Partenza!" he called out in a whisper, as though he were speeding a train, the usual phrase used in Italian depots at the departure of trains,—and the chambermaids, choking with silent laughter, let their heads sink on each other's shoulder.

Thereupon, hopping softly, he ran up to the very door, gave it the merest tap, and, inclining his head to one side, in a low voice, asked with the utmost deference:

"Ha sonato signore?"

And, squeezing his throat, thrusting out his lower jaw, in a grating voice, slowly and sadly, he answered his own question, as though from the other side of the door:

"Yes, come in. ..." *

And at dawn, when it had become light beyond the [306] window of room number forty-three, and a humid wind had begun to rustle the tattered leaves of the banana tree; when the blue sky of morning had lifted and spread out over the Island of Capri, and the pure and clear-cut summit of Monte Solaro had grown aureate against the sun that was rising beyond the distant blue mountains of Italy; when the stone masons, who were repairing the tourists' paths on the island, had set out to work,—a long box that had formerly been used for soda water was brought to room number forty-three. Soon it became very heavy, and was pressing hard against the knees of the junior porter, who bore it off briskly on a one horse cab over the white paved highway that was sinuously winding to and fro over the slopes of Capri, among the stone walls and the vineyards, ever downwards, to the very sea. The cabby, a puny little man with reddened eyes, in an old, wretched jacket with short sleeves and in trodden-down shoes, was undergoing the after effects of drink,—he had diced the whole night through in a *trattoria,* and kept on lashing his sturdy little horse, tricked out in the Sicilian fashion, with all sorts of little bells livelily jingling upon the bridle with its tufts of coloured wool, and upon the brass points of its high pad; with a yard-long feather stuck in its cropped forelock,—a feather that shook as the horse ran. The cabby kept silent; he was oppressed by his shiftlessness, his vices,—by the fact that he had, that night, lost to the last mite all those coppers with which his pockets had been filled. But the morning was fresh; in air such as this, with the sea all around, under the morning sky, the after effects of drink quickly evaporate, and a man is soon restored to a carefree [307] mood, and the cabby was furthermore consoled by that unexpected sum, the opportunity to earn which had been granted him by some gentleman from San Francisco, whose lifeless head was bobbing from side to side in the box at his back. ... The little steamer,—a beetle lying far down below, against the tender and vivid deep-blue with which the Bay of Naples is so densely and highly flooded,—was already blowing its final whistles, that reverberated loudly all over the island, whose every bend, every ridge, every stone, was as distinctly visible from every point as if there were absolutely no such thing as atmosphere. Near the wharf the junior porter was joined by the senior, who was speeding with the daughter and wife of the gentleman from San Francisco in his automobile,—they were pale, with eyes hollow from tears and a sleepless night. And ten minutes later the little steamer was again chugging through the water, again running toward Sorrento, toward Castellamare, carrying away from Capri, for all time, the family from San Francisco. ... And again peace and quiet resumed their reign upon the island.

Upon this island, two thousand years ago, had lived a man who had become completely enmeshed in his cruel and foul deeds, who had for some reason seized the power over millions of people in his hands, and who, having himself lost his head at the senselessness of this power and from the fear of death by assassination, lurking in ambush behind every corner, had committed cruelties beyond all measure,—and humankind has remembered him for all time; and those who, in their collusion, just as incomprehensively and, in substance, just as cruelly as he, reign [308] at present in power over this world, gather from all over the earth to gaze upon the ruins of that stone villa where he had dwelt on one of the steepest ascents of the island. On this splendid morning all those who had come to Capri for just this purpose were still sleeping in the hotels, although, toward their entrances, were already being led little mouse-gray burros with red saddles, upon which, after awaking and sating themselves with food, Americans and Germans, men and women, young and old, would again clamber up ponderously this day, and after whom would again run the old Caprian beggar women, with sticks in their gnarled hands,— would run over stony paths, and always up-hill, up to the very summit of Mount Tiberio. Set at rest by the fact that the dead old man from San Francisco, who had likewise been planning to go with them but instead of that had only frightened them with a *memento mori,* had already been shipped off to Naples, the travellers slept on heavily, and the quiet of the island was still undisturbed, the shops in the city were still shut. The market place on the *piazetta* alone was carrying on traffic,—in fish and greens; and the people there were all simple folk, among whom, without anything to do, as always, was standing Lorenzo the boatman, famous all over Italy,—a tall old man, a care-free rake and a handsome fellow, who had served more than once as a model to many artists; he had brought, and had already sold for a song, two lobsters that he had caught that night and which were already rustling in the apron of the cook of that very hotel where the family from San Francisco had passed the night, and now he could afford to stand in calm idleness even until the evening, looking about [309] him with a kingly bearing (a little trick of his), consciously picturesque with his tatters, clay pipe, and a red woolen *beretta* drooping over one ear.

And, along the precipices of Monte Solaro, upon the ancient Phœnician road, hewn out of the crags, down its stone steps, two mountaineers of Abruzzi were descending from Anacapri. One had bag-pipes under his leathern mantle,—a large bag made from the skin of a she-goat, with two pipes; the other had something in the nature of wooden Pan's-reeds. They went on,—and all the land, joyous, splendid, sunflooded, spread out below them: the stony humps of the island, which was lying almost in its entirety at their feet; and that faery-like deep-blue in which it was aswim; and the radiant morning vapours over the sea, toward the east, under the blinding sun, that was now beating down hotly, rising ever higher and higher; and, still in their morning vagueness, the mistily azure massive outlines of Italy, of her mountains near and far, whose beauty human speech is impotent to express. ... Half way down the pipers slackened their pace: over the path, within a grotto in the craggy side of Monte Solaro, all illumed by the sun, all bathed in its warmth and glow, in snowy-white raiment of gypsum, and in a royal crown, golden-rusty from inclement weathers, stood the Mother of God, meek and gracious, her orbs lifted up to heaven, to the eternal and happy abodes of Her thrice-blessed Son. The pipers bared their heads, put their reeds to their lips,—and there poured forth their naïve and humbly-jubilant praises to the sun, to the morning, to Her, the Immaculate Intercessor for all those who suffer in this evil and beautiful world, and to Him Who had been born of Her womb in a cavern at Bethlehem,[310] in a poor shepherd's shelter in the distant land of Judæa. ...

Meanwhile, the body of the dead old man from San Francisco was returning to its home, to a grave on the shores of the New World. Having gone through many humiliations, through much human neglect, having wandered for a week from one port warehouse to another, it had finally gotten once more on board that same famous ship upon which but so recently, with so much deference, he had been borne to the Old World. But now he was already being concealed from the quick,—he was lowered in his tarred coffin deep into the black hold. And once more the ship was sailing on and on upon its long sea voyage. In the night time it sailed past the Island of Capri, and, to one watching them from the island, there was something sad about the ship's lights, slowly disappearing over the dark sea. But, upon the ship itself, in its brilliant *salons* resplendent with lustres and marbles, there was a crowded ball that night, as usual.

There was a ball on the second night also, and on the third,— again in the midst of a raging snow storm, whirling over an ocean booming like a funeral mass, and heaving in mountains trapped out in mourning by the silver spindrift. The innumerable fiery eyes of the ship that was retreating into the night and the snow gale were barely visible for the snow to the Devil watching from the crags of Gibraltar, from the stony gateway of two worlds. The Devil was as enormous as a cliff, but the ship was still more enormous than he; many-tiered, many-funnelled, created by the pride of the New Man with an ancient heart. The snow gale smote upon its rigging and wide-throated funnels, hoary from the snow, but the [311] ship was steadfast, firm, majestic—and awesome. Upon its topmost deck were reared, in their solitude among the snowy whirlwinds, those snug, dimly-lit chambers where, plunged in a light and uneasy slumber, was its ponderous guide who resembled a heathen idol, reigning over the entire ship. He heard the pained howlings and the ferocious squealings of the storm-stifled siren, but soothed himself by the proximity of that which, in the final summing up, was incomprehensible even to himself, that which was on the other side of his wall: that large cabin, which had the appearance of being armoured, and was being constantly filled by the mysterious rumbling, quivering, and crisp sputtering of blue flames, flaring up and exploding around the pale-faced operator with a metal half-hoop upon his head. In the very depths, in the under-water womb of the *Atlantida,* were the thirty-thousand-pound masses of boilers and of all sorts of other machinery—dully glittering with steel, hissing out steam and exuding oil and boiling water,—of that kitchen, made red hot from infernal furnaces underneath, wherein was brewing the motion of the ship. Forces, fearful in their concentration, were bubbling, were being transmitted to its very keel, into an endlessly long catacomb, into a tunnel, illuminated by electricity, wherein slowly, with an inexorability that was crushing to the human soul, was revolving within its oily couch the gigantean shaft, exactly like a living monster that had stretched itself out in this tunnel. Meanwhile, amidship the *Atlantida,* its warm and luxurious cabins, its dining halls and ball rooms, poured forth radiance and joyousness, were humming with the voices of a well-dressed gathering, were sweetly odorous with fresh flowers, and the strains of the stringed orchestra [312] were their song. And again excruciatingly writhed and at intervals came together among this throng, among this glitter of lights, silks, diamonds and bared feminine shoulders, the supple pair of hired lovers: the sinfully-modest, very pretty young woman, with eye-lashes cast down, with a chaste coiffure, and the well-built young man, with black hair that seemed to be pasted on, with his face pale from powder, shod in the most elegant of patent-leather foot-gear, clad in a tight-fitting dress coat with long tails,—an Adonis who resembled a huge leech. And none knew that, already for a long time, this pair had grown wearied of languishing dissembling in their blissful torment to the sounds of the shamelessly-sad music,—nor that far, far below, at the bottom of the black hold, stood a tarred coffin, in close proximity to the sombre and sultry depths of the ship that was toilsomely overpowering the darkness, the ocean, the snow storm. ...[313]

ALDOUS HUXLEY

FROM *Brave New World* by Aldous Huxley. New York: Harper & Brothers, 1950. Copyright 1932 by Aldous Huxley. Reprinted by permission of Harper & Brothers and Chatto and Windus Ltd.

A squat grey building of only thirty-four stories. Over the main entrance the words, CENTRAL LONDON HATCHERY AND CONDITIONING CENTRE, and, in a shield, the World State's motto, COMMUNITY, IDENTITY, STABILITY.

The enormous room on the ground floor faced towards the north. Cold for all the summer beyond the panes, for all the tropical heat of the room itself, a harsh thin light glared through the windows, hungrily seeking some draped lay figure, some pallid shape of academic goose-flesh, but finding only the glass and nickel and bleakly shining porcelain of a laboratory. Wintriness responded to wintriness. The overalls of the workers were white, their hands gloved with a pale corpse-coloured rubber. The light was frozen, dead, a ghost. Only from the yellow barrels of the microscopes did it borrow a certain [1] rich and living substance, lying along the polished tubes like butter, streak after luscious streak in long recession down the work tables.

"And this," said the Director opening the door, "is the Fertilizing Room."

Bent over their instruments, three hundred Fertilizers were plunged, as the Director of Hatcheries and Conditioning entered the room, in the scarcely breathing silence, the absent-minded, soliloquizing hum or whistle, of absorbed concentration. A troop of newly arrived students, very young, pink and callow, followed nervously, rather abjectly, at the Director's heels. Each of them carried a notebook, in which, whenever the great man spoke, he desperately scribbled. Straight from the horse's mouth. It was a rare privilege. The D.H.C. for Central London always made a point of personally conducting his new students round the various departments.

"Just to give you a general idea," he would explain to them. For of course some sort of general idea they must have, if they were to do their work intelligently—though as little of one, if they were to be good and happy members of society, as possible. For particulars, as every one knows, make for virtue and happiness; generalities are intellectually necessary evils. Not philosophers but fret-sawyers and stamp collectors compose the backbone of society.

"To-morrow," he would add, smiling at them with a slightly menacing geniality, "you'll be settling [2] down to serious work. You won't have time for generalities. Meanwhile ..."

Meanwhile, it was a privilege. Straight from the horse's mouth into the notebook. The boys scribbled like mad.

Tall and rather thin but upright, the Director advanced into the room. He had a long chin and big rather prominent teeth, just covered, when he was not talking, by his full, floridly curved lips. Old, young? Thirty? Fifty? Fifty-five? It was hard to say. And anyhow the question didn't arise; in this year of stability, A. F. 632, it didn't occur to you to ask it.

"I shall begin at the beginning," said the D.H.C. and the more zealous students recorded his intention in their notebooks: *Begin at the beginning*. "These," he waved his hand, "are the incubators." And opening an insulated door he showed them racks upon racks of numbered test-tubes. "The week's supply of ova. Kept," he explained, "at blood heat; whereas the male gametes," and here he opened another door, "they have to be kept at thirty-five instead of thirty-seven. Full blood heat sterilizes." Rams wrapped in theremogene beget no lambs.

Still leaning against the incubators he gave them, while the pencils scurried illegibly across the pages, a brief description of the modern fertilizing process; spoke first, of course, of its surgical introduction— "the operation undergone voluntarily for the good of Society, not to mention the fact that it carries a [3] bonus amounting to six months' salary"; continued with some account of the technique for preserving the excised ovary alive and actively developing; passed on to a consideration of optimum temperature, salinity, viscosity; referred to the liquor in which the detached and ripened eggs were kept; and, leading his charges to the work tables, actually showed them how this liquor was drawn off from the test-tubes; how it was let out drop by drop onto the specially warmed slides of the microscopes; how the eggs which it contained were inspected for abnormalities, counted and transferred to a porous receptacle; how (and he now took them to watch the operation) this receptacle was immersed in a warm bouillon containing free-swimming spermatozoa—at a minimum concentration of one hundred thousand per cubic centimetre, he insisted; and how, after ten minutes, the container was lifted out of the liquor and its contents re-examined; how, if any of the eggs remained unfertilized, it was again immersed, and, if necessary, yet again; how the fertilized ova went back to the incubators; where the Alphas and Betas remained until definitely bottled; while the Gammas, Deltas and Epsilons were brought out again, after only thirty-six hours, to undergo Bokanovsky's Process.

"Bokanovsky's Process," repeated the Director, and the students underlined the words in their little notebooks.[4]

One egg, one embryo, one adult—normality. But a bokanovskified egg will bud, will proliferate, will divide. From eight to ninety-six buds, and every bud will grow into a perfectly formed embryo, and every embryo into a full-sized adult. Making ninety-six human beings grow where only one grew before. Progress.

"Essentially," the D.H.C. concluded, "bokanovskification consists of a series of arrests of development. We check the normal growth and, paradoxically enough, the egg responds by budding."

Responds by budding. The pencils were busy.

He pointed. On a very slowly moving band a rack-full of test-tubes was entering a large metal box, another rack-full was emerging. Machinery faintly purred. It took eight minutes for the tubes to go through, he told them. Eight minutes of hard X-rays being about as much as an egg can stand. A few died; of the rest, the least susceptible divided into two; most put out four buds; some eight; all were returned to the incubators, where the buds began to develop; then, after two days, were suddenly chilled, chilled and checked. Two, four, eight, the buds in their turn budded; and having budded were dosed almost to death with alcohol; consequently burgeoned again and having budded—bud out of bud out of bud—were thereafter—further arrest being generally fatal—left to develop in peace. By which time the original egg was in a fair way to [5] becoming anything from eight to ninety-six embryos—a prodigious improvement, you will agree, on nature. Identical twins—but not in piddling twos and threes as in the old viviparous days, when an egg would sometimes accidentally divide; actually by dozens, by scores at a time.

"Scores," the Director repeated and flung out his arms, as though he were distributing largesse. "Scores."

But one of the students was fool enough to ask where the advantage lay.

"My good boy!" The Director wheeled sharply round on him. "Can't you see? Can't you *see?*" He raised a hand; his expression was solemn. "Bokanovsky's Process is one of the major instruments of social stability!"

Major instruments of social stability.

Standard men and women; in uniform batches. The whole of a small factory staffed with the products of a single bokanovskified egg.

"Ninety-six identical twins working ninety-six identical machines!" The voice was almost tremulous with enthusiasm. "You really know where you are. For the first time in history." He quoted the planetary motto. "Community, Identity, Stability." Grand words. "If we could bokanovskify indefinitely the whole problem would be solved."

Solved by standard Gammas, unvarying Deltas, uniform Epsilons. Millions of identical twins. The [6] principle of mass production at last applied to biology.

"But, alas," the Director shook his head, "we *can't* bokanovskify indefinitely."

Ninety-six seemed to be the limit; seventy-two a good average. From the same ovary and with gametes of the same male to manufacture as many batches of identical twins as possible—that was the best (sadly a second best) that they could do. And even that was difficult.

"For in nature it takes thirty years for two hundred eggs to reach maturity. But our business is to stabilize the population at this moment, here and now. Dribbling out twins over a quarter of a century— what would be the use of that?"

Obviously, no use at all. But Podsnap's Technique had immensely accelerated the process of ripening. They could make sure of at least a hundred and fifty mature eggs within two years. Fertilize and bokanovskify—in other words, multiply by seventy-two—and you get an average of nearly eleven thousand brothers and sisters in a hundred and fifty batches of identical twins, all within two years of the same age.

"And in exceptional cases we can make one ovary yield us over fifteen thousand adult individuals."

Beckoning to a fair-haired, ruddy young man who happened to be passing at the moment. "Mr. Foster," he called. The ruddy young man [7] approached. "Can you tell us the record for a single ovary, Mr. Foster?"

"Sixteen thousand and twelve in this Centre," Mr. Foster replied without hesitation. He spoke very quickly, had a vivacious blue eye, and took an evident pleasure in quoting figures. "Sixteen thousand and twelve; in one hundred and eighty-nine batches of identicals. But of course they've done much better," he rattled on, "in some of the tropical Centres. Singapore has often produced over sixteen thousand five hundred; and Mombasa has actually touched the seventeen thousand mark. But then they have unfair advantages. You should see the way a negro ovary responds to pituitary! It's quite astonishing, when you're used to working with European material. Still," he added, with a laugh (but the light of combat was in his eyes and the lift of his chin was challenging), "still, we mean to beat them if we can. I'm working on a wonderful Delta-Minus ovary at this moment. Only just eighteen months old. Over twelve thousand seven hundred children already, either decanted or in embryo. And still going strong. We'll beat them yet."

"That's the spirit I like!" cried the Director, and clapped Mr. Foster on the shoulder. "Come along with us, and give these boys the benefit of your expert knowledge."

Mr. Foster smiled modestly. "With pleasure." They went.[8]

In the Bottling Room all was harmonious bustle and ordered activity. Flaps of fresh sow's peritoneum ready cut to the proper size came shooting up in little lifts from the Organ Store in the sub-basement. Whizz and then, click! the lift-hatches flew open; the bottle-liner had only to reach out a hand, take the flap, insert, smooth-down, and before the lined bottle had had time to travel out of reach along the endless band, whizz, click! another flap of peritoneum had shot up from the depths, ready to be slipped into yet another bottle, the next of that slow interminable procession on the band.

Next to the Liners stood the Matriculators. The procession advanced; one by one the eggs were transferred from their test-tubes to the larger containers; deftly the peritoneal lining was slit, the morula dropped into place, the saline solution poured in ... and already the bottle had passed, and it was the turn of the labellers. Heredity, date of fertilization, membership of Bokanovsky Group—details were transferred from test-tube to bottle. No longer anonymous, but named, identified, the procession marched slowly on; on through an opening in the wall, slowly on into the Social Predestination Room.

"Eighty-eight cubic metres of card-index," said Mr. Foster with relish, as they entered.

"Containing all the relevant information," added the Director.[9]

"Brought up to date every morning."

"And co-ordinated every afternoon."

"On the basis of which they make their calculations."

"So many individuals, of such and such quality," said Mr. Foster.

"Distributed in such and such quantities."

"The optimum Decanting Rate at any given moment."

"Unforeseen wastages promptly made good."

"Promptly," repeated Mr. Foster. "If you knew the amount of overtime I had to put in after the last Japanese earthquake!" He laughed goodhumouredly and shook his head.

"The Predestinators send in their figures to the Fertilizers."

"Who give them the embryos they ask for."

"And the bottles come in here to be predestined in detail."

"After which they are sent down to the Embryo Store."

"Where we now proceed ourselves."

And opening a door Mr. Foster led the way down a staircase into the basement.

The temperature was still tropical. They descended into a thickening twilight. Two doors and a passage with a double turn insured the cellar against any possible infiltration of the day.

"Embryos are like photograph film," said Mr. [10] Foster waggishly, as he pushed open the second door. "They can only stand red light."

And in effect the sultry darkness into which the students now followed him was visible and crimson, like the darkness of closed eyes on a summer's afternoon. The bulging flanks of row on receding row and tier above tier of bottles glinted with innumerable rubies, and among the rubies moved the dim red spectres of men and women with purple eyes and all the symptoms of lupus. The hum and rattle of machinery faintly stirred the air.

"Give them a few figures, Mr. Foster," said the Director, who was tired of talking.

Mr. Foster was only too happy to give them a few figures.

Two hundred and twenty metres long, two hundred wide, ten high. He pointed upwards. Like chickens drinking, the students lifted their eyes towards the distant ceiling.

Three tiers of racks: ground floor level, first gallery, second gallery.

The spidery steel-work of gallery above gallery faded away in all directions into the dark. Near them three red ghosts were busily unloading demijohns from a moving staircase.

The escalator from the Social Predestination Room.

Each bottle could be placed on one of fifteen racks, each rack, though you couldn't see it, was [11] a conveyor traveling at the rate of thirty-three and a third centimetres an hour. Two hundred and sixty-seven days at eight metres a day. Two thousand one hundred and thirty-six metres in all. One circuit of the cellar at ground level, one on the first gallery, half on the second, and on the two hundred and sixty-seventh morning, daylight in the Decanting Room. Independent existence—so called.

"But in the interval," Mr. Foster concluded, "we've managed to do a lot to them. Oh, a very great deal." His laugh was knowing and triumphant.

"That's the spirit I like," said the Director once more. "Let's walk around. You tell them everything, Mr. Foster."

Mr. Foster duly told them.

Told them of the growing embryo on its bed of peritoneum. Made them taste the rich blood-surrogate on which it fed. Explained why it had to be stimulated with placentin and thyroxin. Told them of the *corpus luteum* extract. Showed them the jets through which at every twelfth metre from zero to 2040 it was automatically injected. Spoke of those gradually increasing doses of pituitary administered during the final ninety-six metres of their course. Described the artificial maternal circulation installed in every bottle at Metre 112; showed them the reservoir of blood-surrogate, the centrifugal pump that kept the liquid moving over the placenta and drove it through the synthetic lung and waste [12] product filter. Referred to the embryo's troublesome tendency to anæmia, to the massive doses of hog's stomach extract and foetal foal's liver with which, in consequence, it had to be supplied.

Showed them the simple mechanism by means of which, during the last two metres out of every eight, all the embryos were simultaneously shaken into familiarity with movement. Hinted at the gravity of the so-called "trauma of decanting," and enumerated the precautions taken to minimize, by a suitable training of the bottled embryo, that dangerous shock. Told them of the test for sex carried out in the neighborhood of Metre 200. Explained the system of labelling—a T for the males, a circle for the females and for those who were destined to become freemartins a question mark, black on a white ground.

"For of course," said Mr. Foster, "in the vast majority of cases, fertility is merely a nuisance. One fertile ovary in twelve hundred—that would really be quite sufficient for our purposes. But we want to have a good choice. And of course one must always have an enormous margin of safety. So we allow as many as thirty per cent of the female embryos to develop normally. The others get a dose of male sex-hormone every twenty-four metres for the rest of the course. Result: they're decanted as freemartins—structurally quite normal (except," he had to admit, "that they *do* have the slightest [13] tendency to grow beards), but sterile. Guaranteed sterile. Which brings us at last," continued Mr. Foster, "out of the realm of mere slavish imitation of nature into the much more interesting world of human invention."

He rubbed his hands. For of course, they didn't content themselves with merely hatching out embryos: any cow could do that.

"We also predestine and condition. We decant our babies as socialized human beings, as Alphas or Epsilons, as future sewage workers or future ..." He was going to say "future World controllers," but correcting himself, said "future Directors of Hatcheries," instead.

The D.H.C. acknowledged the compliment with a smile.

They were passing Metre 320 on Rack 11. A young Beta-Minus mechanic was busy with screw-driver and spanner on the blood-surrogate pump of a passing bottle. The hum of the electric motor deepened by fractions of a tone as he turned down the nuts. Down, down ... A final twist, a glance at the revolution counter, and he was done. He moved two paces down the line and began the same process on the next pump.

"Reducing the number of revolutions per minute," Mr. Foster explained. "The surrogate goes round slower; therefore passes through the lung at longer intervals; therefore gives the embryo less [14] oxygen. Nothing like oxygen-shortage for keeping an embryo below par." Again he rubbed his hands.

"But why do you want to keep the embryo below par?" asked an ingenuous student.

"Ass!" said the Director, breaking a long silence. "Hasn't it occurred to you that an Epsilon embryo must have an Epsilon environment as well as an Epsilon heredity?"

It evidently hadn't occurred to him. He was covered with confusion.

"The lower the caste," said Mr. Foster, "the shorter the oxygen." The first organ affected was the brain. After that the skeleton. At seventy per cent of normal oxygen you get dwarfs. At less than seventy eyeless monsters.

"Who are no use at all," concluded Mr. Foster.

Whereas (his voice became confidential and eager), if they could discover a technique for shortening the period of maturation what a triumph, what a benefaction to Society!

"Consider the horse."

They considered it.

Mature at six; the elephant at ten. While at thirteen a man is not yet sexually mature; and is only full-grown at twenty. Hence, of course, that fruit of delayed development, the human intelligence.

"But in Epsilons," said Mr. Foster very justly, "we don't need human intelligence."

Didn't need and didn't get it. But though the [15] Epsilon mind was mature at ten, the Epsilon body was not fit to work till eighteen. Long years of superfluous and wasted immaturity. If the physical development could be speeded up till it was as quick, say, as a cow's, what an enormous saving to the Community!

"Enormous!" murmured the students. Mr. Foster's enthusiasm was infectious.

He became rather technical; spoke of the abnormal endocrine coordination which made men grow so slowly; postulated a germinal mutation to account for it. Could the effects of this germinal mutation be undone? Could the individual Epsilon embryo be made a revert, by a suitable technique, to the normality of dogs and cows? That was the problem. And it was all but solved.

Pilkington, at Mombasa, had produced individuals who were sexually mature at four and full-grown at six and a half. A scientific triumph. But socially useless. Six-year-old men and women were too stupid to do even Epsilon work. And the process was an all-or-nothing one; either you failed to modify at all, or else you modified the whole way. They were still trying to find the ideal compromise between adults of twenty and adults of six. So far without success. Mr. Foster sighed and shook his head.

Their wanderings through the crimson twilight had brought them to the neighborhood of Metre [16] 170 on Rack 9. From this point onwards Rack 9 was enclosed and the bottles performed the remainder of their journey in a kind of tunnel, interrupted here and there by openings two or three metres wide.

"Heat conditioning," said Mr. Foster.

Hot tunnels alternated with cool tunnels. Coolness was wedded to discomfort in the form of hard X-rays. By the time they were decanted the embryos had a horror of cold. They were predestined to emigrate to the tropics, to be miners and acetate silk spinners and steel workers. Later on their minds would be made to endorse the judgment of their bodies. "We condition them to thrive on heat," concluded Mr. Foster. "Our colleagues upstairs will teach them to love it."

"And that," put in the Director sententiously, "that is the secret of happiness and virtue—liking what you've *got* to do. All conditioning aims at that: making people like their unescapable social destiny."

In a gap between two tunnels, a nurse was delicately probing with a long fine syringe into the gelatinous contents of a passing bottle. The students and their guides stood watching her for a few moments in silence.

"Well, Lenina," said Mr. Foster, when at last she withdrew the syringe and straightened herself up.

The girl turned with a start. One could see that, for all the lupus and the purple eyes, she was uncommonly pretty.[17]

"Henry!" Her smile flashed redly at him—a row of coral teeth.

"Charming, charming," murmured the Director and, giving her two or three little pats, received in exchange a rather deferential smile for himself.

"What are you giving them?" asked Mr. Foster, making his tone very professional.

"Oh, the usual typhoid and sleeping sickness."

"Tropical workers start being inoculated at Metre 150," Mr. Foster explained to the students. "The embryos still have gills. We immunize the fish against the future man's diseases." Then, turning back to Lenina, "Ten to five on the roof this afternoon," he said, "as usual."

"Charming," said the Director once more, and, with a final pat, moved away after the others.

On Rack 10 rows of next generation's chemical workers were being trained in the toleration of lead, caustic soda, tar, chlorine. The first of a batch of two hundred and fifty embryonic rocket-plane engineers was just passing the eleven hundred metre mark on Rack 3. A special mechanism kept their containers in constant rotation. "To improve their sense of balance," Mr. Foster explained. "Doing repairs on the outside of a rocket in mid-air is a ticklish job. We slacken off the circulation when they're right way up, so that they're half starved, and double the flow of surrogate when they're upside down. They learn to associate topsy-turvydom with well-being; in fact,[18] they're only truly happy when they're standing on their heads.

"And now," Mr. Foster went on, "I'd like to show you some very interesting conditioning for Alpha-Plus Intellectuals. We have a big batch of them on Rack 5. First Gallery level," he called to two boys who had started to go down to the ground floor.

'They're round about Metre 900," he explained. "You can't really do any useful intellectual conditioning till the foetuses have lost their tails. Follow me."

But the Director had looked at his watch. "Ten to three," he said. "No time for the intellectual embryos, I'm afraid. We must go up to the Nurseries before the children have finished their afternoon sleep."

Mr. Foster was disappointed. "At least one glance at the Decanting Room," he pleaded.

"Very well then." The Director smiled indulgently. "Just one glance." [19]

PHILIP WYLIE

Common Women

FROM *Generation of Vipers* by Philip Wylie. New York: Holt, Rinehart and Winston, Inc., 1942. Copyright 1942, © 1955 by Philip Wylie. Reprinted by permission of Holt, Rinehart and Winston, Inc.

Mom Is the End Product of She

She is Cinderella . . . the shining-haired, the starry-eyed, the ruby-lipped virgo æternis, of which there is presumably one, and only one, or a one-and-only for each male, whose dream is fixed upon her deflowerment and subsequent perpetual possession. This act is a sacrament in all churches and a civil affair in our society. The collective aspects of marriage are thus largely compressed into the rituals and social perquisites of one day. Unless some element of mayhem or intention of divorce subsequently obtrudes, a sort of privacy engulfs the union and all further developments are deemed to be the business of each separate pair, including the transition of Cinderella into mom, which, if it occasions any shock, only adds to the huge, invisible burthen every man carries with him into eternity. It is the weight of this bundle which, incidentally, squeezes out of him the wish for death, his last positive biological resource.

Mom is an American creation. Her elaboration was necessary because she was launched as Cinderella. Past generations of men have accorded to their mothers, as a rule, only such honors as they earned by meritorious action in their individual daily lives. Filial *duty* was recognized by many sorts of civilizations and loyalty to it has been highly regarded among most peoples. But I cannot think, offhand, of any civilization except ours in which an entire division of living men has been used, during wartime, or at any time, to spell out the word "mom" on a drill field, or to perform any equivalent act.

The adoration of motherhood has even been made the basis of [184] a religious cult, but the mother so worshipped achieved maternity without change in her virgin status—a distinction worthy of contemplation in itself—and she thus in no way resembled mom.

Hitherto, in fact, man has shown a considerable qui vive to the dangers which arise from momism and freely perceived that his "old wives" were often vixens, dragons, and Xanthippes. Classical literature makes a constant point of it. Shakespeare dwelt on it. Man has also kept before his mind an awareness that, even in the most lambent mother love, there is always a chance some extraneous current will blow up a change, and the thing will become a consuming furnace. The spectacle of the female devouring her young in the firm belief that it is for their own good is too old in man's legends to be overlooked by any but the most flimsily constructed society. . . .

Megaloid momworship has got completely out of hand. Our land, subjectively mapped, would have more silver cords and apron strings crisscrossing it than railroads and telephone wires. Mom is everywhere and everything and damned near everybody, and from her depends all the rest of the U. S. Disguised as good old mom, dear old mom, sweet old mom, your loving mom, and so on, she is the bride at every funeral and the corpse at every wedding. Men live for her and die for her, dote upon her and whisper her name as they pass away, and I believe she has now achieved, in the hierarchy of miscellaneous articles,[185] a spot next to the Bible and the Flag, being reckoned part of both in a way. . . .

Mom is something new in the world of men. Hitherto, mom has been so busy raising a large family, keeping house, doing the chores, and fabricating everything in every home except the floor and the walls that she was rarely a problem to her family or to her equally busy friends, and never one to herself. Usually, until very recently, mom folded up and died of hard work somewhere in the middle of her life. Old ladies were scarce and those who managed to get old did so by making remarkable inner adjustments and by virtue of a fabulous horniness of body, so that they lent to old age not only dignity but metal.

Nowadays, with nothing to do, and tens of thousands of men . . . to maintain her, every clattering prickamette in the republic survives for an incredible number of years, to stamp and jibber in the midst of man, a noisy neuter by natural default or a scientific gelding sustained by science, all tongue and teat and razzmatazz. The machine has deprived her of social usefulness; time has stripped away her biological possibilities and poured her hide full of liquid soap; and man has sealed his own soul beneath the clamorous cordillera by handing her the checkbook and going to work in the service of her caprices.[186] . . .

Satan, we are told, finds work for idle hands to do. There is no mistaking the accuracy of this proverb. Millions of men have heaped up riches and made a conquest of idleness so as to discover what it is that Satan puts them up to. Not one has failed to find out. But never before has a great nation of brave and dreaming men absent-mindedly created a huge class of idle, middle-aged women. Satan himself has been taxed to dig up enterprises enough for them. But the field is so rich, so profligate, so perfectly to his taste, that his first effort, obviously, has been to make it self-enlarging and self-perpetuating. This he has done by whispering into the ears of girls that the only way they can cushion the shock destined to follow the rude disillusionment over the fact that they are not really Cinderella is to institute momworship. Since he had already infested both male and female with the love of worldly goods, a single step accomplished the entire triumph: he taught the gals to teach their men that dowry went the other way, that it was a weekly contribution, and that any male worthy of a Cinderella would have to work like a piston after getting one, so as to be worthy, also, of all the moms in the world.[187] . . .

Mom got herself out of the nursery and the kitchen. She then got out of the house. She did not get out of the church, but, instead, got the stern stuff out of it, padded the guild room, and moved in more solidly than ever before. No longer either hesitant or reverent, because there was no cause for either attitude after her purge, she swung the church by the tail as she swung everything else. In a preliminary test of strength, she also got herself the vote and, although politics never interested her (unless she was exceptionally naïve, a hairy foghorn, or a size forty scorpion), the damage she forthwith did to society was so enormous and so rapid that even the best men lost track of things. Mom's first gracious presence at the ballot-box was roughly concomitant with the start toward a new all-time low in political scurviness, hoodlumism, gangsterism, labor strife, monopolistic thuggery, moral degeneration, civic corruption, smuggling, bribery,[188] theft, murder, homosexuality, drunkenness, financial depression, chaos and war. Note that.

The degenerating era however, marked new highs in the production of junk. Note that, also.

Mom, however, is a great little guy. Pulling pants onto her by these words, let us look at mom.

She is a middle-aged puffin with an eye like a hawk that has just seen a rabbit twitch far below. She is about twenty-five pounds overweight, with no sprint, but sharp heels and a hard backhand which she does not regard as a foul but a womanly defense. In a thousand of her there is not sex appeal enough to budge a hermit ten paces off a rock ledge. She none the less spends several hundred dollars a year on permanents and transformations, pomades, cleansers, rouges, lipsticks, and the like—and fools nobody except herself. If a man kisses her with any earnestness, it is time for mom to feel for her pocketbook, and this occasionally does happen.

She smokes thirty cigarettes a day, chews gum, and consumes tons of bonbons and petit fours. The shortening in the latter, stripped from pigs, sheep and cattle, shortens mom. She plays bridge with the stupid voracity of a hammerhead shark, which cannot see what it is trying to gobble but never stops snapping its jaws and roiling the waves with its tail. She drinks moderately, which is to say, two or three cocktails before dinner every night and a brandy and a couple of highballs afterward. She doesn't count the two cocktails she takes before lunch when she lunches out, which is every day she can. On Saturday nights, at the club or in the juke joint, she loses count of her drinks and is liable to get a little tiddly, which is to say, shot or blind. But it is her man who worries about where to acquire the money while she worries only about how to spend it, so he has the ulcers and colitis and she has the guts of a bear; she can get pretty stiff before she topples.

Her sports are all spectator sports.[189]

She was graduated from high school or a "finishing" school or even a college in her distant past and made up for the unhappiness of compulsory education by sloughing all that she learned so completely that she could not pass the final examinations of a fifth grader. She reads the fiction in three women's magazines each month and occasionally skims through an article, which usually angers her so that she gets other moms to skim through it, and then they have a session on the subject over a canister of spiked coffee in order to damn the magazine, the editors, the author, and the silly girls who run about these days. She reads two or three motion-picture fan magazines also, and goes to the movies about two nights a week. If a picture does not coincide precisely with her attitude of the moment, she converses through all of it and so whiles away the time. She does not appear to be lecherous toward the movie photographs as men do, but that is because she is a realist and a little shy on imagination. However, if she gets to Hollywood and encounters the flesh-and-blood article known as a male star, she and her sister moms will run forward in a mob, wearing a joint expression that must make God rue his invention of bisexuality, and tear the man's clothes from his body, yea, verily, down to his B.V.D.'s.

Mom is organization-minded. Organizations, she has happily discovered, are intimidating to all men, not just to mere men. They frighten politicians to sniveling servility and they terrify pastors; they bother bank presidents and they pulverize school boards. Mom has many such organizations, the real purpose of which is to compel an abject compliance of her environs to her personal desires. With these associations and committees she has double parking ignored, for example. With them she drives out of the town and the state, if possible, all young harlots and all proprietors of places where "questionable" young women (though why they are called that—being of all women the least in question) could possibly foregather, not because she competes with such creatures but because she contrasts so unfavorably with them. With her clubs (a solid term!) she causes bus lines to run where [190] they are convenient for her rather than for workers, plants flowers in sordid spots that would do better with sanitation, snaps independent men out of office and replaces them with clammy castrates, throws prodigious fairs and parties for charity and gives the proceeds, usually about eight dollars, to the janitor to buy the committee some beer for its headache on the morning after, and builds clubhouses for the entertainment of soldiers where she succeeds in persuading thousands of them that they are momsick and would rather talk to her than take Betty into the shrubs. All this, of course, is considered social service, charity, care of the poor, civic reform, patriotism, and self-sacrifice. . . .

Knowing nothing about medicine, art, science, religion, law, sanitation, civics, hygiene, psychology, morals, history, geography, poetry, literature, or any other topic except the all-consuming one of momism, she seldom has any especial interest in *what,* exactly, she is doing as a member of any of these endless organizations, so long as it is *something.*[191] . . .

In churches, the true purpose of organized momhood is to unseat bishops, snatch the frocks off prelates, change rectors just for variety, cross-jet community gossip, take the customary organizational kudos out of the pot each for each, bestow and receive titles, and short-circuit one another.

Mom also has patriotism. If a war comes, this may even turn into a genuine feeling and the departure of her son may be her means to grace in old age. Often, however, the going of her son is only an occasion for more show. She has, in that case, no deep respect for him. What he has permitted her to do to him has rendered him unworthy of consideration—and she has shown him none since puberty. She does not miss him—only his varletry—but over that she can weep interminably.[192] . . .

But, peace or war, the moms have another kind of patriotism that, in the department of the human spirit, is identical to commercialized vice, because it captures a good thing and doles it out for the coin of unctuous pride—at the expense of deceased ancestors rather than young female offspring. By becoming a Daughter of this historic war or that, a woman makes herself into a sort of madam who fills the coffers of her ego with the prestige that has accrued to the doings of others. A frantic emptiness of those coffers provides the impulse for the act. There are, of course, other means of filling them, but they are difficult, and mom never does anything that is difficult—either the moving of a piano or the breaking of a nasty habit.[193] . . .

In the matter of her affiliation of herself with the Daughters of some war the Hitler analogue especially holds, because these sororities of the sword often constitute her Party—her shirtism. Ancestor worship, like all other forms of religion, contained an instinctual reason and developed rituals thought to be germane to the reason. People sedulously followed those rituals, which were basically intended to remind them that they, too, were going to be ancestors someday and would have to labor for personal merit in order to be worthy of veneration. But mom's reverence for her bold forebears lacks even a ritualistic significance, and so instructs her in nothing. She is peremptory about historical truth, mandates, custom, fact, and point. She brushes aside the ideals and concepts for which her forebears perished fighting, as if they were the crumbs of melba toast. Instead, she attributes to the noble dead her own immediate and selfish attitudes. She "knows full well what they would have thought and done," and in that whole-cloth trumpery she goes busting on her way.

Thus the long-vanished warriors who liberated this land from one George in order to make another its first president guide mom divinely as she barges along the badgering boulevard of her life, relaying fiats from the grave on birth control, rayon, vitamins, the power trust, and a hundred other items of which the dead had no knowledge. To some degree most people, these days, are guilty of this absurd procedure. There has been more nonsense printed lately detailing what Jefferson would say about matters he never dreamed of than a sensible man can endure. (I do not have any idea, for instance, and I am sure nobody has any idea, what Jefferson would think about the giddy bungle of interstate truck commerce; but people, columnists especially, will tell you.)

Mom, however, does not merely quote Thomas Jefferson on modern topics: she *is* Thomas Jefferson. This removes her twice from sanity. Mom wraps herself in the mantle of every canny man [194] and coward who has drilled with a musket on this continent and reproduced a line that zigzagged down to mom. In that cloak, together with the other miters, rings, scepters, and power symbols which she has swiped, she has become the American pope.

People are feebly aware of this situation and it has been pointed out at one time or another that the phrase "Mother knows best" has practically worn out the staircase to private hell. Most decriers of matriarchy, however, are men of middle age, like me.

Young men whose natures are attuned to a female image with more feelings than mom possesses and different purposes from those of our synthetic archetype of Cinderella-the-go-getter bounce anxiously away from their first few brutal contacts with modern young women, frightened to find their shining hair is vulcanized, their agate eyes are embedded in cement, and their ruby lips case-hardened into pliers for bending males like wire. These young men, fresh-startled by learning that She is a chrome-plated afreet, but not able to discern that the condition is mom's unconscious preparation of somebody's sister for a place in the gynecocracy—are, again, presented with a soft and shimmering resting place, the bosom of mom. . . .

"Her boy," having been "protected" by her love, and carefully, even shudderingly, shielded from his logical development through his barbaric period, or childhood (so that he has either to become [195] a barbarian as a man or else to spend most of his energy denying the barbarism that howls in his brain—an autonomous remnant of the youth he was forbidden), is cushioned against any major step in his progress toward maturity. Mom steals from the generation of women behind her (which she has, as a still further defense, also sterilized of integrity and courage) that part of her boy's personality which should have become the love of a female contemporary. Mom transmutes it into sentimentality for herself.[196] . . .

As men grow older, they tend to become more like women, and vice versa. Even physically, their characteristics swap; men's voices rise, their breasts grow, and their chins recede; women develop bass voices and mustaches. This is another complementary, or opposite, turn of nature. It is meant to reconcile sexuality and provide a fountainhead of wisdom uncompromised by it, in the persons of those individuals who are hardy enough and lucky enough to survive to old age in a natural environment. But survival, as I have said, no longer depends on any sort of natural selection, excepting a great basic one which our brains are intended to deal with, and which, if allowed to go brainlessly on, will have to reduce our species to savagery in order to get back to a level on which instinct itself can rule effectively.[197] . . .

I have explained how the moms turned Cinderellaism to their advantage and I have explained that women possess some eighty per cent of the nation's money (the crystal form of its energy) and I need only allude, I think, to the statistical reviews which show that the women are the spenders, wherefore the controlling consumers of nearly all we make with our machines. The steel puddler in Pittsburgh may not think of himself as a feminine tool, but he is really only getting a Chevrolet ready for mom to drive through a garden wall. I should round out this picture of America existing for mom with one or two more details, such as annual increase in the depth of padding in vehicles over the past thirty years due to the fact that a fat rump is more easily irritated than a lean one, and the final essential detail of mom's main subjective preoccupation, which is listening to the radio. The radio is mom's soul; a detail, indeed.

It is also a book in itself, and one I would prefer to have my reader write after he has learned a little of the art of catching overtones as a trained ear, such as mine, catches them. But there must be a note on it.

The radio has made sentimentality the twentieth century Plymouth Rock. As a discipline, I have forced myself to sit a whole morning listening to the soap operas, along with twenty million moms who were busy sweeping dust under carpets while planning to drown their progeny in honey or bash in their heads. This filthy and indecent abomination, this trash with which, until lately, only moron servant girls could dull their credulous minds in the tawdry privacy of their cubicles, is now the national saga. Team after team of feeble-minded Annies and Davids crawl from the loudspeaker into the front rooms of America. The characters are impossible, their adventures would make a saint spew, their morals are lower than those of ghouls, their habits are uncleanly, their humor is the substance that starts whole races grinding bayonets,[201] they have no manners, no sense, no goals, no worthy ambitions, no hope, no faith, no information, no values related to reality, and no estimate of truth. They merely sob and snicker—as they cheat each other. . . .

The radio is mom's final tool, for it stamps everybody who listens with the matriarchal brand—its superstitions, prejudices, devotional rules, taboos, musts, and all other qualifications needful to its maintenance. Just as Goebbels has revealed what can be done with such a mass-stamping of the public psyche in his nation, so our land is a living representation of the same fact worked out in matriarchal sentimentality, goo, slop, hidden cruelty, and the foreshadow of national death. That alone is sinister enough, but the process is still more vicious, because it fills in every crack and cranny of mom's time and mind—and pop's also, since he has long ago yielded the dial-privilege to his female; so that a whole nation of people lives in eternal fugue and never has to deal for one second with itself or its own problems. Any interior sign of worry, wonder, speculation, anxiety, apprehension—or even a stirring of an enfeebled will to plan sanely- can be annihilated by an electrical click whereby the populace puts itself in the place, the untenable place—of somebody called Myrt—and never has even to try to *be* itself alone in the presence of this real world.

This is Nirvana at last. It is also entropy. For here the spirit of man, absorbed, disoriented, confused, identified with ten thousand spurious personalities and motives, has utterly lost itself. By this [202] means is man altogether lost. The radio, in very truth, sells soap. We could confine it to music, intelligent discourse, and news—all other uses being dangerous—but mom will not let us. Rather than study herself and her environment with the necessary honesty, she will fight for this poisoned syrup to the last. Rather than take up her democratic responsibility in this mighty and tottering republic, she will bring it crashing down simply to maintain to the final rumble of ruin her personal feudalism. Once, sentimentalism was piecework, or cost the price of a movie or a book; now it is mass produced and not merely free, but almost compulsory.

I give you mom. I give you the destroying mother. I give you her justice—from which we have never removed the eye bandage. I give you the angel—and point to the sword in her hand. I give you death— the hundred million deaths that are muttered under Yggdrasill's ash. I give you Medusa and Stheno and Euryale. I give you the harpies and the witches, and the Fates. I give you the woman in pants, and the new religion: she-popery. I give you Pandora. I give you Proserpine, the Queen of Hell. The five-and-ten-cent-store Lilith, the mother of Cain, the black widow who is poisonous and eats her mate, and I designate at the bottom of your program the grand finale of all the soap operas: the mother of America's Cinderella.

We must face the dynasty of the dames at once, deprive them of our pocketbooks when they waste the substance in them, and take back our dreams which, without the perfidious materialism of mom, were shaping up a new and braver world. We must drive roads to Rio and to Moscow and stop spending all our strength in the manufacture of girdles: it is time that mom's sag became known to the desperate public; we must plunge into our psyches and find out there, each for each, scientifically, about immortality and miracles. To do such deeds, we will first have to make the conquest of momism, which grew up from male default.

Our society is too much an institution built to appease the rapacity of loving mothers. If that condition is an ineluctable experiment of nature, then we are the victims of a failure. But I [203] do not think it is. Even while the regiments spell out "mom" on the parade grounds, I think mom's grip can be broken by private integrity.[204] . . .

SUGGESTIONS FOR STUDY

To arrive at satisfactory conclusions about the nature of satire, one must ask and answer necessary questions about the interrelationships among such elements as plot, setting, character, image, and symbol. Only then can one approach the three essential questions about satire: (1) What is satirized? (2) What methods—invective, burlesque, irony, allegory, etc.—help accomplish the satire? (3) What is the dominant tone—grim, cheerful, sardonic, optimistic, etc.?

The brief "Introductions" to the life and work of each author represented in Part Two of this volume are designed to urge the reader to explore beyond the works reprinted here. The "Problems for Discussion and Writing" and the "Topics for Research and Evaluation" are presented to encourage both the student and the instructor to formulate their own pertinent questions about the language, form, and meaning of the materials in Parts One and Two.

For those interested in exploring the latest scholarly materials about the works in this book, the "Annual Bibliography" in the April issues of *PMLA (Publications of the Modern Language Association)* and other current periodical bibliographies are helpful.

Part One: Theory

Problems for Discussion and Writing

1. Abstract each of the theories of satire. Try to capture each author's main ideas in a few sentences.

2. Vice (or evil) and folly are, broadly speaking, the two main objects of satirical attack. Which of these was the main concern of Horace? of Juvenal? What are the main concerns of the other writers represented here?

3. By general agreement, instruction and pleasure are accepted as the two aims of literature. Instruction, or the moral improvement of humanity and human society, is often regarded as the more important aim of satire. Among these theorists do you find any who speaks for pleasure? Can you think of any satire that seems to have pleasure as its main objective? Do you prefer to read for pleasure or instruction—or both? Explain.

4. Horace says he writes without malice, and several other writers, including Swift, favor the laugh instead of the lash. Yet one does not laugh in reading Gulliver's Travels, particularly Book IV; and Juvenal boils with anger and indignation. Which of the two attitudes do you consider more likely to be successful as a corrective of evil or folly?

5. Is humor essential to satire? Among other remarks, see those by Richard Garnett, Edgar Johnson and Northrop Frye on this subject. Also see Abrams' glossary.

6. Edward Young states, "Laughing at the misconduct of the world will, in a great measure, ease us of any more disagreeable passion about it. One passion is more effectually driven out by another than by reason. . . ." Do you agree? Explain.

7. Do you agree with Henry Fielding that "The only source of the true Ridiculous . . . is affectation"? To what extent does Edgar Johnson agree?

8. George Meredith makes a distinction between comedy and satire. Do you agree with his definition of comedy, or do you feel that he is also describing satire? Compare the views of Johnson and Frye on this subject, and see also Comedy in Abrams' glossary.

9. When Johnson insists that satire is "criticism getting around or overcoming an obstacle, . . . the Censor," is he introducing a concept ignored by the other theorists? Is Johnson speaking of the social or the Freudian censor?

10. Frye defines satire as a kind of writing that breaks up "things which impede the free movement of society." Does he imply, then, that satire is revolutionary? May it not be conservative, or even reactionary?

11. Frye speaks of satire as "the seamy side of the tragic vision"; at its most concentrated, "a universal negation that cheapens and belittles everything, . . . an art of nihilism." Is he condemning satire? What does he mean by his concluding reference to Satan, who seems to be upright but turns out to be standing on his head?

12. Is it important to be aware of possible differences between the actual personality of the writer and the personality of his satirist? (See the selection from Alvin Kernan's The Cankered Muse.) Why? Try to describe the satirist as he appears in several works included in this text.

13. Manifestly satire has been written in many different forms—verse, story, play, etc. Does the form in any way limit or determine the meaning? How?

14. Would you say that Richard Garnett holds a strict or a relaxed definition of satire? Cite evidence from his text to support your opinion.

15. Having considered these definitions and theories, and having explored the above questions, write your own definition of satire in an essay.

Topic for Research and Evaluation

Using the definitions and statements of theory given above, and any others you can find, prepare a research paper evaluating the areas of agreement and disagreement about the language, method, and meaning of satire.

Part Two: Practice

Aesop, Horace, La Fontaine, James Thurber:
The Town Mouse and the Country Mouse—Four Versions

Although both Herodotus (born *c.* 484 B.C.) and Plutarch (late first century A.D.) wrote in considerable detail about the fabulist Aesop, only two facts are established with certainty. The people of Athens believed Aesop to be the author of the compact satires, and they commissioned one of their famous sculptors, Lysippus (fourth century B.C.), to create and set up a statue to honor Aesop's memory. Whether Aesop really lived and wrote, or whether the fables attributed to him are but the polished results of a long Indo-European oral tradition of beast tales, is perhaps a question not worth arguing. What is important is that the world chooses to believe in Aesop as the author of the fables. Almost two hundred of them, about half of the total, were translated and collected by S. A. Handford in his *Fables of Aesop* (Penguin Classics, 1954), a book with a concise but valuable introduction.

Quintus Horatius Flaccus (65 B.C.–8 B.C.), the most genial and tolerant of the Roman satirists, lived a serene and stoic life dedicated to friendship and literature. Although he is perhaps best known for his lyric odes, Horace's finest accomplishments are found in his two books of satires, both of which are intimate revelations of Roman society and of the poet himself. For a lively and scholarly introduction to Horace and his works, and for a translation in contemporary idiom, see Smith Palmer Bovie, *Satires and Epistles* (Chicago: University of Chicago Press, 1959).

Of the fables of Jean de La Fontaine (1621–1695), one of the most witty and accomplished of poets, Madame de Sévigné has written: "[they] are like a basket of strawberries. You begin by selecting the largest and best, but, little by little, you eat, first one, then another, till at last the basket is empty." It is a copious basket, heaped with about 240 fables, varying in length from a few lines to several hundred. A recent translation, *The Fables of La Fontaine* (New York: The Viking Press, 1954), by the distinguished contemporary American poet Marianne Moore, is excellent. A concise and easily accessible article about La Fontaine's life and work is found in the 1959 edition of the *Encyclopaedia Britannica*.

Everyone knows James Thurber, or should know him. Born in 1894 in Columbus, Ohio, he joined the staff of *The New Yorker* in 1927 and has been famous ever since. One could do worse than to read every word Thurber has written and to collect every drawing he has drawn. Don't read about Thurber. Just read him, especially *Fables for Our Time* (1940) and *Further Fables for Our Time* (1956). James Thurber died in November 1961.

At first glance, the town and country mouse fables and many others may not appear satiric. But one need only consider "Folly's Companions," as Desiderius Erasmus enumerates them in his classic satire, *The Praise of Folly* (1511): "Self-Love, Flattery, Laziness, Wantonness, Intemperance," and so on. These are the follies and vices most likely to defeat the self-indulgent animal characters of an Aesop or a La Fontaine. And so, by implication, the folk wisdom of the fabulists condemns greed and recommends moderation; exposes disloyalty or ingratitude and commends their opposites. Like most satirists, the fabulists ridicule excess and extol the common-sense virtues.

The animal portraits in the fables have some distinctively beast-like traits, but the characters are really little more than disguised human beings—men in the guise of fur and feathers. During the late Renaissance, this ancient tradition became perhaps a trifle tiresome for reader and author alike. Thus certain writers, such as Ben Jonson (1573–1637), began to experiment in new directions. Jonson almost reverses the Aesop tradition: instead of showing animals with predominantly human qualities, he gives us men with reprehensible animal traits. In *Volpone,* perhaps the best satirical drama in English literature, the characters not only act like beasts but are labeled with such names as fox and parrot. The recent play *Rhinoceros,* by Eugene Ionesco, is a direct descendant of *Volpone.*

In one of the greatest of animal stories, Book IV of *Gulliver's Travels,* Jonathan Swift (1667–1745) fiercely attacks man's folly and vice by contrasting the corrupt European society with a "civilized" society—a race of superior horses. The direction set by the embittered but passionately hopeful Swift has been further explored by such moderns as Garcia Lorca in his two-act play *El Maleficio de la Mariposa;* by James Agee in his story about intelligent cattle, "A Mother's Tale"; and by C. S. Lewis in his space fiction, *Out of the Silent Planet.* Many other provocative plays, stories, and novels use animal or animal-like characters for the purposes of satire—notably, Aristophanes' *The Birds;* Anatole France's *Penguin Island;* and Karel Capek's *War with the Newts.* There is also George Orwell's *Animal Farm,* a novel which, among other things, shows pigs becoming greedy men.

Problems for Discussion and Writing

1. What, in your opinion, is the main difference between Aesop's and Horace's treatment of the fable?
2. What possible artistic reasons might La Fontaine have for reversing the order of the visits between the two rats?
3. Does La Fontaine's verse (insofar as you can judge it through Marianne Moore's translation) seem to you a better medium for the fable than prose?
4. Which of the four writers is most interested in his characters as animals?

5. Why do you think Thurber departs radically from the conventional narrative and moral? Is the departure possibly a parody (see Abrams' glossary)?

6. Write your own fable about the two mice, either in prose or in verse.

Topic for Research and Evaluation

A history of the fable from Aesop to Thurber.

Geoffrey Chaucer: *The Nun's Priest's Tale*

Geoffrey Chaucer (*c.* 1340–1400), except for several trips to France and Italy, spent most of his life in London as a royal favorite and courtier. As a servant to the king, he performed many duties of a business and diplomatic nature. Married and a father, a collector of books and an eager reader, a man of good cheer and humor, he was above all a great poet. Among his poems are *The House of Fame, The Parliament of Fowls, Troilus and Criseyde,* and *The Legend of Good Women.* His most famous work, *The Canterbury Tales,* was probably composed in the late 1380s.

"If we may trust the *Prologue,*" remarks Nevill Coghill in his edition of the *Tales,* "Chaucer intended that each of some thirty pilgrims should tell two tales on the way to Canterbury and two on the way back. He never completed this immense project, and what he wrote was not finally revised even so far as it went. . . . The idea of a collection of tales diversified in style to suit their tellers and unified in form by uniting the tellers in a common purpose is Chaucer's own." However, the subject matter for most of the narratives is largely derivative. Probably Chaucer was acquainted with several versions of the cock and fox story that was popular throughout medieval Europe. As he reworked it, the narrative became one of the choicest of animal stories, and a fine example of mock-heroic satire (see Abrams' glossary). There are three major characters: the gaudy gentleman rooster; his plump and loving wife; their wily enemy, the fox, in color "betwixe yellow and reed."

The student will also enjoy reading two other satires from the Canterbury series, "The Pardoner's Tale" and "The Summoner's Tale." An informal and readable biography, and reliable enough as an introduction, is Marchette Chute, *Geoffrey Chaucer of England* (New York: E. P. Dutton and Co., Inc., 1946).

Problems for Discussion and Writing

1. Does the priestly narrator interject his satiric opinions into the tale? Where and how?

2. Pertelote, fashionably up to date, believes dreams are caused by the natural humors and complexions of the body; Chanticleer, arguing from the ancients, attributes a supernatural origin to dreams. With which character does the narrator-priest seem to be more

sympathetic? Is this imbalance of sympathy a means of obtaining satire?

3. What are the main personality traits of the rooster, the hen, and the fox? To what extent is each of them fallible? Is the revelation of fallibilities a method of obtaining satire?

4. The poem is in the mock-heroic tradition. Describe as specifically as possible the mock-heroic effects.

Topics for Research and Evaluation

1. The "cock and the fox" story from ancient to modern times.
2. The sources for "The Nun's Priest's Tale."
3. Reflections of fourteenth-century English society in "The Nun's Priest's Tale."

Molière: *Love Is the Best Doctor*

Molière (1622–1673), whose real name was Jean-Baptiste Poquelin, was born into a bourgeois family whose head, his father, was *tapissier* or upholsterer to the King of France. At a time when an actor was still so disreputable that simply by virtue of his calling he was excommunicated by the Catholic Church, Molière renounced middle-class security and chose the stage. He became the most popular comic actor of his time and one of the greatest comic writers of all time. After twelve years as actor-manager-writer in the provincial regions of France, he returned to Paris with his theatrical company in 1658 and there, under the patronage of Louis XIV, he wrote and produced a series of brilliant comedies.

L'Amour Médicin, or *Love Is the Best Doctor*, was first presented on September 15, 1665, at the court in Versailles, probably with Molière in the role of Sganarelle. In a preface he states that the play was sketched, written, learned, and acted in five days. It was chosen for this volume partly because of its brevity, but though it is a minor play—*The School for Husbands, The School for Wives, The Misanthrope, Tartuffe*, and others are more important—it is representative of Molière's skill in comic satire. And it displays a theme that interested him strongly toward the end of his life: satire of the faculty of medicine. More devastating and thoroughgoing attacks on the physicians are to be found in *The Doctor in Spite of Himself, Monsieur de Pourceaugnac*, and, best of all, his last play, *Le Malade Imaginaire*, or *The Imaginary Invalid*, written and acted when Molière must have known that he was dying of tuberculosis.

The text used here observes a stage convention of Molière's time: subdivision into scenes defined by entrance and exit of a principal character. This had little effect on the play's staging, and the student should understand that the movement within each act was continuous. The comedy-ballet, included at the beginning and end, was a popular form of the day, and can be compared to our musical comedy.

The student who wishes to learn more about Molière's life and work would do well to read his *Plays*, with an introduction by Francis

Fergusson (New York: Modern Library, 1950); *Molière's Comedies,* Everyman edition with an introduction by F. C. Green (New York: E. P. Dutton & Co., Inc., 1929, 1956); Ramon Fernandez, *La Vie de Molière,* translated by Wilson Follett (New York: Hill and Wang, 1958); W. G. Moore, *Molière, A New Criticism* (Oxford: Clarendon Press, 1949).

Problems for Discussion and Writing

1. Does the play seem to you mainly a farce comedy (see Abrams' glossary)? Discuss the play as farce.

2. Molière is also a master of "high comedy" or "comedy of manners" (see Abrams' glossary). Analyze the play as an example of comedy of manners.

3. In *Laughter* (see Bibliography), Henri Bergson says that "a comic character is generally comic in proportion to his ignorance of himself. The comic person is unconscious." Is this true of the physicians? Of Sganarelle? How important is it to comedy that the audience or reader know more than the characters?

4. Marcel Pagnol, in *Notes sur le rire* (Paris: Nagel, 1947), writes: "Laughter is a song of triumph. It expresses the laugher's sudden discovery of his own momentary superiority over the person he laughs at." If true, would this account for some of the delight we feel in comic satire? Analyze your reactions to the humor of the play.

5. Do you think a play satirizing physicians would be acceptable to the public today? (Consider Bernard Shaw's *The Doctor's Dilemma.*) If not, why not?

Topic for Research and Evaluation

Molière's career as satirist.

Jonathan Swift: *A Modest Proposal*

As his pamphlets *The Drapier's Letters* (1724), *A Modest Proposal* (1729), and other writings abundantly demonstrate, Jonathan Swift (1667–1745), born and bred in Dublin, furiously defended the Irish against the misrule and economic exploitation of the English. He became Dean of St. Patrick's Cathedral in Dublin in 1713, soon became a national hero, and was granted "Freedom of the City of Dublin" by a grateful people. A professed hater of mankind in the mass, Swift was nevertheless a friend of individual men, including such literary wits as Joseph Addison, John Gay, and Alexander Pope.

His most famous satire, *Travels into Several Remote Nations of the World . . . By Captain Lemuel Gulliver* (1726), is also his best work. As Carl Van Doren has noted, *Gulliver's Travels,* along with *Pilgrim's Progress* and *Robinson Crusoe,* is often considered a children's book and is therefore among the most widely read in the language. But all three, beyond the level of their adventures, reflect "the plight and fate of man." As its complete title, *A Modest Proposal for Preventing the Children of Poor People from Being a Burthen to Their Parents or Country, and for Making Them Beneficial to the Public,* immediately implies, the Swift selection included here contains a brilliantly sustained irony. Throughout the essay the animal smell hangs in the air almost as heavily as in the fables, "The Nun's Priest's Tale," or Book IV of *Gulliver.* Why?

A lively introduction to Swift's life and work is Carl Van Doren, *The Portable Swift* (New York: Viking Press, 1948). The biography by Sir Henry Craik (*Jonathan Swift,* 2 vols., London: John Murray, 1882) is still the most complete and accurate.

Problems for Discussion and Writing

1. Apparently misinterpreting the essay, William Makepeace Thackeray (nineteenth-century English novelist, author of *Vanity Fair*) called Swift "an inhuman monster." How did you feel about the author when you first read this essay?

2. The essay has the appearance of being a straight-faced tract in economics. Examine the text closely for devices used to create satire. Is there irony? Invective? Burlesque? If there is burlesque, is it high or low? (See Abrams' glossary.) Is there anything grotesque? Is there antithesis? Can you determine the chief target of the satire? Other targets?

3. Reread Swift's own comment on the function of humor in satire. Do you think Swift is primarily "laughing" or "lashing" in *A Modest Proposal?* Do you receive a clear picture of the personality advocating the proposal? How would you characterize him: benevolent, objective, embittered, etc.?

4. Using only *A Modest Proposal* as a source, what evidence can you find that might indicate Swift's attitudes toward war, racial equality, materialism, work, death, education, and women and marriage? Would you label Swift—on the basis of the evidence in this essay— a probable conservative, liberal, or radical in his political opinions?

Topics for Research and Evaluation

1. The economic, social, and religious conditions in eighteenth-century Ireland.

2. English policies toward Ireland in Swift's time.

Alexander Pope: The Rape of the Lock

Although he was a Roman Catholic—therefore subject to the political and social restrictions on people of that faith in the England of his time—and a hunchback who once described his life as one long disease, Alexander Pope (1688–1744) used his literary talent to gain financial independence and acceptance in high social circles. The fact that he was largely self-educated did not prevent him from translating Homer's *Iliad* and *Odyssey* into English verse and reaping unprecedented profits from their publication. More to the point, he became the foremost poet and man of letters of his time.

Much of his verse was critical, argumentative, didactic, but he was far from being an original thinker. Most readers today are likely to be less interested in poems like *An Essay on Criticism, An Essay on Man,* or *Moral Essays*—though they express in highly skilled form many of the characteristic ideas and attitudes of the time—than in "The Rape of the Lock" and *The Dunciad.* Of these two satires, the former usually has more appeal, for a variety of reasons. Although *The Dunciad* is written with great skill and biting wit, its satire—aimed at certain individuals who had incurred Pope's wrath—is personal, caustic, even virulent. "The Rape of the Lock" is another matter. William Hazlitt, early nineteenth-century English essayist, called the poem "the perfection of the mock heroic." It is doubtful whether a more perfect example of the type can be found. Indeed, there are good grounds for calling this the most brilliant poetic work of the entire neo-classical period and an outstanding exemplar for all time of the poetry of wit and intellect.

A quarrel which broke out among some of Pope's friends when Lord Petre cut off one of Lady Arabella Fermor's curls furnished the poet with the trivial incident which he enlarged, in mock style, to epic proportions. Urbane, charming, ironical, rendered in highly polished heroic couplets, the poem shows Pope in his lightest vein. The first version, published in two cantos (1712), did not contain supernatural "machinery" such as the sylphs and gnomes. This was added in the second version, published in 1714, in five cantos as reprinted in this text.

A good one-volume edition of Pope's poems is *The Complete Poetical Works of Alexander Pope,* edited by Henry W. Boynton (Boston and New York: Houghton Mifflin Co., 1931); also useful is *The Best of Pope,* edited and with an introduction by George Sherburn (New York: The Ronald Press, 1940). Among others, Bonamy Dobree, *Alexander Pope* (London: Sylvan Press, 1951), and Edith Sitwell, *Alexander Pope* (London: Faber and Faber, 1930), are readable biographies. Of the wealth of critical material, the student will profit by consulting Austin Warren, *Alexander Pope as Critic and Humanist* (Princeton: Princeton University Press, 1929); and Geoffrey Tillotson, *On the Poetry of Pope* (Oxford: Clarendon Press, 1950).

Problems for Discussion and Writing

1. Discuss the poem as an example of "mock epic" or "mock heroic" (see Abrams' glossary).

2. The poem has often been called a masterpiece of wit and irony. Do you agree? Find evidence in specific passages to support your opinion. Consider, for example, the effect of the juxtaposition of incongruities as in:

   Not louder shrieks to pitying heav'n are cast,
   When husbands, or when lapdogs breathe their last.

3. The word "rape" obviously means "theft," but are there implications of a sexual nature? Consider such lines as these:

Whether the nymph shall break Diana's law,
Or some frail China jar receive a flaw;
Or stain her honor, or her new brocade.

4. Consider the use Pope makes of the military metaphor. Is he commenting on the "war between the sexes"? Give examples.

5. Do you think Pope means the poem to be mainly a moral corrective? If not, what other interpretation do you favor?

Topics for Research and Evaluation

1. The mock epic as used by several poets (Chaucer, Pope, Byron, etc.).

2. Pope's career as a satirist.

Voltaire: *Memnon the Philosopher*

François Marie Arouet was born in Paris in 1694. He added de Voltaire to his name in 1717 and began a long and brilliant career as historian, Biblical scholar, businessman, philosopher, and literary artist. As a satirist and as a humanitarian, he was often in trouble with the church and state—and was usually a hero among his fellow intellectuals. His many volumes were highly influential in his own time and for years after his death in 1778. Today, however, Voltaire's reputation mainly stands on a few pieces of short fiction; a few poems; and his masterpiece, *Candide,* a short novel about the misadventures of a guileless young man in a guileful world.

The short story "Memnon," published in 1750—nine years before *Candide*—foreshadows the language, form, and theme of the longer work. There is the same simplicity and clarity of language, the same witty and urbane tone. There is the same humorous method of piling catastrophe on catastrophe. There is something of the same quarrel with Pope and Leibnitz's easy optimism that insists, "Whatever is, is right."

For a brief introduction to his life and work, see Ben Ray Redman, *The Portable Voltaire* (New York: The Viking Press, 1949). For longer studies, see H. N. Brailsford, *Voltaire* (New York: Henry Holt, 1935), and S. G. Tallentyre, *The Life of Voltaire,* 3rd ed. (London: Smith, Elder & Co., 1935).

Problems for Discussion and Writing

Having isolated the primary object of this satire, the dominant satirical tone, and the methods of developing the satire, ask and answer the following questions:

1. What, if any, social censor (see Edgar Johnson in Theory) is Voltaire trying to overcome?

2. Note Frye's observation about the prevalence of obscenity in great satire; does "Memnon" seem to lend substance to Frye's observation?

3. Note Frye's paragraph beginning with the sentence: "Now both humor and attack depend on certain conventions which are assumed

to be in existence before the satirist begins to write. . . ." Do you think readers of two hundred years ago would have found "Memnon" more humorous than today's readers?

Topic for Research and Evaluation

Comparison of "Memnon" and *Candide*. What incidents, scenes, characters, and ideas in "Memnon" are similar to those in the novel? Compare the satirical language, method, and theme of the two works. (*Candide* is readily available in inexpensive paperback editions.)

Samuel Langhorne Clemens: from *The Adventures of Huckleberry Finn*

Samuel Langhorne Clemens (1835–1910), more familiarly known as Mark Twain, grew up in Hannibal, Missouri, by the Mississippi River, and in rapid succession became a printer, steamboat pilot, soldier, hard-rock miner, newspaperman, lecturer, and by about 1870 a well-established author. *The Adventures of Huckleberry Finn*, published in 1885, is generally regarded as Twain's best work, despite the foolishness of the last ten chapters. It is also one of America's best-known novels. With the quiet summer days and the dark flow of the river, the book is often warm and sensuous in its treatment of nature. The language and form—with the central symbol of the river, with the nice balance of violent and idyllic episodes, and with the sustained use of Huck's point of view and inimitable dialect—combine to fashion an entertaining and searching probe into the world's good and evil. *Huck Finn* demands several readings to unlock its successes and its failures; naturally, therefore, it fascinates each generation of critics. For a balanced and cautious study of Twain's life and work, and also for a copious, up-to-date bibliography, see Edward Wagenknecht, *Mark Twain: The Man and His Work* (Norman: The University of Oklahoma Press, 1935; rev. ed., 1961). For those interested in the sources of *Huckleberry Finn*, Walter Blair's *Mark Twain and Huck Finn* (Berkeley: University of California Press, 1960) will prove fascinating.

The excerpt from *Huckleberry Finn*, taken from Chapters 21 and 22, represents the grimmest satire in the novel and foreshadows the embittered attacks against "the damned human race" found in *The Man That Corrupted Hadleyburg* (1900) and *The Mysterious Stranger* (1916).

Problems for Discussion and Writing

1. What attitudes, customs, institutions are satirized? How would you characterize the satire—light, angry, bitter, etc.? What methods—allegory, burlesque, caricature, sarcasm, etc.—does Twain use to accomplish his satire?

2. What details do you find witty or humorous? How does this piece of writing help justify Frye's assertion that wit and humor are essential to satire?

Topic for Research and Evaluation

The major objects of satire in *The Man That Corrupted Hadley-burg, The Mysterious Stranger,* or *Huckleberry Finn.* (What methods or strategies does Twain use to accomplish his satire?)

Ivan Bunin: *The Gentleman from San Francisco*

Ivan Bunin, born of noble parents in the Russian village of Voronezh in 1870, began writing as a student at the University of Moscow. Winner of the Pushkin Prize for poetry in 1903, elected to the Russian Academy in 1909, he became an exile in 1917 with the advent of the revolution. He produced little of importance after his immigration to western Europe. His best-known novel is *The Village* (1910); his best-known story is the one reprinted here, first published in 1915. He was awarded the Nobel Prize for literature in 1933 and died in Paris in 1953.

After a first reading, one may wonder why "The Gentleman" is included in this collection of satire, but a second reading and reflection will reveal that the story is an Horatian thrust at a universal failing: "Alas, alas, that great city Babylon, that mighty city!" Like much great satire, this story is fundamentally a moral comment on nature, man, and God; on good and evil; on the meanings of life and death.

For estimates of Bunin's life and work see G. Struve, "The Art of Ivan Bunin," *Slavonic Review* (1933); Renato Poggioli, "The Art of Ivan Bunin," *Harvard Slavic Studies,* I (1953); Jacques Croise, "Ivan Bunin: 1870–1953," *Russian Review,* XIII (1954); C. H. Bedford, "The Fulfillment of Ivan Bunin," *Canadian Slavonic Papers,* I (1956); A. G. Colin, "Ivan Bunin in Retrospect," *Slavonic and East European Review,* XXXIV (1956). For critical analyses of "The Gentleman," see Question 7 of the "Problems for Discussion and Writing."

Problems for Discussion and Writing

1. Consider the following characters: the "Gentleman," the wife and daughter, the captain of the *Atlantida,* the Devil at Gibraltar, the hotel proprietor and his employees at Capri, the hired lovers on the ship, the Asiatic prince, the vignettes of Tiberius Caesar, Lorenzo, and especially the two mountaineers from Abruzzi. Contrast and compare their significance. Do they tend to establish an underlying meaning? State this meaning as briefly as possible.

2. Make a brief outline of the various events and happenings of the story. Do they tend to establish an underlying meaning? Explain briefly.

3. Consider the significance of the story's other details, such as the gongs and bells, the clothes worn by the gentleman and the other members of his class, the storms at sea, and the ship's hold. Do the meanings of the details and images tend in any way to reinforce, modify, or qualify the meanings of the events and happenings and characterization? Explain.

4. The story contains a great amount of irony. What kinds of irony do

you discover? Give examples of each kind. One commentator speaks of "the peculiar ironic tone" of the piece. How does the tone support or modify the meanings discovered in your analyses of character, action, and other detail?

5. Try to state as carefully as possible the story's total underlying theme, using your discoveries about character, action, tone, and miscellaneous detail and image. Is the final theme primarily pessimistic or optimistic? To what extent is it satiric?

6. Would Bunin probably agree with Van Wyck Brooks (Bibliography) that satire should be "a criticism of the spirit of one's age"?

7. In about 200-300 words, abstract one of the following evaluations of the story: Seymour L. Gross, "Nature, Man, and God in Bunin's 'The Gentleman from San Francisco,'" *Modern Fiction Studies*, IV (Summer 1960), 153–163; Cleanth Brooks, John Thibaut Purser, and Robert Penn Warren, *An Approach to Literature*, 3rd ed. (New York: Appleton-Century-Crofts, 1952), pp. 174–177; Ray B. West and Robert Wooster Stallman, *The Art of Modern Fiction* (New York: Rinehart, 1949), pp. 117–120; M. B. McNamee, *Reading for Understanding* (New York: Rinehart, 1952), pp. 454–457. To what extent do you agree or disagree with the thought of the evaluation which you have abstracted? Give evidence to support your opinion.

Topic for Research and Evaluation

Using the four evaluations listed in Question 7 above, and the articles mentioned in the biographical introduction (if most of them are available in your libraries), write a criticism of the story. Rely primarily on your own insight, but use the secondary materials whenever they can help strengthen your case, lend variety to your style, or perform some other function, such as introducing a note of humor or irony. Citations will usually work better than quotations; when you do quote, the passages should be brief and usually incorporated into your own sentence. Follow the bibliography and footnote forms suggested by your instructor.

Aldous Huxley: from *Brave New World*

Grandson of a distinguished English scientist, Thomas Henry Huxley, and relative of an equally distinguished poet-critic, Matthew Arnold, Aldous Huxley (1894–   ) has had a brilliant career. After an education at Eton and Oxford—despite poor eyesight, which at times has approached total blindness—he began a writing career that has resulted in the publication of some thirty-five books—novels, short stories, essays, poetry, plays. Since the late 1930s he has lived in the United States, recently in Hollywood, where he has written several movie scenarios in addition to many other works.

Of his novels, *Crome Yellow* (1921), *Antic Hay* (1923), *Point Counter Point* (1928), and *Brave New World* (1932) are perhaps outstanding. Huxley's critical examination of man and civilization has been at once subtle and far-reaching, iconoclastic and sympathetic, despairing and amused. The work of his young manhood was dominated by sardonic amusement and caustic despair; as he has grown older, he has at times seemed to turn to mysticism.

"It is astonishing," writes Charles J. Rolo (in an introduction to the edition of the novel used in this text), that *Brave New World* "should have lost so little, if any, of its challenge and delight. . . . When Aldous Huxley wrote this singular novel, it seemed to him that science and technology were leading mankind toward the soulless, mass-produced contentment—the 'death-without-tears'—of a wholly materialist Utopia." Huxley himself in 1947 commented: "All things considered, it looks as though Utopia were far closer to us than anyone, only fifteen years ago, could have imagined. Then, I projected it six hundred years into the future. Today it seems quite possible that the horror may be upon us within a single century. That is, if we refrain from blowing ourselves to smithereens in the interval."

Problems for Discussion and Writing

1. Huxley places his "brave new world" in the sixth century "After Ford." Ford is the god of this society. (Note, for instance, the assembly-line technique used in the hatchery.) But Huxley also refers to "Bokhanovsky groups," which were associated with Communist Russia in the 1920s. Is Huxley satirizing both the United States and Russia—or more? Explain your answer.

2. Assuming that you have read the complete novel, can you determine whether Huxley is condemning science and technology without reservations? When, later in the novel, the Savage appears as an alternative to Utopia, is Huxley saying that the irrational, unstable Savage and his unstable society are preferable to the people and society of this Utopia? Explain.

3. What are the implications of the Director's statement: "No time for the intellectual embryos, I'm afraid"?

4. Does Northrop Frye's remark (see Theory) that satire is "the seamy side of the tragic vision" apply to *Brave New World?* Is Frye's reference to Satan, who seems to be standing upright but is actually on his head, applicable in any way? Explain.

5. Note in the Theory section the statements by Alvin Kernan, and see also Maynard Mack's "The Muse of Satire" (Bibliography), with reference to the function or "ethos" of the fictive narrator, or *persona.* How would you characterize the *persona* who reveals himself in the first chapter of *Brave New World?*

Topics for Research and Evaluation

1. A comparison of several utopias such as Plato's *Republic,* Thomas More's *Utopia,* Samuel Butler's *Erewhon,* Eugene I. Zamiatin's *We,* C. S. Lewis's *Out of the Silent Planet,* George Orwell's *1984.*

2. *Brave New World* and *Brave New World Revisited* (Harper & Brothers, New York, 1958): a study of Huxley's reappraisal after twenty-six years.

Philip Wylie: *Common Women*

Philip Wylie (1902–   ) has been, at various times, a member of the staff of *The New Yorker,* a newspaper columnist, an editor, a motion-picture writer. Above all, he has been a professional writer. He has contributed many articles and stories to popular magazines such as *Redbook* and *Saturday Evening Post,* and his list of published books, many of them novels, is lengthy.

He states that he has written largely for entertainment—"a euphemism for saying I have written for money." But *Generation of Vipers* was written out of his conviction that much is wrong with us and our civilization. The opening sentences proclaim the book's serious purpose: "It is time for man to make a new appraisal of himself. His failure is abject. His plans for the future are infantile. The varied forms of his civilization in this century are smashing each other." The book was a *succès de scandale,* widely read—and as widely attacked—mainly because of its treatment of sex and its satire of American women. It has had much to do with making "momism," and all its connotations, a part of our vocabulary and our thinking.

Problems for Discussion and Writing

1. This essay is obviously a diatribe in the Juvenalian tradition. Were you shocked or repelled? Would Wylie's satire be more effective if it were less caustic? Explain.

2. Compare "Common Women" with Pope's "The Rape of the Lock" in regard to their treatment of women. Which do you prefer? Why?

3. Though an extreme example, this is only one of many attacks on American women in recent years. How much truth is there in it? List and analyze Wylie's charges in detail, arguing for or against them and citing evidence where possible.

4. Wylie claims a serious purpose in writing *Generation of Vipers.* From reading this selection, do you feel that he intends it as a moral corrective? Cite reasons for your answer. (You may wish to read the entire book.)

5. The remarks about radio programs were written before the advent of television. Are the charges against radio applicable to television? How acceptable do you find them?

6. How effective is Wylie's use of such things as imagery, metaphor, wit, and irony? Find examples of each.

Topics for Research and Evaluation

1. Other American writers' satirical attacks on women. (In what respects do they agree or disagree with Wylie's attack?)

2. Satire of women in other periods of history, such as the Middle Ages; or by other writers, such as Juvenal, Chaucer, La Fontaine, and Pope.

BIBLIOGRAPHY

In addition to following up the references in the Suggestions for Study, the student who wishes to read other critical discussions of the theory and practice of satire will find ample material in the following sources. Selections included in Part One of the text are not included in this list. Brief notations are provided for certain items whose titles are misleading or unspecific.

Alden, Raymond. *The Rise of Formal Satire in England under Classical Influence.* Philadelphia: University of Pennsylvania Press, 1899.

Beerbohm, Max. "Laughter," in *And Even Now.* New York: E. P. Dutton & Co., Inc., 1921. Amusing treatment of the subject by a clever writer.

Bergson, Henri. *Laughter: An Essay on the Meaning of the Comic,* trans. by Cloudesley Brereton and Fred Rothwell. London: Macmillan & Co., Ltd., 1911. Defines laughter as an intellectual force and a social corrective.

Bond, R. P. *English Burlesque Poetry, 1700–1750.* Cambridge: Harvard University Press, 1932. Includes discussion of the mock heroic as found in Chaucer, Samuel Butler, Boileau, and Pope.

Brooks, Van Wyck. "Mark Twain's Satire," *The Dial,* LXVIII (April 1920), 424–443.

Bullitt, John M. *Jonathan Swift and the Anatomy of Satire.* Cambridge: Harvard University Press, 1953.

Campbell, Oscar J. *Shakespeare's Satire.* London: Oxford University Press, 1943.

——————. *Comicall Satyre and Shakespeare's Troilus and Cressida.* Los Angeles: Adcraft Press, 1938.

Cannan, Gilbert. *Satire.* London: M. Secker, 1914.

Cazamian, Louis. *The Development of English Humor.* Durham: Duke University Press, 1952. Thorough survey of humor in English literature.

Davis, Herbert J. *The Satire of Jonathan Swift.* New York: The Macmillan Co., 1947.

Dempster, Germaine. *Dramatic Irony in Chaucer.* London: Oxford University Press, 1932.

Dryden, John. "A Discourse Concerning the Original and Progress of Satire," in *Essays of John Dryden,* ed. W. P. Ker. London: Oxford University Press, 1925. Important pioneering statement.

Eastman, Max. *Enjoyment of Laughter.* New York: Simon & Schuster, 1948. Regards laughter as an instinct: "The comic is the unpleasant taken playfully."

Elliott, Robert C. *The Power of Satire: Magic, Ritual, Art.* Princeton: Princeton University Press, 1960. Valuable study of the origins of satire in magic and ritual and its development as an art.

Feibleman, James. *In Praise of Comedy.* New York: The Macmillan Co., 1939.

Ford, James L. "The Guns of Satire," *The Bookman,* LXV (June 1927), 390–396.

Freud, Sigmund. *Wit and Its Relation to the Unconscious,* in *The Basic Writings of Sigmund Freud,* trans. by A. A. Brill. New York: Random House, Inc., 1938. The comic diagnosed as an antisocial impulse which sneaks past the "censor" in disguise.

Frye, Northrop. *Anatomy of Criticism.* Princeton: Princeton University Press, 1947. Further observations on satire by a first-rate critic.

Geismar, Maxwell. *Writers in Crisis.* Boston and New York: Houghton Mifflin Co., 1942. Includes discussion of Ring Lardner.

Grotjahn, Martin. *Beyond Laughter.* New York: McGraw-Hill Book Co., Inc., 1957. Competent statement by a post-Freudian psychiatrist.

Highet, Gilbert. "Satire," in *The Classical Tradition.* London. Oxford University Press, 1949, 1957. Useful history of satire from beginnings through neoclassical period.

Holden, William P. *Anti-Puritan Satire, 1572–1642.* New Haven: Yale University Press, 1954.

Hopkins, Kenneth. *Portraits in Satire.* London: Barrie Books, 1958. Discusses work of Charles Churchill, Christopher Anstey, William Gifford, etc.

Kitchin, George. *A Survey of Burlesque and Parody in English.* Edinburgh and London: Oliver & Boyd, 1931. Discusses burlesque from medieval to recent times, with many amusing examples.

Knox, Edmund G. V. *The Mechanism of Satire.* Cambridge, England: Cambridge University Press, 1951.

Kronenberger, Louis. *The Thread of Laughter.* New York: Alfred A. Knopf, Inc., 1952.

Langer, Susanne K. *Feeling and Form.* New York: Charles Scribner's Sons, 1953. Important critical-philosophical statement.

Lewis, Wyndham. *Men Without Art.* London: Cassell & Co., 1934. Prefers the objective point of view in satire, where "the eye is supreme."

Leyburn, Ellen. *Satiric Allegory: Mirror of Man.* New Haven: Yale University Press, 1956.

Lowell, James Russell. "Humor, Wit and Satire," *The Century Magazine,* XXV (November 1893), 124–131.

Mack, Maynard. "The Muse of Satire," *The Yale Review,* XLI (Autumn 1951), 80–92. Competent discussion of the "ethos" or *persona* of the satirist.

Peter, John Desmond. *Complaint and Satire in Early English Literature.* Oxford: Clarendon Press, 1956. A study of pre-Elizabethan satire.

Previté-Orton, C. W. *Political Satire in English Poetry.* Cambridge, England: Cambridge University Press, 1910.

Repplier, Agnes. *In Pursuit of Laughter.* Boston and New York: Houghton Mifflin Co., 1936. Glances now and again at satire.

Rourke, Constance. *American Humor.* New York: Harcourt, Brace & Co. 1931. Standard critical-historical work on the subject.

Russell, Frances. *Satire in the Victorian Novel.* New York: The Macmillan Co., 1920.

Sedgewick, Garnett G. *Of Irony, Especially in the Drama.* Toronto: University of Toronto Press, 1935.

Snider, Rose. *Satire in the Comedies of Congreve, Sheridan, Wilde, and Coward.* Orono: Maine University Press, 1937.

Sutherland, James R. *English Satire.* Cambridge, England: Cambridge University Press, 1958. A competent survey.

Thomson, J. A. K. *Irony.* Cambridge: Harvard University Press, 1927.

Tiddy, R. J. E. "Satura and Satire," in *English Literature and the Classics.* Oxford: The Clarendon Press, 1912.

Tucker, Samuel M. *Verse Satire in England before the Renaissance.* New York: Columbia University Press, 1908.

Turner, Francis McD. C. *The Element of Irony in English Literature.* Cambridge, England: Cambridge University Press, 1926.

Vines, Sherard. *Georgian Satirists.* London: Wishart & Co., 1934.

Vulliamy, Colwyn E. *The Anatomy of Satire.* London: Joseph, 1950.

Walker, Hugh. *English Satire and Satirists.* New York: E. P. Dutton & Co., 1925.

Wolfe, Humbert. *Notes on English Verse Satire.* New York: Harcourt, Brace & Co., 1929.

Worcester, David. *The Art of Satire.* New York: Russell & Russell, 1960. Discusses invectives, burlesque, and irony.

Besides the examples of satire in the text, we mention various satirical works in the Suggestions for Study. The following list does not pretend to include all of the world's best satirists, but it gives a representative selection of these writers and their outstanding works not already mentioned. The arrangement is chronological—that is, according to the time in which the writers lived. The form—tale, verse, play, novel, essay—is either common knowledge or can easily be ascertained. Most of these works are available in several good editions.

Aristophanes (*c.* 448–385 B.C.)	*The Clouds; The Birds; Lysistrata;* other plays
Horace (65–8 B.C.)	*Satires*
Ovid (43 B.C.–17 A.D.)	*The Art of Love*
Juvenal (*c.* 60–140)	*Satires*
Petronius (1st cent. A.D.)	*Satyricon*
Lucian (*c.* 125–*c.* 190)	*The Dialogues of the Gods; The Dialogues of the Dead*
Anonymous	*Gesta Romanorum (The Deeds of the Romans)*
Anonymous	*Reynard the Fox*
Boccaccio (1313–1375)	*Decameron*

illiam Langland (c. 1332–c. 1400)   *Piers Plowman*
inçois Villon (1431–c. 1463)   *Grand Testament*
)astian Brant (1457–1521)   *The Ship of Fools*
siderius Erasmus (c. 1466–1536)   *The Praise of Folly*
omas More (1478–1535)   *Utopia*
vantes (1547–1616)   *Don Quixote*
kespeare (1564–1616)   *Love's Labour's Lost; Troilus and Cressida*

n Jonson (c. 1573–1637)   *Volpone*
ohn Donne (1573–1631)   "The Flea"; "The Will"
Mathurin Régnier (1573–1613)   *Satires*
Francisco Quevedo (1580–1645)   *Los Sueños (The Visions)*
Samuel Butler (1612–1680)   *Hudibras*
John Dryden (1631–1700)   *Absalom and Achitophel; Mac Flecknoe; The Medal*

Nicolas Boileau (1636–1711)   *Satires; Le Lutrin (The Lectern)*
William Wycherley (c. 1640–1715)   *The Plain Dealer*
Jonathan Swift (1667–1745)   *The Battle of the Books; The Tale of a Tub*

William Congreve (c. 1670–1729)   *The Way of the World*
Joseph Addison (1672–1719) and
Richard Steele (1672–1729)   *Spectator* papers
John Gay (1685–1732)   *The Beggar's Opera*
Voltaire (1694–1778)   *Satirical Dictionary*
Henry Fielding (1704–1754)   *Tom Thumb the Great; Jonathan Wild; Joseph Andrews; Tom Jones*
Samuel Johnson (1709–1784)   *London; The Vanity of Human Wishes*

Laurence Sterne (1713–1768)   *Tristram Shandy*
Tobias Smollett (1721–1771)   *Roderick Random*
Richard Brinsley Sheridan (1751–1816)   *The Rivals; The School for Scandal*
Robert Burns (1759–1796)   "Holy Willie's Prayer"; "Is There for Honesty Poverty"
Jane Austen (1775–1817)   *Sense and Sensibility; Pride and Prejudice*
Lord Byron (1788–1824)   *English Bards and Scotch Reviewers; Don Juan*

Heinrich Heine (1797–1856)   *Pictures of Travel*
Nicolai Gogol (1809–1852)   *The Inspector General*
William M. Thackeray (1811–1863)   *Vanity Fair*
Charles Dickens (1812–1870)   *Pickwick Papers; American Notes*
George Meredith (1828–1909)   *The Egoist*
Lewis Carroll (1832–1898)   *Alice in Wonderland; Through the Looking Glass*

Samuel Butler (1835–1902)   *Erewhon; The Way of All Flesh*
W. S. Gilbert (1836–1911)   *The Mikado; Iolanthe; Patience*
Thomas Hardy (1840–1928)   *Satires of Circumstance*
Anatole France (1844–1924)   *Penguin Island*
Oscar Wilde (1854–1900)   *The Importance of Being Earnest*
H. C. Bunner (1855–1896)   "Home Sweet Home"

G. Bernard Shaw (1856–1950)	*Arms and the Man; Major B bara; Man and Superman*
H. G. Wells (1866–1946)	*The Time Machine; The F Men on the Moon*
Norman Douglas (1868–1952)	*South Wind*
Saki (H. H. Munro) (1870–1916)	*Beasts and Superbeasts*
Max Beerbohm (1872–1956)	*Seven Men;* other stories and es
G. K. Chesterton (1874–1936)	*Manalive;* other stories and es
James Branch Cabell (1879–1958)	*Jurgen*
H. L. Mencken (1880–1956)	*Prejudices*
Jean Giraudoux (1882–1944)	*The Madwoman of Chaillot*
Franz Kafka (1883–1924)	*The Trial; The Castle*
Eugene I. Zamiatin (1884–1937)	*We*
Sinclair Lewis (1885–1951)	*Main Street; Babbitt; Elmer Gantry*
Ring Lardner (1885–1933)	*Round up* (collected stories)
Eugene O'Neill (1888–1953)	*Marco Millions*
Karel Capek (1890–1938)	*R. U. R.*
Elmer Rice (1892–)	*The Adding Machine*
Louis-Ferdinand Celine (1894–)	*Journey to the End of the Night*
E. E. Cummings (1894–)	*Collected Poems*
Stringfellow Barr (1897–)	*Purely Academic*
Bertolt Brecht (1898–1956)	*The Threepenny Opera; The Threepenny Novel*
C. S. Lewis (1898–)	*Screwtape* essays
John Collier (1901–)	*Fancies and Goodnights; Presenting Moonshine*
Nathanael West (1902–1940)	*The Day of the Locust*
Evelyn Waugh (1903–)	*Vile Bodies; The Loved One*
S. J. Perelman (1904–)	*Crazy Like a Fox; The Road to Miltown*
Christopher Fry (1907–)	*A Phoenix Too Frequent; The Lady's Not for Burning*
Jean Genet (1910–)	*The Balcony*
Eugene Ionesco (1912–)	*The Chairs*
Mary McCarthy (1912–)	*The Groves of Academe*
Kingsley Amis (1922–)	*Lucky Jim*